Anthony Holt MBE was a pilot in the Royal Navy for 30 years, leaving as a Commander in 1992 to run the Naval and Military Club in Piccadilly, and then the Army and Navy Club in Pall Mall.

His naval service took him around the world including a two year spell on secondment to the Australian Navy where he and his family encountered 'Spoofy'.

He is married and lives in Dorset, where he now spends his time writing, sailing his yacht, working as a volunteer Coast Watcher and as a member of the Weymouth Harbour Board, as well as entertaining his four grandchildren.

SPOOFY

Anthony Holt

SPOOFY

for Naomi,

Anthony Holt

Vanguard Press

VANGUARD PAPERBACK

© Copyright 2012
Anthony Holt

A CIP catalogue record for this title is
available from the British Library.

ISBN 978 1 84386 886 6

Vanguard Press is an imprint of
Pegasus Elliot MacKenzie Publishers Ltd.
www.pegasuspublishers.com

First Published in 2012

Vanguard Press
Sheraton House Castle Park
Cambridge England

Printed & Bound in Great Britain

Disclosure

The story of Spoofy is based on often vivid memories, surviving photographs and documents. But some of his early life before we met him is inevitably drawn from third hand information. However, I have no reason to doubt the general accuracy of my description of these early years.

The incidents and events described all happened and where I have given an opinion it is only an opinion drawn from the information available to me and from my impressions at the time. There is no attempt to imply criticism of individuals nor to do anything other than act as an honest reporter of events. In a few cases however, the names of some characters in the story have been changed. The story is primarily about a unique dog but set against the background of my young family and the excitement, humour, friendships and occasional pressures that came with flying naval aircraft in Australia forty years ago.

Acknowledgements

I am indebted to Gordon Edgecombe for his help in answering my questions, providing photographs and in telling me how Spoofy spent his final days; also to my son Richard for his never-ending patience in resolving the many technical problems produced by an old and seemingly vindictive computer.

My daughter Rebecca was a precise and accurate proof reader and finally I could not have completed this work without the constant support, advice and home research given unstintingly to me by my wife Irene.

To the late Mrs Serpa (Sip) Edgecombe and Commander Gordon Edgecombe RAN without whom we might never have known Spoofy.

Prologue

Man and dog. This theme has been entwined throughout the development of the human race almost from the time men emerged from their caves. There are many stories of dogs – clever dogs, working dogs, rescue dogs, brave dogs, aggressive dogs, heroic dogs. Dogs have starred in films and have been the companionable heroes of stories all over the world.

The difference with this story is that it is real. The events depicted actually happened, not always in the order described but they are real events although in some cases it has been necessary to be discreet with the identities of some of my cast. Not so with Spoofy. Spoofy was, to the casual observer, nothing special. But to me, to my wife and to my daughter, his impact, his presence provides the overwhelming and all embracing flavour to our experience of Australia.

Australia was still growing up in the 1970s. It was emerging from the aura of a pioneering colony. The state capitals had achieved urban sophistication but we spent very little time in them. Our Australia, the one we learned to love, was the Australia of small towns, rural districts, pubs with sawdust on the floor and spittoons in the corners. It was a country of massive proportions with awe inspiring scenery, populated by ordinary folk whose lives rotated around the need to survive and eat. They were people who built their own houses with their own hands rather than buying them off the shelf. They were people who carved a livelihood out of an often unforgiving land, taking in their stride all the dramas that their sometimes savage environment could throw at them.

In very many instances, the progress through life was done with the companionship, hard work and support of dogs. Most of the dogs in the country districts of Australia at this time were as tough and resilient as their owners. They had to be.

Spoofy grew up in this hard, tough and unforgiving environment. He learned to look out for himself but at the same time he gave out his doggy love in companionship, support and protection to his many owners. Although the reason for my presence in Australia had nothing to do with dogs, the arrival of Spoofy made my family more rounded, more wholesome and provided the diversion necessary to move us to view the successes and failures we experienced as the modest events they really were. We had been deposited in a strange country with many variations from the lifestyle and climate we had been used to. My story starts with Bobby, our first dog, who circumstances had forced us to leave behind in England, leaving a difficult gap in our family life. It was Spoofy who filled that gap. Spoofy somehow seemed to connect us with the family arrangements we had known and seemed to make it all more normal. Spoofy always seemed to be with us or near us, and if he was unable to join us on our tours of distant parts, he was always there to greet us on return and managed to give the double impression of having waited patiently through the whole time of our absence, and to reproach us for actually going away.

We knew a bit about dogs before we went to Australia but it is no overstatement to say that Spoofy, more than anything else made my family's time in that country the memorable, fulfilling and enjoyable experience it became. Even forty years on, we cannot think of Australia without Spoofy popping into mind. I was there to fly helicopters and make my mark in an exacting, sometimes dangerous and always demanding profession. Additional pressures and difficulties had to be accepted by my wife, and to some degree, by my daughter. For all of us life was made better by Spoofy.

Here is his story, and our story.

Chapter 1
Learning to Live with a Dog

Spoofy was a free spirit. He didn't have owners, just companions; supporters who provided his limited needs; friends or, perhaps as he saw them humano-dog colleagues. His origins were uncertain. He had no smart kennel name, nor any papers to identify him or his breed. We knew he was a Labrador because he looked like a Labrador. Big, black, with a flash of white on his shirt front and expressive brown eyes that could plead, play, sympathise, beg or glare. He lived for the moment and for the most part ambled amiably through life without any apparent cares.

In some way or other he changed the lives of everyone with whom he came into contact. He was a dog never to be forgotten which is why he is the subject of my story forty years after my family first met him.

Spoofy seemed to make his own decisions. He could be fiercely loyal, to people or objects and he seemed to have an uncanny ability to be able to predict, or perhaps guide the future – or at least his future. In the chilly winter evenings I have often wondered about our first meeting and the quite remarkable co-incidents involved. Did he really know that he needed a new home – or perhaps he would have thought of it as a new base. I even wondered if he sat up late at night, pawing through the private papers of his owners – his current companions and supporters – and had worked out that they were going away and that he would have to move on. Well, that is just bizarre, but he knew. He really knew.

When he entered the life of my family we were adjusting to a new location in a country far from home where the small differences outranked the similarities. We had no real friends around us, we had parted sadly from our own dog, we had no relatives within thousands of miles but we did have a few local acquaintances. It was into this void that Spoofy projected himself – a grubby, friendly, haphazard, bohemian companion and comforter.

There is no doubt that Spoofy adopted us and not the other way around. He could not have known that in answering the call of my duty and travelling to the other side of the world we had left behind a dog we had grown to love and who had been an essential part of our small and new family. But I think he knew that in some way we were out of our depth and yet to acclimatise to a life that he recognised. Perhaps he detected an underlying stress and sadness in us. If this was so it might account for his determined attachment to my family from the very start – or maybe he foresaw his own coming isolation and was seeking soulmates.

I had been sent to Australia to do a job – a fairly demanding job flying naval helicopters in sometimes exacting circumstances with all the ups and downs, triumphs and problems that go with any job and with unavoidable pressures placed on my family, who, immediately following the birth of our daughter, had been wrenched from the comfortable routine of shore based life in England, in a newly purchased house with the trappings of home-building already surrounding us.

****

In the late 1960s somewhere in the bush country of southern New South Wales, on a small homestead of three hundred acres or so a litter of Labrador pups was born. There were seven or perhaps eight to start with but certainly fewer as time went on. The mother was a working dog on the farm but the identity of the father was not known for certain. It was reckoned that he was also a black Labrador because that appeared to be the breed of his abandoned family. He could have come from any one of half a dozen similar farms nearby but nobody could summon up the effort to discover his identity. Life was not easy on the small homestead farms many of which had been established to provide employment for returning soldiers after the Second World War.

All the dogs lived on scraps, slept in a barn and hunted rats and other small vermin for their livelihood. As the pups developed and were weaned it became apparent that there were too many for either the farmer or the farm to support. Two at the most might remain – the rest, one way or another, would have to go.

A notice was placed in the post office. This was in the township sixteen miles away. A couple of enquiries from families looking for a pet and a neighbouring farmer seeking a replacement rat catcher reduced the litter to three. Two bitches were to be kept on the farm but the future for the dog was looking short and grim.

Rescue came in the shape of a battered Holden utility truck of uncertain vintage that appeared from the trees, bumped down the single track dirt road in a cloud of red dust and came to a standstill between the barn and the single storey wooden house. The occupant was a young English woman in her early twenties. She was one of the hundreds of young people who roamed around the country districts of Australia, taking work when it was available and soaking up the unique experience of wandering through a massive, under-populated semi wilderness; living in a car or truck and occasionally taking a bed in an austere room, with three square meals in return for a session of hard and long work on the farm.

The young woman called herself 'Cathy' and had been on the road for more than six months. She was heading north with a view to stopping and settling in one of the growing towns along the coastal strip south of Sydney.

Cathy had intended to stay for three or four days, but the room was comfortable and the food was good, if somewhat plain, so she stayed on. There was no television, few books and two radios, one, erratic at best and usually tuned to a 'Country' music station, in Cathy's old Holden and the other in the farmhouse kitchen. Cathy had little to amuse herself with in the warm evenings and so fell to playing with the growing pups. About two weeks after her arrival the subject of the remaining pups came up over supper. There had been no takers for the third pup. The farmer and his wife agreed that the dog puppy would be put down, probably the next day. Cathy had formed an affinity with the pups and she was really upset by this. Later, without thinking much about it but having shed some tears she said, "I'll have him."

Agreement was immediate and so Cathy took charge of the little dog. She stayed a further three weeks on the farm before moving on, this time with a small black companion on the seat beside her.

****

It was about the same time but twelve thousand miles and a hemisphere away that we acquired our first dog. Recently married, I was approaching the end of my flying training as a Royal Navy helicopter pilot and with my wife Irene we were cosily settled in a charming old red brick bungalow surrounded by semi wild gardens of shrubs, flowers and wild birds in the then tiny fishing village of Porthleven in the west of Cornwall. Even with flying pay and Irene's work as a midwife, we didn't have much money and so holidays and luxuries were out of the question but something seemed to be missing and since the uncertain future offered by naval employment meant that starting a family would need to be deferred we decided to get ourselves a dog.

We scanned the local papers and Irene asked questions of the villagers she met on the way down to the harbour to collect a fresh John Dory or some mackerel when the boats came in. We examined the postcard notices pinned up in the Post Office cum village shop or in the ramshackle harbour side garage, all to no avail until, with the arrival of the autumn evenings we spotted an advertisement for Border Collie puppies – good working stock – for sale in Mawnan Smith near Falmouth. We talked about this for a while, then rang the farm just to ask about the puppies and in no time at all we were heading off in our station wagon to drive through the typically penetrating Cornish rain and almost impenetrable mist all the way around the huge expanse of Falmouth harbour down ever smaller country lanes, eventually with grass growing in the middle and great dollops of mud cast like the droppings of some ancient beast but only marking the progress of tractors and farm vehicles going about their business.

The dull October afternoon had passed into a black, wet and cold evening by the time we saw the lighted windows ahead which seemed to suggest our destination. The farm yard was typical of the small, chaotic West Country farms which dot this maritime landscape. The wind whistled in off the sea, the rain grew heavier and the mud more glutinous as we tentatively navigated towards what appeared to be a kitchen door. There was no bell or knocker so I hammered on the door which was jerked open almost immediately by a large woman swathed in jerseys, housecoats and other paraphernalia. Without providing us the opportunity to speak she bellowed over her shoulder, "Arthur, there's more come about them dogs."

From somewhere further within the depths of the house came a rumbling indecipherable male voice, while the woman let go of the door to turn urgent attention to a spitting smoking stove to her left. As her bulk cleared the doorway we were treated to the wonderful aroma of frying sausages mixed with the confused smell of onions, bacon and other culinary delights.

We waited. The sound of heavy boots being manoeuvred into position occupied the next few minutes and then the man of the house emerged. He was as wiry and spare as his wife was large and if he got his fair share of sausages and mash he must have been in the habit of converting it immediately into the energy needed to work the farm. He jammed an old sweat stained cloth cap on his head, stuck an equally ancient pipe in the side of his mouth and followed the cloud of rich brown tobacco smoke out through the kitchen and into the yard. He didn't seem to notice the rain.

"Evenin', come about the dogs?" he said, striding past our two damp forms.

"Er, yes," I responded, beginning to wonder whether we had made a sensible decision. He set off across the yard, hunching his head and shoulders into the slanting penetrating rain. We squelched along behind.

We came to an ancient wooden building with a stable door set into the nearest end, the bulk of which provided some protection from the now almost horizontal rain which had eased to a thin drizzle but had become even colder and more penetrating, as only Cornish rain could. Our guide opened the top half of the stable door, shone a torch inside and, peering around him we saw a small black and white collie bitch surrounded by a nest of about eight enthusiastic pups. The whole scene appeared comfortable and warm despite the weather. The sudden light together with our presence didn't seem to bother the mother or her pups so we concluded that we were not the first visitors.

The farmer opened the lower door and stepped into the small straw filled space, bending and picking up one small struggling bundle of black and white fur for our inspection. "You want a dawg or'n a bitch?" We didn't know.

We both eased into the comparative warmth of the shed and tentatively fondled a couple of the pups. There seemed to be eight of them and one or two were bolder than the others in moving towards us and allowing themselves to be handled. Irene said, "We'll have this one." I didn't know that we had actually decided to have one at all but it looked as though we had a done deal.

Our selected pup was loosely wrapped in a piece of whitish cloth and we headed back to the farmhouse kitchen, this time with the rain on our backs. A few minutes later we had paid the few pounds necessary for the purchase of our new friend and we were back in the car, three point turning it through the mud and the slurry to start the long journey home. Irene nursed the puppy while I negotiated the narrow Cornish lanes, bordered on each side by a mixture of high vegetation which was really only there to disguise the granite walls that typically bordered these roads.

Our troubles began soon after we left the farm. The tiny bundle, shivering and squeaking in Irene's arms clearly didn't fancy being driven in a car at all. His reaction to his new circumstances first showed itself by his most recent meal being vomited all over Irene, the car seat, the floor and everything within range.

"My God, what is he doing?" I yelled. Before Irene could offer the obvious answer, an intense and foul smell filled the car as the terrified pup emptied his other end. This was very hard to take. Irene, still clutching the pup in his now disgusting swaddling cloth wound down the car window which merely added a burst of cold rain to our discomfort.

We travelled on through the night and every time we thought our little dog had emptied himself, one end or the other – or both – he proved us wrong. It took over an hour to get back and when we pulled up outside the garage at the back of our bungalow we were all stinking, wet and very uncomfortable.

We hurried inside, glad to get out of the now heavy drizzle; Irene took the pup to the bathroom to clean him up. I went back out to put the car away then we made as cosy a dog bed as we could manage before stripping off our filthy clothes and heading into the bathroom.

When we emerged, cleaner and in different clothes but still tainted with the recollection of our recent ordeal we looked into the kitchen where our new friend was curled up on his makeshift bed looking as though he belonged. A tiny tail wagged and we bonded.

The next requirement was for a name that would suit the little black and tan and white face looking up at us. After not very much discussion, he became 'Bobby'.

Bobby was to make a considerable difference to our lives. Despite the uninspiring journey on that first evening he was a quick learner and was soon housetrained. Constantly alert, he became Irene's four-legged shadow and was never far from her side. His learning process was not always smoothness and light however. The peace of an early Sunday morning was destroyed by a yell of horror as I stumbled, half asleep and barefoot from the bedroom to the kitchen with the intention of producing our morning tea, when one foot after the other landed in a squishy deposit left just inside the kitchen door. While I was hopping about, spreading further the ordure, Irene realized the cause of the drama and she arrived, unbidden, cloth in hand to clean up the mess and keep dog and master apart. I went to the bathroom to clean my feet and she made the tea. Bobby made himself scarce by disappearing into the garden.

Bobby left us with another ever-lasting impression of a different sort when he started to intercept the mail as it was pushed through the letter box. Irene had sent off our marriage certificate to the Royal College of Midwives so she could be re-registered in her married name. We were also expecting the arrival of a substantial cheque at about the same time, so imagine our consternation when we encountered a trail of little fragments of official looking paper leading towards the letter box in the kitchen door. On the floor just inside the door, lay a chewed brown envelope with, thankfully, the bulk of its contents still inside. This, on examination, proved to be the marriage certificate – or at least about four fifths of it. We gathered all of the scraps of paper and carefully reassembled the certificate with the aid of sellotape, all the while casting reproachful glances towards the now placid Border Collie who was resting in his bed, comfortable with having protected his new family from the dangers being thrust through the hole in the kitchen door – a job well done!

The learning process continued – for both dog and owners – over the coming months, with highs and lows of training on both sides but with an overall coming together of understanding between the three of us, and eventually an impressive improvement in the behaviour and manners of our now not so new arrival.

We had one or two more problems such as the occasion when Irene was preparing sirloin steaks for our supper and I telephoned to say that I was scheduled for night flying and would be late home. Although my flying training programme was carefully laid out, the notoriously unpredictable Cornish weather would frequently entail changes to the plan.

Our telephone conversation was continuing with me attempting to explain the likely flying requirements for the next few days when Irene became aware of a howling coming from the kitchen. She asked me to hold, put the phone down and popped down the passage to see what the problem was. When she came back on the line it was to tell me that our supper was to be a little more modest than we had expected. Bobby had been able to reach up to the kitchen table and managed to eat one of the steaks. He had then set up an affronted howl because he couldn't reach the second one. Pay was pretty low in the navy at that time, particularly for young officers under training and steak was expensive so the loss of our treat was a real blow.

We learned from that, as they say, and our culinary precautions were reinforced considerably.

Chapter 2
Moving On

Time moved on, summer moved into autumn and my flying training graduated from Basic to Advanced courses. I had a worrying and nasty series of problems to overcome before this was achieved. Basic Flying Training at the Royal Naval Air Station at Culdrose was divided into two parts. The first part was carried out on Hiller two seat training helicopters where the large Perspex 'bubble' cockpit provided the best possible visibility for the trainee pilot. We young tyros were all quite proud of our newfound skills as fixed wing pilots, capable of driving the light Chipmunk trainer around the sky and through all the standard aerobatics safely and stylishly. So it was a very considerable shock to discover just how difficult it was to get the Hiller off the ground and achieve a hover – this being defined as remaining within the confines of a fairly large field whilst simultaneously preventing the aircraft from going up or down.

When this had been accomplished and we had mastered the highly manoeuvrable little Hiller it was time to move on to the Whirlwind which was a bigger, more difficult, and more complex aircraft to fly. We were taken systematically through a series of exercises using all of the capabilities of this aircraft which had been the workhorse of the early helicopter fleet. The programme of exercises culminated in night flying and then instrument flying aiming to qualify for our first instrument rating and thus become the proud owners of a "White" instrument rating card. This was where my problems began and where my embryo flying career almost came to an ignominious end.

I should explain that the statistics then (and probably now) identified an overall failure rate during the two years necessary to become a qualified front line pilot in the Fleet Air Arm of about 70%. My course had started with nearly fifteen pilots and we were already down to about ten – although not all of the departures had been caused by flying problems.

About half way through the Whirlwind course, one of our number, a tough character who had started out as a Royal Marine before being transferred from RM to RN for flying training, fell madly in love. Harry and his fiancée decided that they should marry without delay so that they would have time together before Harry was appointed away, almost inevitably to an aircraft carrier in the Far East and probably for at least nine months. The more immediate problem was that newly wedded bliss would not always sit easily with the demands imposed on a young aviator seeking to come to terms with the increasing pressures of an intense and exacting training regime.

The training moved on and the wedding date was set for about the middle of the Whirlwind course, shortly before the second set of ground school exams. On a brisk clear Saturday in early March the whole course motored off to a village on the edge of Dartmoor, north of Plymouth where the wedding was to take place.

As well as the young naval aviators, the guests included a largish group of Royal Marines. The small village church was packed and the ceremony went off without a hitch. The newlyweds emerged from the church through an arch of swords, mostly borrowed, held by the rest of the course and the whole party then headed for the village hotel cum pub where the wedding reception was to take place. The wine flowed and the party got into its stride but after the first hour it became apparent that the bride, whilst circulating among her guests, was becoming increasingly anxious about the possibility of

29

'decorations' being applied to the car in which she and her new husband were to depart on their short honeymoon. This was like a red rag to a bull for some of the guests who began to plot what was deemed to be an appropriate send-off.

The car, however, was nowhere to be seen. It had been hidden away. A surreptitious search began and after some time the car was located, packed and ready to go, hidden behind the doors of a wooden garage around the side of the hotel. The drinks continued to flow and a plan was hatched. It was decided that when the time for departure approached the guests should gather near to the garage and one sub lieutenant would wait in his car, strategically placed, ready to rush forward and block the passage of the honeymoon car, delaying it long enough to be suitably daubed and adorned. Inevitably, of course, considering the environment of its construction, the plan was doomed.

The bride and groom disappeared to change. The drinks continued to flow and the conspirators grew bolder. Eventually Harry and his bride appeared, said goodbye to their close family and friends and made a dash for a side door leading to the garage. Clearly the anxiety of the bride had infected the groom and the unexpected appearance of their course mates and colleagues around the garage entrance did nothing to improve the situation.

The garage doors were flung wide, the open topped car surged forward but its progress was arrested by a bunch of Royal Marines who lifted the back of the car off the ground. The engine roared, the blocking car shot into position, and the bride leaned backwards out of her seat screaming and shouting at the straining marines while simultaneously beating their heads and shoulders with what appeared to be a wrapped wedding present. Harry, still pressing the accelerator, leaned around and joined in the verbal and physical attack on the marines. The marines dropped the car, the wheels bit the gravel, driver and passenger continued to direct their rage towards the back of the car and the car surged forward, colliding with a resounding thud into the side of the blocking car. A cry of anguish came from within the now heavily damaged blocking car, giving us all to understand that the car actually belonged to the mother of the driver.

The crowd were shocked into a brief dusty silence punctuated by the ripe language still coming from the happy couple as well as a cacophony of groans and clangs as Harry tried to kick and heave the bent bonnet and wings back towards their original shape. It was an impossible task and within a few minutes the little open tourer went clanging and grinding up the track to disappear from view along the road.

This was really the beginning of the end for Harry. His domestic pressures started to weigh heavily on him and his flying began to suffer. His ground school results were little better and this combined to cause him to spend more time in the training squadron and less time at home. His new wife took a dim view of this and was eventually given to telephoning the squadron demanding that her husband return home immediately. This came to a head about the time we all went into the Whirlwind night flying phase, when Harry's absence from home by day as well as during a large part of the night became just too much. He failed to turn up for work – which in a disciplined Service can be viewed as desertion. We trainees were not party to precisely what happened but Harry was removed from training and we didn't see him again. A promising career prematurely ended.

****

In Australia, Cathy had continued on her route heading north. She was now accompanied by a handsome, glossy coated black dog with a small white blaze on his chest. He had no registration but he had acquired a name – Spoofy. He had become almost as adept as his owner at foraging and making the best of whatever circumstances he encountered. He was a tough dog, and a lucky dog, the constant companion of his resourceful and hard working mistress.

As Cathy travelled further north along the coast the settlements became bigger and busier and the subsistence agriculture gave way to more mechanised, bigger units. Work for casual itinerant labourers became more difficult to find and accommodation was not so readily available to a woman travelling with a dog.

Cathy had grown to love Spoofy but she realised that soon, when she stopped her travelling she would need to find permanent employment and then, in all likelihood, she would return to a different life in England. In these circumstances it would be almost impossible to look after Spoofy properly, even allowing that the dog was undemanding in care and attention.

Cathy arrived in the small settlement of Batemans Bay towards the end of the summer tourist season. The holiday shacks were being closed up for the winter and the fishing and tour boats were being tied up in the inner harbour. There were two or three small shops, each mostly selling anything and everything as well as a garage cum filling station with a small café attached. The season's end offered the opportunity to the locals, who had been working all summer to serve the visiting population, to head off for their own holidays. Traditionally these would be extended into a couple of months and those who could afford it would head north to the Queensland Gold Coast where the sun shone all year round and the cash registers continued ringing accordingly.

Cathy had the option of two jobs – an assistant in the general store and a waitress – in fact the only waitress in the garage café. As well as serving meals this could involve checking oil levels and cleaning windscreens. She lasted three months altogether before deciding that there must be better jobs, so she loaded her possessions and her dog into the utility and headed north up the Princes Highway.

Thirty miles on she rode into Nowra, then a small but expanding country town at the estuary of the Shoalhaven River. Here she was in luck. The town had a largish modern supermarket which was short of staff and was prepared to pay above the odds to fill the gaps. Cathy found lodgings that would take her for as long as she wanted but would only take her dog for a limited few weeks.

Spoofy, for his part, rather took to Nowra. It had miles of small residential streets with grass edged pavements, beaches, shaded riverside groves of eucalyptus, parkland and bush for him to roam in. He was in dog heaven. He became known around the town as a friendly, happy go lucky dog who was no threat to anyone and who was thought of as a bit of a character.

It couldn't last. The reminders from Cathy's landlady became more frequent and had reached the level of "that dog has got to go".

Only a week or so later a letter arrived at the post office for Cathy 'to await collection'. It had been sent from England, not by airmail and so had taken six weeks over the sea journey. It had then passed through the post offices of about eleven small towns in Victoria and New South Wales and had now been forwarded from the post desk at the Batemans Bay Hardware Store. It stayed on the 'collect' board at Nowra for another week before another checkout girl in the supermarket spotted Cathy's name and told her about it.

No one knows the content of that letter but it had the decisive effect of resolving Cathy's intention for her future. Her travelling days were over and she would stay only long enough to pay for her return journey to England. The problem of Spoofy loomed large.

The easiest and quickest way to attempt a resolution to the problem of Spoofy was to put an ad in the bulletin board just inside the main doors of the supermarket. She wrote out a notice: *Friendly and well trained dog, free to a good home.* Underneath, she attached one of her few photographs of Spoofy. It showed him standing proudly on top of a huge boulder with a small stand of gum trees behind him. She called it her 'King of the Jungle' picture.

Within three days the ad had taken effect. Mrs Sip Edgecombe, Finnish born wife of Lieutenant Gordon Edgecombe spotted the photograph as she was completing her weekly shopping trip with two of her three children. In fact it was four-year-old Buffy who saw the picture and asked what it was about. "It's a dog looking for a home." For anyone not serious about providing Spoofy with a new home, that unthinking remark would have been a mistake. As it was, within the week, Gordon having been convinced, Spoofy was being introduced to his new home. Spoofy was a fun loving, adventure seeking, gregarious dog with no shred of malice towards humans and a great affinity for children so his change of base was an immediate success. He still enjoyed his daily and sometimes nightly patrols but he had a comfortable new dog basket, two meals a day, a supply of scraps and ready made playmates. Dog heaven had just improved.

Cathy stayed a further three months working at the supermarket, taking all the overtime she could get, and then she left Nowra, presumably to return to England. She left no acquaintances behind, or a forwarding address, and her only companion was now enjoying a life of comparative luxury with the Edgecombe family.

Chapter 3
Wings

In Cornwall, the flying training programme ploughed inexorably forward. One or two other trainee pilots fell by the wayside but not in such a spectacular style as Harry. As night flying moved into instrument flying I very nearly joined the failures. The Whirlwind Mk 7 was a bitch to try to fly accurately on instruments. Indeed, when originally introduced into service it had been regarded as impossible to fly on instruments. The navy would never stand for such a limitation and techniques were developed. The trouble was that there was no aerodynamic or mechanical 'feel' to the control column – known in helicopters as the 'cyclic'. This meant that if the pilot let go of the cyclic in flight, it would flop into the corner of the cockpit – rather like a pencil stood on end. Of course the helicopter would then follow the direction of the cyclic, with dramatic and frightening results. There is a second major control in the cockpit of a helicopter which must also be constantly held by the pilot. This is the 'collective' which, simplistically, is used to move the helicopter vertically up and down while the cyclic controls horizontal motion. In the Whirlwind the collective control also incorporates the engine throttle – rather like a motorcycle throttle – which must be constantly adjusted to maintain steady engine and hence rotor speed. Add to this the need to adjust various instrument settings and the problem becomes almost insurmountable – or so it seemed to me at the time. The course was coming to its end and I had failed several attempts at my Instrument Rating

Test. My flying career seemed to be approaching a cliff edge when it was decided that I would be given one last chance and I was to be given an hour or two of special instruction by the Chief Instrument Rating Instructor. I waited in dismal trepidation for this god-like individual, further depressed in the knowledge that the course 'Wings' parade was only two days away and contemplating my failure as a General List officer while all the younger and more junior short service officers who I had been expected to lead would pass the course, leaving me cast aside to go back to general service as a failure.

I was given one day and two, possibly three, sorties to overcome my problems. I sat in the crew room morosely, desperately, studying my Pilot's Notes. In walked a tall thin Lieutenant Commander with an impressive array of squadron badges sown on his flying overalls. He peered at me over a huge black beard and said, "Well let's get going shall we." This was John Marshall, a naval aviator with a renowned reputation extending back to the Second World War, when he had been a Walrus pilot, launched by catapult and frequently landing in the sea. He was also an incredibly skilled helicopter pilot and a superb instructor.

Within a matter of minutes after the first take-off and instrument climb-out John had identified the simple problem which was giving me so much trouble and ruining each sortie. It was all caused by the need to reset the altimeter on climb-out at the same time as keeping the cyclic under control. We spent an hour practising this followed by one more sortie and then success with the Instrument Rating Test.

To my huge relief I was then able to complete the course, collect my 'Wings' – presented by the permanently irascible Rear Admiral David Kirk, and start the Advanced Flying Training course on the 'state of the art' Wessex Mk 1.

After another ten weeks or so we graduated from 706 Squadron and were posted to HMS Osprey, the naval air station at Portland in Dorset for Advanced Flying Training. We felt almost like old hands.

This move away from Culdrose introduced a family dilemma. Would I be appointed to a flight operating from Portland or, more likely, would I return to Cornwall to join one of the big carrier squadrons based at Culdrose? This likelihood led to a decision whereby Irene, and I – and our faithful Bobby would take up temporary accommodation in Weymouth pending the move back west.

Of course it didn't happen like this and I was appointed to the ship's flight of *HMS Fife*, a relatively new County Class guided missile destroyer. The ship was destined to undergo a series of sea trials for the next year and a half before deploying for a nine month long cruise to the other side of the world.

This provided a splendid opportunity to bond with our still relatively new family pet. Bobby had already proved remarkably easy to train and was very responsive to our needs and thoughts. He was an intelligent dog who could now be trusted in most circumstances and his brief criminal record dissolved into the past. He was in fact very much a one person dog – in this case a one woman dog. He was fiercely protective of Irene whilst treating me more or less as a friendly equal. His greatest achievement was in teaching us how to live with and get the best out of a family dog.

His ancestry as a working dog gave Bobby the necessary skills and instincts to respond quickly to our expectations and training requirements. He seemed to be able to think on the same plane as us and even to anticipate our demands. This, of course, was because of his ability to detect and interpret all the little clues that we inadvertently offer when we set out to do something such as leave the house, drive the car, dig the garden, go for a walk, or feed ourselves or the dog. Bobby was possessed of seemingly unbounded energy, endless patience, earnest enthusiasm and a protective instinct for his home and his people.

It was this instinct that nearly got him and us into trouble. We had purchased a small house in Weymouth and had set about putting it into suitable order. The house was situated on a relatively new estate and, in the fashion of the time, sported an open plan front garden laid mostly to lawn.

One Saturday morning I was digging out a small circle in the centre of the lawn in preparation for the planting of a lilac tree when a Post Office van drew up outside and a burly postman – not our usual friendly man – marched directly across the lawn and, without speaking, thrust a small package at me. I dropped the spade in order to clutch the package and at the same time, Bobby who had been 'on duty' sitting a few feet behind me, sprang into action. I have a vivid recollection of the look of surprise replacing the surly truculence which had previously occupied the face of the intruder as his arm, still held horizontal, pointing towards me, was suddenly adorned with a dog hanging by its teeth from the elbow. "Down," I yelled. Bobby responded instantly. The postman, still without a word, turned on his heel and stalked away. I made placatory remarks and so far as I could see there was no damage either to the sleeve or to the individual. The arm seemed to be performing much as it had done before so I took a break and we both went inside for a cup of coffee and a slurp of water.

About two weeks later we received a terse little note from the Post Office, written as these things so often are by a faceless bureaucrat with only a thin grasp of English grammar. The note alleged, or rather asserted, that we were the owners of a vicious dog who was in the habit of attacking innocent passing postmen. So much for being innocent until proven guilty! Worse was to follow. Another note from a different source informed us that a complaint had been received and we were to receive a visit from the local constabulary who would investigate the alleged behaviour of our dog. Despite our faith in our four footed protector, we were worried.

In due course, a small police 'panda car' pulled up outside and curtains twitched along the street. It was late in the afternoon so we invited the constable to have a cup of tea and a biscuit. He was a youngish man with a friendly open face and an easy manner. As he settled himself down in the armchair with his cup of tea and his biscuit he was joined by a sleek black, white and brindle dog, who was clearly on his best behaviour and determined to charm his new friend. We chatted. Eventually our guest, while stroking Bobby, who was cosying up alongside him, took out his notebook and asked "Where's the dangerous dog then? I'd better see him," he said.

"He's right alongside you," I answered, "sharing your biscuit," which was indeed the case.

"But that can't be right. He's not dangerous. He's a friend," he said, ruffling a pair of warm black ears. I swear that Bobby actually smirked.

We all decided that was the end of the matter, more tea was served, Bobby continued to be the perfect host, we chatted some more and the policeman eventually went on his way with a happy tail-wagging dog escorting him all the way to his car.

"Bobby"

Chapter 4
To See the World

Even though *HMS Fife* was still struggling with her programme of sea and harbour trials it was deemed necessary for her helicopter to embark and this meant that I was going to be away at sea for several periods of a month or so at a time. During these early deployments, a new Flight Commander joined. It was John Marshall, my mentor who had helped me to qualify as a pilot. He had only been with the flight for about three weeks when tragedy struck. John had asked me to stand down from a programmed flight over the sea while a colleague took my place. While I was having a snack lunch, still in my immersion flying suit, the aircraft blew up and John was killed. The navy lost a man of remarkable skill and experience who had, during his long career, helped so many others.

I had to continue with the trials flying on my own and so I was absent from home more frequently. While I was away Bobby and Irene formed an even closer affinity and when she was not out at work or shopping they were inseparable.

This was the common lot of naval families when the lives of wives, children and pets were frequently disrupted by the sometimes short notice comings and goings of the master of the house. In our case we adapted to the lifestyle with little problem but this was not always so with other families.

We had some naval friends who were also near neighbours. They owned a huge Alsatian who took his protection duties fairly seriously even at normal times but when the husband was away at sea he stepped up a gear or so and became so intense that only his mistress could manage him. He meant no harm but he was just big and quite intense. He was given the run of the home which meant that when a passer-by was deemed to be passing too close to the house he became agitated and developed the ability to appear almost simultaneously behind every door and window.

One day I was deputed to deliver some shopping which my wife had collected for Judy, our Alsatian owning friend, and when I expressed some concern over the renowned protective instinct of the dog I was told that he was really a great big softy. I headed down the road with increasing concern competing with a more rational determination to appear laid back and unafraid. It was important to set the right relationship, I thought as I pressed the doorbell.

All hell broke loose. A noise akin to thunder emanated seemingly from all over the house and I realised the legend was true. The enormous hairy brute really could appear simultaneously behind every opening in the house. My resolve was actually in the process of folding its tent and fleeing from the scene when the door started to open. I heard Judy's welcoming voice when a whirlwind struck and I was flung back against the wall inside the door with a giant paw on each shoulder and a black nose inches from mine assaulting the immediate atmosphere with his own distinct version of dog breath. It was not a pleasant experience. I was a dog master but I was not in control. I heard Judy say "he likes you" or something equally trite. My distraught mind paused in its prayers for salvation from the immediate peril just long enough to register that I was still alive and my lower face was now being investigated by a hot wet tongue. I made 'my excuses' as they say in the Sunday newspapers, and left.

Some time later, Judy's husband Arthur returned from a fairly long period away at sea in the Far East and arrived home as the third member of the happy duo that Charlie the dog believed had been established. A state of careful neutrality seemed to dominate the domestic scene as Arthur and Judy settled in together. This lasted until bed time when Charlie, following the couple upstairs at a discreet distance, saw that Arthur was getting into bed with Judy – and he disapproved. As Arthur attempted to settle into bed alongside his wife he was hit by a hundred pounds of dog and flung to the floor. Further attempts were equally unsuccessful until later that night Arthur had to spend his first night home in the spare bedroom. This situation could not continue but Charlie was not to be budged. Sadly this meant eventually that Charlie had to go to a new and more appropriate home to accommodate his size and his interesting little ways.

The trials programme was moving steadily but sluggishly to its conclusion and the ship's operational deployment plans were outlined. For a young naval officer looking for adventure it was a fabulous opportunity but it also brought closer the difficult prospect for a relatively newly married couple of enforced separation for a period of at least nine months.

We sailed from Portsmouth in April. The morning was sunny and as the ship passed serenely out of Portsmouth Harbour to the accompaniment of a piper on the Bridge roof I was just able to make out the small group among the crowds standing waving by the 'Still and West' pub on the eastern side of the harbour entrance. My wife was accompanied by my parents as well as the ever attendant Bobby. They all waved furiously with arms and tail as the ship sailed out into the early morning sunshine. The tears came later.

We crossed the Atlantic in a leisurely eight days or so, exercising with our sister ship *HMS Glamorgan*. Flying operations filled the days and nights until we arrived in Washington. Intense interest in these revolutionary new ships together with a full programme of entertainment and hospitality left little time for anything else. Telephone communication between ships and home was difficult and very expensive in those days so the arrival of mail from home was really important. I tried always to ensure that I wrote from every port we visited but correspondence was frequently disrupted or confused by letters arriving in the wrong order. Not every letter brought good news and the strain became apparent in some of the recipients. Sometimes it was just confusing, such as when I received a telegram saying: 'don't worry, all is now well'. This arrived in the middle of the Indian Ocean, about two weeks since leaving our last port. The only way to resolve the mystery thus presented was to embark on the expensive and uncertain rigmarole of a ship to shore telephone call.

This had to be booked well in advance, to take place when the ship was not occupied on any demanding or warlike activity, as well as being set to take into account the time difference between us and Britain so that the call would not be received in the middle of the night. When a high frequency radio link had been established between the ship and the Post Office shore station at Niton Radio an announcement would come over the main broadcast for the men who had booked calls to go to the Main Communications Office. There, we would wait patiently as each call was connected and carried out, sometimes against the difficult and disruptive background of atmospheric static and interference from other stations. Calls were limited to an initial three minutes unless there was no one else waiting either in the ether or in the Communications Office. A look at the face of the last caller would show instantly whether the attempt at communication had been a success or had consisted of two and a half minutes of indecipherable static. Also on some occasions the conversation would end up being broadcast around the office to be heard by the dozen or so occupants. This lack of local privacy needed to be considered relative to the fact that every word transmitted and received could also be heard by any other vessel tuned to the same frequency as well as the operators in

44

the receiving station – often more clearly than the intended recipient.

We passed down the Eastern Seaboard of the United States, across the Caribbean and through the Panama Canal – a singularly over-rated experience where it was necessary to bribe the customs officials to obtain release of important spares for the aircraft, which had been consigned for collection at Panama City. Of even more concern, the ship's doctor, a very senior officer, had to be bailed out of the filthy, stinking Panamanian jail in which he had spent most of the night. He had made the mistake of arguing with his taxi driver over the extortionate fare for the trip from the city to the ship, and doing so, against the advice of our US Navy hosts, before the taxi had entered into the base area. The argument became heated and the taxi driver promptly turned the car round and headed for a police station conveniently being run by the driver's brother-in-law.

After Panama we sailed up the coast of Oregon and California, out over the Pacific and, via Hawaii, down to Australia. I was really impressed with the vibrant and modern city that was Sydney and took all the opportunities within the means of my meagre funds to experience everything I could. This included walking from Garden Island (the Royal Australian Naval Base on the South side of the harbour near the not yet complete Opera House) up over the Sydney Harbour Bridge, about four miles along the North Harbourside to Taronga Park Zoological Gardens where I spent the afternoon wandering around and viewing the animals before heading back along the North Shore, back over the bridge and through the Botanical Gardens to the ship. I also had the unforgettable experience of being able to fly our helicopter along the coast and around the harbour. I was greatly tempted to fly under the bridge but chickened out, worried that there may have been cables hanging down from the bridge towards the water. I had another three weeks or so to continue to enjoy from the air and from the sea what Australia had to offer. Little did I realise that within about three years I would be back there as a resident.

****

One hundred miles to the south, Spoofy was now a firm member of the Edgecombe family, growing up with the children, protecting what he thought of as 'his' property, carrying out his daily routine patrols and maintaining an easy-going dominance of most of the canine population of Nowra.

He had also, unfortunately succumbed to the severe summer climate and developed eczema, which meant having his back shaved from time to time prior to daily treatment with a special shampoo provided by the vet – whose surgery was conveniently located one block along Berry Street from the Edgecombe's house.

Chapter 5
Home

We arrived home to Portsmouth just before Christmas in one of the worst snowstorms ever experienced in the south of England. Our arrival had been delayed by a diversion towards the coast of Nigeria where we were told that we would be providing the venue for yet another attempt at negotiations between the British government and the unilaterally independent Rhodesia. When this happened the combined prospect of missing Christmas at home after nine months away and having to entertain the Prime Minister onboard, as well as the inevitable host of flunkies and hangers-on caused morale throughout the ship's company to plummet to rock bottom.

Fortunately, after changing course and heading in towards the Nigerian coast we received another signal telling us that no further negotiations would take place and the whole operation was cancelled. As the ship turned back to the northwest and increased to maximum speed the onboard gloom was replaced by hope hanging on the possibility that we were going to get home for Christmas. We were not out of the wood yet though, because, having rounded the western bulge of Africa it became increasingly evident that a major storm system was building up ahead of us. We passed the entrance to the Mediterranean and paused in a rising sea to take on fuel from a Royal Fleet Auxiliary Tanker specially sent out from Gibraltar. Refuelled and propelled by the wishes of every sailor onboard we increased speed once again and headed north into the storm. We had about five days to go and so preparations continued as best they could for our arrival and for the departure of those crew members who would be moving on to other ships or shore jobs on arrival. The navy always seems to be like that, with people constantly coming and going.

The weather worsened and as the ship pounded into a force 9 gale the Captain embarked on his programme of saying farewell personally to those officers who would be leaving. This included me. I am a good sailor and rarely feel affected by seasickness but as I made my way unsteadily forward and up towards the Captain's Cabin I was already not enjoying the experience.

The Captain's Cabin in the County Class guided missile destroyers was a fairly grand arrangement in comparison to those usually found in a warship. The ships had been designed by Lord Louis Mountbatten to be able to operate as flagships and to carry an admiral and his staff. This meant that a huge admiral's day cabin had been constructed immediately below the bridge, stretching right across the width of the ship, with large square windows arranged from side to side and all around the front. Just aft of this cabin was a somewhat smaller and much less grand cabin on the port side which was designated for the Captain but with the Captain occupying the big cabin, this was often used as a convenient meeting room or accommodation for important guests.

I knocked on the narrow, already open, door. The familiar reedy voice invited me unenthusiastically to enter and as I did so the tall, angular – and to my young eyes, somewhat elderly form detached itself from the small desk on the far side of the cabin and moved towards a group of comfortable chairs, gesturing me to follow. I headed in the general direction of the chairs, staggering and swallowing compulsively as the carpeted deck rose beneath my feet like a demented roller coaster. At the same time the noise of a thunderclap accompanied the sudden whiteout of all the windows which seemed to last for several minutes but was probably only twenty or thirty seconds until replaced by curtains of descending foam followed by torrents of green water. Falling into the nearest chair my eye was caught by the repeater instruments showing the course and speed of the ship as well as the depth of water and some tactical information. The dial showing speed through the water was showing a fairly steady 36 knots! The Petty Officer Steward danced skilfully across the skittish heaving deck and I found myself clutching a large dry sherry – pretty standard refreshment for the circumstances.

"Well Holt," began the Captain... Christian names were rarely used at that time in the relationship between the Master under God and his minions. He rambled on about where we had been what we had done and what I was going to do, with oblique references to his perceived shortcomings in my character and professional ability while I sipped at the sherry, tried desperately to avoid being hurled around the room complete with chair, observed the regular crash of green or foamy waves as they hit the windows and counted the seconds when the ship seemed to be entirely submerged. I didn't really care what he said because I knew he hadn't a clue as to the duties of embarked helicopter pilots nor the capabilities of the sophisticated anti-submarine helicopter we carried. I recognised that he had considerable skill as a ship-handler but was otherwise, I believed, a complete bloody fool – unemployable outside the cocoon of the navy. I was also much more concerned with our progress towards home and therefore pleased to see the steady 36 knots being maintained despite all that the elements could throw at us and I continued to maintain my mask of polite interest until the fifteen minute interview was over and we could both forget each other's existence.

****

We sailed slowly into the Solent on 23rd of December in a driving snowstorm and nil visibility. The whiteout meant that Portsmouth Harbour would remain closed until conditions improved and so everyone onboard fretted at the final hurdle preventing the completion of our journey from the other side of the world. A large dockyard tug managed to get out of the harbour and, finding us in the fog and swirling snow, brought us mail and some essential bits and pieces before leaving for shore with a few of the ship's company who for some reason or other were deemed to have pressing reasons for being delivered ashore. It was all fairly pointless really because most of the South of England was paralysed and Portsmouth was cut off by road and rail from the rest of the country. Most of the 'essential shore party' were waiting, shivering, on the jetty when we finally entered harbour a few hours later.

For me, the wait was not over. Unexpectedly there was no one to meet me and since there were no mobile phones in those days I had to wait several hours before discovering that my wife – accompanied by our dog – had been stranded in her car for eight or nine hours, mostly sitting unmoving on the same New Forest roundabout.

The system which had produced such appalling weather conditions with very little warning was known as a 'polar low'. This can occur when the country is covered by strong northerly winds and a small area of low pressure develops within the northerly air flow. This will move quickly south whilst deepening until it produces the rapid onset of the very severe wintry storm we had experienced.

Chapter 6
A New Job

Eventually, following a short stay with my parents, we drove off down to Weymouth for Christmas, relaxation and a couple of weeks to learn to be a family again.

In mid January I was sent off to RAF Ternhill to do an instructors' course. I hated every minute of it. I hated being away from home so soon after returning from sea, I was depressed by the long drive back to Weymouth from Shropshire every weekend, I worried about the wear and tear on the car and I loathed the pedantic, humourless patronising attitude of those RAF instructors. After about three months I was posted to 737 squadron at Portland teaching the mysteries of operational anti-submarine flying to new pilots, observers and sonar operators. I could drive to work each morning and head off to our married quarter each evening. We had regular sessions of night flying which in the summer could extend into the early hours of the morning. We would also embark in the helicopter support ship *Engadine* for three weeks or so of offshore operations every three months. Life was so easy I could almost have been in the Air Force.

By mid 1970 I had become well settled into the routine of work and domestic bliss when my world, my concerns and my projections for the future suddenly changed. Irene announced that she was pregnant. We had by this time bought a small comfortable house in Weymouth and moved out of our married quarter, acquired a little old Ford Anglia as a second car and were deep in the land of nest building when the Admiralty produced one of their periodic bombshells. I was to be moved on to a new appointment – and not just any easy to reach local appointment.

Australia was deeply involved in the Vietnam War and most of their helicopter aircrew were being deployed to Vietnam, or were on leave or re-training in the United States. No longer being able to provide sufficient anti-submarine aircrew to meet their other treaty commitments, the Royal Australian Navy had turned to the Royal Navy for help. An arrangement had been agreed whereby four crews, a third of a squadron, of aircrew officers would be sent on loan service for two years to the RAN. This meant four experienced pilots, four newly qualified pilots and four observers, with a mix of experience. Most of the young pilots and some of the observers were from the recent course which I had been training. I was to go as one of the experienced pilots.

I had been deeply impressed with the lifestyle presented during my earlier brief visit to Australia but the problems of such a move seemed intimidating. Irene was now well into her pregnancy, we had recently bought a house, we had two somewhat elderly cars to sell, we had a dog to find a home for and we had no money.

You don't generally have the option of turning down appointments in the Royal Navy, and anyway I wanted to seize this chance of a lifetime so within a few weeks I found myself in Australia House in the Strand being briefed on what awaited me. There were quite a few surprises. Firstly, the helpful and friendly Aussie Commander put me at my ease and said that my appointment would be deferred until after the birth of our child and that since Loan Service meant that technically I would leave the Royal Navy and join the Royal Australian Navy for the duration of the appointment my travel arrangements would be made for me by the RAN. The most interesting aspect of this was that we would be flown first class from London to Sydney and assisted with arrival and accommodation arrangements. The Australians really looked after their people.

As it turned out we had no problem in selling the house, which had the added advantage of giving us a little bit of working capital. The cars took longer to sell but they went eventually, assisted by an attractive price. This left us with the problem of Bobby, our faithful, and now middle aged in doggy years, Border Collie. While I had been away he had been Irene's constant companion and the collective guilt at the knowledge that we would part company for at least two years was heavy to bear. We decided that we could not simply give him away so we advertised for someone to provide him with a home while we would continue to meet all the expenses of food, vet's bills and so forth.

After some false starts we settled on an elderly retired couple who lived in the village of Southwell on Portland. They seemed ideal to our purposes but we had rather ignored the fact that the move from within a young active family to live with a long retired couple who had no transport of their own and who rarely moved off the Isle of Portland would possibly be a very traumatic experience for an active and athletic dog. It was a well intentioned decision but in all the circumstances I believe it was a mistake. We did get Bobby back when we returned and he greeted us ecstatically but he was a different dog with a different character. He had been well looked after but he seemed to have aged almost to match the age of his temporary owners and he was much more nervous and somewhat neurotic. But that story is for another day.

Chapter 7
Heading for Down Under

Our first born was not due until March 1971 and so the navy had to find something to do with me until we were able to fly to Australia. The problem was solved by sending me to the Royal Naval College at Greenwich for the three month 'Lieutenant's Course'. This was in effect a junior staff course, providing an academic break for young officers to discover the world about them. It was sometimes unkindly called the 'idiots reading and writing course' but it was well run, focussed our attention on the world outside the navy and generally broadened the outlook of the young officers. I took every opportunity presented. I learned the mysteries of formal Service writing and how to set out my case in a convincing manner. Presentation skills were covered and we were also sent on visits to interesting places such as the Old Bailey, the House of Commons, the House of Lords, national newspapers and various others.

Leaders of industry, the armed forces, the trades unions and politicians came to speak to us, some more successfully than others. A junior defence minister, a very uninspiring left wing hack lost his temper and stormed off the stage and Ray Buckton, leader of the train drivers union also became very stroppy and accused his hosts – us – of being feather bedded wealthy playboys. This was a bit rich bearing in mind that his train driving members had salaries about three times the level of a young naval officer. I also learnt the rudiments of oil painting and managed to give up smoking!

After Greenwich, Irene still had a few months to go so I was sent back to 737 squadron, flying the now obsolescent

Wessex I which was being replaced by the technologically sophisticated Wessex III. One of my pupils at this time was Ian Stanley, one of the last pilots to complete his training on the Wessex I. Ian was later to distinguish himself with his brilliant and courageous rescue of the stranded Royal Marines and crashed Commando Wessex crews from the glacier on South Georgia. It was to be the first success in the Falklands War and Ian richly deserved his DSC.

****

At last the time for our departure drew near. Our daughter, Rebecca, was born, our cars and house were sold and our faithful dog was re-homed. The removal van turned up to take most of our furniture into store and prepare the remainder of our possessions for the long sea journey to Australia. We then locked up the house to spend the last few days before departure with my parents. The Australians also provided us with a generous allowance of baggage to be sent by air in advance and an even more generous allowance to go by sea. With a new baby to care for, and the need to take my bulky flying kit, we had to be very careful indeed in deciding what would travel with us, what would go in advance by air and what would spend three months travelling by sea.

One small incident during our preparations for departure bears relating. Our new daughter was just one week old and was generally quiet and peaceful, spending a lot of time in her carrycot which was all that was left for baby transport. Irene was not very well and recovering slowly from the birth so I was left supervising the transfer of our possessions into the removal van. Inevitably all the doors of the house were open to allow the men to come and go. Suddenly there was a cry of motherly distress. Where was the baby? The removal process stopped and a frantic search commenced throughout the house. There was no baby. The stress level was climbing and we were thinking of calling the police when there was an exclamation from inside the removal van. Baby and carry cot had been packed away with the other boxes in the middle of the van. The baby was recovered, the van packing was completed and we all celebrated with a cup of tea. Later that day we left to begin our big adventure.

We drove the remaining car to Fareham where it was to pass to its new owner and spent three days with my parents after which they drove us to Heathrow.

****

In Nowra, Gordon Edgecombe, who had recently returned from a three month deployment to what the Australians describe as 'the Near North' in *HMAS Melbourne*, Australia's only remaining aircraft carrier, was holding in his hand a small slip of thin blue paper. He had just received confirmation of his appointment on exchange duty to the Fleet Air Arm of the Royal Navy. This was a wonderful opportunity but it also raised a lot of family problems for him, each of which could be difficult to resolve. Among these were what he was going to do about his home in Nowra (should he sell it or let it?) how the children would adjust to being taken away from their schools and their friends and not least, what was to become of Spoofy?

As soon as she heard the news, Sip started work on the problem of Spoofy, which she thought might be most difficult and take longest to resolve. He couldn't go back to his previous owner. She was no longer there.

Sip made a list of all their friends in and around Nowra who she thought she might be able to persuade to help. The list started as quite a long one but as the responses and excuses came in it shortened quickly. The 'turn off' point often came when potential boarders were told of Spoofy's medical problems. In vain Sip explained that she would meet the vet's bills, that there was no risk from Spoofy's conditions and that they were relatively easy to deal with. Friends were sympathetic but reluctant. The list became five possibles, then two, then one.

The last hope was a childless couple who lived in North Nowra near the golf course and indeed, the two families had first become acquainted through the game and the social life surrounding golf – which in a remote country town was considerable.

Arrangements were made for Spoofy to meet his new foster-owners. This went well and each side seemed relaxed and easy. It was agreed that the final transfer to the North Nowra home should take place a fortnight before the Edgecombe family departed to start their long journey to Britain.

Chapter 8
Australia

We boarded the BOAC 707 and were seated in the front row of the first class section with our daughter Rebecca, still sleeping peacefully in her carrycot in the space in front of us. The rest of the ample space was occupied by a Philips tape recorder and an Elna electric sewing machine. These had been purchased free of purchase tax and duty as we passed through the airport and had to be exported as part of our personal luggage in order to obtain the tax concession. We also each carried an umbrella, a topcoat, an in-flight bag as well as, between us, a 'baby box' packed with essentials for the journey. As the aircraft taxied out the steward asked if we would like anything to drink and, not wishing to waste the opportunity, I was soon holding a generous Bell's whisky in my hand – with just a touch of water. With over 1500 hours of flying under my belt I mused that this was the first time I had enjoyed a dram of whisky during take-off.

The flight was very comfortable but long and tiring. Fortunately our new daughter slept through most of it, producing a relieved congratulatory comment from an initially worried looking businessman occupying the row opposite. His parting shot on leaving the aircraft at Singapore was "Madam, you have a wonderful baby." The relief in not being exposed to several hours of close quarters baby noise showed in his face.

In fact it seemed to take about 36 hours to reach Sydney, with more stops than a rural bus service, including a couple of hours in Singapore while the aircraft was serviced and refuelled. All of the passengers got off and wandered around the terminal during which we made the mistake of buying a few more attractively priced knick-knacks to help us set up our new home. The problem with this was that, when we came finally to leave the aircraft in Sydney, it took the entire cabin crew to remove us, our baby and the host of items we seemed to have acquired along the way.

On arrival at our destination these items were all carefully placed in front of the immigration and customs officers' desk. They were perplexed but resorted to the traditional first question posed to everyone entering Australia.

"Have you got any food products in there?"

"We certainly have," I replied, "baby food, loads of it."

"You can't bring food into Australia." The response was tight lipped, grim faced, unhelpful.

"Well you better find it," I said, indicating the huge pile of boxes, clothes and the baby all of which was now preventing access to the desk. The disembarking crowd of passengers was getting bigger and clearly growing impatient. A hasty whispered discussion took place between the customs officers, and our antagonist looked up, jerked his head in the direction of the exit and said, none too kindly, "Yeah, O.K. Get that stuff outa here."

Welcome to Australia, I thought, as we piled everything onto two trolleys and headed for the fresh air.

As we passed through into the outer concourse I spotted an Australian Leading Seaman – or 'Leading Sailor' as I was to learn they were called. He was scanning the emerging crowds and holding a card with our name on it. He saw and intercepted us – and with a big cheery grin, said, "G'day sir, welcome to Oz!" Things were looking up.

Our one man welcoming party proved remarkably efficient. He had a large grey painted RAN utility vehicle parked outside rather challengingly occupying a couple of parking spaces marked 'Authorised vehicles only'. We placed our cabin luggage in the open back of the 'Ute' under the watchful eye of the Leading Sailor, who said his name was 'Ray' and furrowed our way back into the depths of the Kingsford Smith arrival hall to collect the rest of our worldly goods which had travelled in the aircraft hold. Surprisingly this didn't take long and we were soon loading it into the back of the Ute.

I explained that we should have some more baggage which had been sent by air in advance and it should be collectable from the freight terminal. Ray was sceptical since it was a Sunday. Nevertheless he disappeared to find a telephone while we waited and cooked in the rising temperature beside the Ute. Ray was back quite quickly with his engaging grin fixed in place. "Bonzer!" he exclaimed, "No worries," which I took to mean good news. I was right. Ray had located the advance baggage and determined that it could be collected up to four p.m. We had a short conference and decided that since it was still only late morning, we would drive Irene and baby Rebecca into the city where we had been booked into the Travelodge Hotel and then come back and collect the remaining luggage.

We drove into the city, located the towering multi-storey Travelodge, deposited Irene, the baby and the baby box and headed back out to the airport, round to the freight terminal on the far side, picked up the luggage consisting of a huge aircrew holdall, an officer's 'tin trunk' and a set of folding pram wheels which when attached to the carrycot would provide efficient baby transport. The whole exercise was liberally scattered with "No worries", "she'll be right", "bonzer" and "g'day, how are you?" I was learning a whole new vocabulary.

We completed the round trip in just under two hours with very easy traffic flow, helped by it being a Sunday and one week after Easter. Ray helped me into the hotel foyer with the luggage and with a cheery wave strode off to the vehicle and the remainder of his weekend.

As I turned around from the luggage I was shocked to see Irene still sitting in the small entrance hall desperately trying to calm an increasingly fretful baby. The receptionist or manager or whatever he was had refused to allow her access to the room despite the fact that a confirmed booking had been made and paid for by the Australian Navy, she had identified herself with her passport and had practically begged to be allowed into the room to feed the baby.

I picked up the gist of this while we were being led into the lift by a lazy obsequious porter who, when we reached our room, had the cheek to hold out his hand for a tip. Tips were not generally given in Australia then, and the offering of one could be taken as an insult. In this case I just stared at the outstretched open palm until it was removed. We were both exhausted from the flight and the inevitable lack of sleep, and our priority was to feed and change our distressed baby, so we let it pass but we resolved to get out of that apology for a hotel as soon as we could. On reflection I should have stormed down to the reception desk, demanded the manager and raised hell. I didn't. I was too tired.

However since that day I have never entered another Travelodge Hotel nor booked anyone else into one. After more than thirty years of travelling the world and sixteen years as a Chief Executive in the hospitality industry I still believe it was the most disgraceful performance that I have ever encountered in any hotel or guest house anywhere in the world.

All three of us slept late the next morning. Ray had explained that guest house accommodation had been arranged for us in the little town of Nowra, our final destination, and we had been provided with train tickets for the hundred mile rail journey from Sydney. We hadn't unpacked much so it did not take long to assemble our goods and chattels, organize a taxi, avoid a demand to pay the bill – which had already been paid – and shake the dust of that horrible hotel off as we headed for the railway station.

Every Australian taxi driver chats away happily and in forthright terms on practically any subject under the sun so our journey through the Monday morning vibrant buzz of Sydney passed quickly and easily and as the driver helped to unload our impressive pile of luggage we seemed to have become old friends. A handshake all round, a cheery wave then off to the rather ancient train which clanked its way out through the southern suburbs to the spectacular coastal and grazing land scenery of New South Wales. The journey only took about two hours and in that time we had not only been shaken and bounced unmercifully by the apparently springless carriage running on a track made of disused scrap iron and cast off agricultural machinery but we had been given our first serious view of rural Australia. We both agreed that it was wonderful and although the British viewed Australia as an extension of Old England, it was unlike anything we had seen at home. The sky was clearer, the colours brighter, the bird and animal life were different, even the sounds were different – and the whole thing was exciting.

One side effect of the journey was that the jolting and bouncing of the carriage had the remarkable effect of sending our little daughter into a deep and contented sleep. For the rest of our stay in Australia we found that the sure way to get Rebecca off to sleep, despite teething, fractiousness and other childish concerns, was to play 'Sydney Trains'. We would take her in her pram or in the car over the roughest, most volatile route we could find. It never failed.

Chapter 9
Nowra

We were booked to stay in 'The White House', a large rambling two storey white painted wooden building with a corrugated iron roof. It was run by a kindly but 'no nonsense' landlady who had learned her trade somewhere in Yorkshire. The rules were detailed, comprehensive and strict but I can't now remember any of them so we must have behaved ourselves.

We were collected from the station by Lieutenant Chris Johnson and his wife Joan in their enormous Holden station wagon into which our trappings seemed to disappear with relative ease. Chris was another Royal Naval officer on exchange duty with the Royal Australian Navy. Exchange duty being technically different from my loan service in that I was removed from the Royal Navy and enrolled in the Royal Australian Navy whereas exchange officers would be exchanged one for one with an officer of the other country but would retain their membership of their parent service. Other differences were that I would be paid by the Australian Navy in dollars and I would pay Australian taxes – and be required to vote (compulsorily) in Australian elections. My wife and I had become temporary Australian citizens.

Nowra was a typical country town. Wide streets were bordered by neat pavements shaded by a variety of decorative trees including many examples of the glorious blue flowering Jacaranda. The town centre was quite compact with a large supermarket and a range of other modern shops and businesses meeting most of the needs of the populace. Anything that Nowra couldn't supply would need to be obtained from the big coastal steel manufacturing town of Wollongong, about thirty miles to the north. The main part of the town was bordered by the Shoalhaven River with a somewhat ancient bridge carrying the Princes Highway across to the small but expanding suburbs of North Nowra, Bomaderry and the immaculate green acres of the Golf Club.

The town was hemmed in on most sides by tall eucalyptus trees and the scrub undergrowth of the eastern coastal forests, having literally been carved out of the bush. To the north of the town the bush had been extensively cleared to produce rich rolling pasture land. The main Princes Highway passed through the centre of the town with an arrow-straight road branching off inland for about five miles through the bush to the Royal Australian Naval Air Station, HMAS Albatross. This name followed the pattern established in Britain whereby every naval air station was named after a particular seabird. Further on from the air station various other roads led inland to isolated farms, and, in one case, to the old gold mining centre of Yalwal – now just a largish lake in a clearing surrounded by the abandoned detritus of gold mining. Almost all of the secondary roads at this time were 'dirt roads'. They were just scraped out of the bush with rough dirt surfaces routinely maintained in a fairly flat condition by big machines called 'road graders'. Despite this, even with only limited traffic these roads soon formed a series of transverse corrugations so driving along them was rather like trying to drive over corrugated iron.

The houses in the town were mostly of the old colonial type, single storey with walls made of wood and corrugated iron roofs. They were kept cool by shaded verandas extending around them on all sides and each building was elevated above the ground by a series of pillars on which it stood. This allowed air to circulate under the building and gave some protection from flash floods. This also, it seemed to me, provided a cool and dark hiding place for all sorts of creatures unfriendly to the occupants. A few miles away to the east lay the coastline and the fabulous scenery of beaches such as Callala and Culburra, contrasting with the charm of the tiny settlements of Huskisson, Vincentia and other similar hamlets.

The bush was everywhere. And of course so were the animals, birds and insects. It was common to encounter kangaroos and wallabies leaping into the road, often sadly evidenced by the bloody carnage left at the roadside. Wild pigs, snakes and all sorts of other animals awaited the unwary traveller. The telegraph lines following the highway looked like a network of black lace where spiders of various sizes and descriptions had woven their webs. With all of the hazards underfoot we were constantly amazed to see children running around barefoot on lawns and parkland. Later on we became used to it and even wandered around in flip-flops ourselves.

Once we had settled into our temporary home in the White House we needed to get on with finding a home of our own to rent for the next two years, open a bank account, register for taxation and buy a car. I would not be required to report for duty for about a week so we were able to tackle our task with alacrity.

We found a house to suit our needs quite quickly and almost immediately managed to buy a nice white, nearly new Holden station wagon. The car was essential to move all the increasingly accumulated brick-a-brac from the White House to our new home. Within a few days we had viewed the single storey house in Berry Street. It was a typical thirty or forty-year-old Australian house, set back from the road and surrounded by lawns on all sides. A wide gravel drive led down to a doorless garage and the whole building was raised about three feet above the ground on a series of concrete stands. It had two generous bedrooms at the front, a large sitting room, dining room and bathroom in the middle and a spacious kitchen leading to a breakfast room and utility rooms at the back. There was a colonial style veranda at the front and side and an open sided, covered raised wooden patio off the kitchen at the back with steps leading down to the garden. It was a nice house.

The necessary arrangements didn't take long to make. A two year rental agreement was drawn up by the local estate agent and we set about moving from the White House guest house which, with all the trappings we were gathering about us, was beginning to feel a little claustrophobic for us. Nowra was a small country town in those days and the guest house on Junction Street was only about ten minutes' stroll through arches of jacaranda to the middle of Berry Street and so the move was pretty straightforward. The house was well furnished and with the things we had brought out with us and what we had acquired on the way, we were comfortable enough to await the arrival of the rest of our possessions by sea. We bought ourselves a television and an oil heater because the house could become surprisingly cold in the evenings. The cupboards and wardrobes seemed to be still full of the dresses and coats of our landlady who, we were informed, was a Sydney taxi driver. The lady was married to a Petty Officer at the air station who, from our only brief meeting turned out to be a handsome and engaging young man. This, together with the modern and youthful array of clothing left behind suggested a rather glamorous young couple. The clothing was collected and removed when we were introduced to the son of our landlady who kindly explained some of the foibles of the house. This included a recommendation to get the 'flick' man in to spray the outside of the house for spiders. We were advised that it was not necessary to spray inside so we should save the money.

Quite a long discussion took place with our landlady's son, Barry, and his friend in our kitchen one evening, about the number and lethality of poisonous snakes and spiders populating that part of New South Wales – and in particular, we were led to believe, our garden! It is fair to say that we were becoming increasingly alarmed at the lurid descriptions of spiders – bird eating, mice eating and so on, when the conversation died away and my attention was caught by Irene, an arachnophobic, who was staring fixedly and with a look of horror towards the kitchen cupboards. I followed her gaze and saw that the object of her attention was several very long spider's legs waving out from the gap between the cupboard and the wall. Our guests, who had been enjoying an Australian pastime of putting the frighteners on newly arrived 'Pommies', were suddenly silenced. The legs continued to wave. We continued to stare fixedly and eventually Barry advanced on the waving appendages and poked a thick piece of straw into the gap. A huge spider, measuring about five inches across the legs fell on to the worktop and thence to the floor. Irene fled. The rest of us stood back as the spider started to move, none too fast, across the floor. This seemed a desperate situation and called for desperate measures. I rushed forward and jumped on the spider with both feet. It was no more, and on measuring the remains we noted that they could just barely be covered with a tea saucer.

Sadly, I was to learn subsequently that this impressively large beast was a Huntsman Spider. These do not spin webs but live within houses and perform the useful task of rushing out of their bolt holes and catching flies. They – and the one I had recently killed – are regarded as pets and my victim had probably lived in the house for years performing his important duty and not harming anyone. I felt a real heel.

The advice to 'Flick' spray only the outside of the house proved spectacularly wrong. Within a few days of the completion of the treatment and while we were still wondering how the 'Flick' man could bring himself to crawl about underneath the house, he was hurriedly summoned back again. Every species of six and eight legged creature imaginable had apparently sought refuge from the external treatment of the house by heading inside.

The only real employment in the town was generated by the air station, the surrounding farming districts and the fact that Nowra formed the centre of an attractive tourist area. The town was divided by the Shoalhaven River and the outlying villages of Huskisson, Vincentia and Ulladulla sat facing the beautiful Callala Beach on the edge of Jervis Bay. It was the sort of place where almost everyone had a nodding acquaintance with almost everyone else. This meant that on walking about through the town one would encounter a series of apparently deeply sincere greetings: "Hi, how are *you?*", with a heavy emphasis on the "*you*". Not being used to such effusive greetings and trained in the polite nod of English reserve, we would assume that this must be someone we had met or been introduced to, or at least someone who knew who we were and who was sincerely enquiring after our welfare, so we would begin to respond politely by answering the question and telling them how we were, only to find that the enquirer/greeter had passed on their way and we were explaining our wellbeing to thin air.

After a short while we discovered that the correct response was merely to repeat the greeting word for word and not bother to pause for a response.

This was the beginning of the process of learning to live with, fit in and understand Australians and Australia. Our initial impression of it being a vibrant, colourful and very different environment to that which we had been used to at home was further enhanced and underlined as we settled in to our new home in Nowra. The bright fresh April mornings, although heralding the onset of winter to the locals, were like early English summer days to us. We took to having our breakfast on the balcony at the back of the house, which made our neighbours think we were slightly unhinged. Days were pleasantly warm and the jacaranda was still in bloom. So we took every opportunity to go out and about during the few days remaining before I was to report for duty. Even the noises surrounding us were new to our ears. We had an embarrassing incident one evening shortly after we had moved in, when we arrived back to the house about sunset. As we entered the garden we could hear a persistent high-pitched note which I soon became convinced meant that we had some electrical problem. We stayed outside and called the estate agent, who appeared, surprisingly, in only a few minutes. He got out of his car, looked at our concerned faces, cocked an ear, and then exploded into gales of laughter. We had experienced cicadas in full chorus for the first time. Clearly our garden was well stocked with them.

We had three sets of immediate neighbours: a young Turkish couple, an elderly man who lived alone in the house backing onto the bottom of our garden, and Mr Booth. Mr Booth typified the tough raw-boned image of the early outback Australians. He was a small wiry man with a brown weather beaten face, usually framed by an ancient slouch hat. He was ninety-six years of age, totally self sufficient and frequently described our septuagenarian neighbour at the bottom of the garden as 'the lad'. Mr Booth, it was said, had journeyed in his ox-wagon over the hills from the agricultural centre of Bowral about the turn of the century. He had set out his claim in the newly established settlement that was to become Nowra, put up his camp, gone into the bush to cut timber, and built his house. He also had a magnificent wooden barn stocked with precisely arranged logs and kindling to provide fuel for cooking and heating. He lived with two spinster daughters who kept house for him and he spent his time either tending his extensive garden full of exotic fruit trees and shrubs or driving his elderly truck out into the bush to gather wood which he then sawed and chopped with military precision. He also gathered wood for his son who lived elsewhere in Nowra and who, he told us, had lost an arm. As various fruits came into season he took to providing us with sacks of oranges and lemons as well as bags of nuts with the hardest shells I have ever encountered.

One Saturday morning we were woken early by the sound of Mr Booth showing 'the lad' at the bottom of our garden how to bang in fence posts! The wiry little man was swinging a huge sledgehammer nearly as big as himself while keeping up a running commentary on the technique of fencing, fruit growing and various other activities in which he thought his seventy-something pupil might be deficient. Mr Booth in reality had a character and personality larger than life.

Chapter 10
The Squadron

All too soon our freewheeling lifestyle came to an end and I had to report for duty at the air station. On Monday morning I joined the line of cars heading up the dead straight road through the bush towards the air station and five miles later was easing through the main gate following the directions I had been given for the squadron dispersal. As I cleared the accommodation area I spotted the distinctive blue and white painted Wessex helicopters of the RAN and so easily followed the perimeter road round to join the collection of cars parked outside the row of low level huts that constituted the base for both the front line and training squadrons.

The anti-submarine helicopter force of the Royal Australian Navy at that time consisted of No 817 Squadron, a 'front line' unit destined to go to sea as part of *HMAS Melbourne's* Air Group, and No 725 Squadron, whose function was to provide training and conversion courses as well as support for offshore exercises taking place nearby. Each squadron was equipped with eight Mk 31B Westland Wessex helicopters. These aircraft were built using the same airframe and engine as the Royal Navy's Wessex's but with a hotch-potch of American, British and home grown operational and avionic equipment. This caused a lot of serviceability headaches, one of the worst being that the British dipping sonar had been removed and replaced with an American sonar set which had the advantage of being able to lower a four hundred and fifty foot long cable into the sea beneath the aircraft, enabling the transmitting sonar body to reach much deeper below the surface. One of the fundamental requirements of every dipping sonar system is a means of cutting the cable in an emergency, so the aircraft can escape. This is invariably done by fitting a cartridge fired steel bolt which can be activated to cut the cable. Unfortunately the only way this sonar could be fitted into the aircraft meant that the trajectory of the bolt was such that after passing through and cutting the sonar cable, the bolt would then pass through the observer's head. Since observer's heads were considered valuable the Australian Navy decided not to fit the cable cutters at all. This meant that if, or more probably, when a problem arose whereby the aircraft could not maintain an accurate hover over the sonar cable at night or in poor visibility, the only recourse was to fly the helicopter vertically up through at least 450 feet, with the sonar swinging like a conker on the end of a very long string.

The two sets of squadron offices were located in four old single storey huts placed side by side, with a short walk to the single large hangar. I was carefully told to avoid the redback spiders who lived above the doors into the main admin hut before being led into the big office which housed the Senior Pilot and the Senior Observer. Next door to this was the C.O.'s office and then a crew room, locker room and various briefing rooms. I learned that the two squadron bosses were known respectively and irreverently as 'Bullfrog' and 'Slug'. As soon as I was introduced to the first one I realised why he had acquired this particular handle. The Senior Observer, who I had flown with while he was on exchange in Britain, was older than most of the aircrew, more worldly wise, easy going and unflappable. The Senior Pilot who was also the squadron's Qualified Flying Instructor was of a different cut entirely.

Most of the men I was to fly with in 725 Squadron were typical of the friendly, laid back, unflustered style redolent of most Australians of that period but I sensed that Jack, the Senior Pilot, was different. Small, wiry, taciturn and quietly spoken he seemed to be particularly reserved towards me. It would be some time before I was to find out why.

My first few days in the squadron were taken up with the usual round of introductions, visits to the Flying Clothing Store, the Safety Equipment Centre, the Pay Office, the Wardroom and all sorts of other places, in each of which a form was ticked off to prove that I had been there and had not rebelled against the inevitably boring round. One important thing I did discover was that everyone was to go on seasonal leave in a few weeks, including me. This should just give me a chance to complete a conversion onto the Wessex 31B before going on leave, as someone put it, to forget everything I had just learnt.

"The Shoalhaven River."

"The House – our home in Nowra"

"Manning up with a dinghy backpack."

"A Wessex Mk 31B."
Photograph by Brian Johnstone

Chapter 11
A New Friend

The Sunday before the station went on leave was a beautiful clear warm autumn day. We had discovered the local church and were making our way back down Berry Street, underneath the vivid blue flowering jacarandas, with an occasional contrasting scarlet bougainvillea wound like a Christmas decoration up through the branches, while we considered what to do with the rest of the day. The stresses associated with moving half way round the world while coping with the life changing process of learning to look after a new baby had taken quite a lot out of both of us, but particularly Irene who had given birth only seven days before travelling twelve thousand miles. We were happy to take the unexpected opportunity to relax and 'nest-build'. Because it was such a lovely day we didn't want to stay inside but we were also concerned about the risks of wandering about in our garden which we were convinced would be teeming with hidden snakes and hordes of deadly funnel-web spiders.

Although New South Wales boasted no less than forty different species of poisonous snakes, it was in fact relatively rare for snakes to be found in domestic gardens within towns and when deaths from snake bite were reported most of these occurred with bush walkers or, more commonly snakes found in or under cars. Most snake bites were readily treatable and so our fears in this respect were somewhat overstated. This was not the case however with the funnel-web spider. This nasty little beast lived in holes in the ground where they constructed an elaborate web in the shape of a funnel, leading down towards the hole. The spider sat in the hole and waited until the web was disturbed by the vibration of passing potential prey.

The spider would then emerge and, very likely, would jump in the direction of the nearest moving object. The funnel-web could spring to a height of nearly three feet and as soon as it landed it would bite. It carried a very virulent nerve poison. There was no known antidote at that time and the only treatment was to attempt to deal with the symptoms as they appeared. Following a funnel-web bite, death was a more common outcome than survival. Our fears were well founded and in the early days at least, we treated our slightly untamed garden with considerable wariness.

We wanted to get out and enjoy the open air and we had been told of several attractive locations in and around Nowra. One of these was the estuary banks of the Shoalhaven River which presented a very attractive option, with grey sandy beaches shaded by groves of the ubiquitous gum trees and people frolicking by the edge of the fresh flowing stream.

There was a problem with this. A matter of days before we had left England two small items were reported in the British newspapers. Both concerned Nowra. In the first case it was reported that a man wading in the shallows of a beach near Nowra had suddenly run screaming from the sea and dropped down dead. This turned out to be something of an overstatement. True a man bathing in the shallows of a nearby beach had died. It was thought he may have been bitten by either a blue ringed octopus – rarely found this far down the coast – or stung by the long tentacles of a 'sea wasp' jellyfish, but it turned out that he had actually died of a heart attack. The second report was slightly more accurate. This declared that a woman had been walking under some trees near the river when a funnel-web spider had fallen from a tree, down the front of her dress and bitten her. She died of the bite. It was true that there was a poor unfortunate woman who had died of a funnel-web bite, but funnel-webs do not live in trees and what had really happened was that the young lady had been swimming in the river and had left her clothes bundled up on the ground. A funnel-web had found its way into her clothes and bitten her as she was dressing.

The notion that funnel-webs might be found in trees caused Irene to insist on walking in the road rather than the tree lined pavements, carefully circumnavigating anything that looked remotely like a tree for the first few months after our arrival. We then spotted that all of the telegraph lines were festooned with millions of spiders' webs making them look like long sheets of black lace strung between the poles. We began to add telegraph poles, telegraph wires and overhanging buildings to our list of places to avoid. I could see that soon the only space deemed safe from falling spiders would be the middle of the road – where we were at greater risk of being run down by a passing truck. The fact that the pavements were not strewn with agonised citizens expiring from spider bites eventually encouraged Irene to take a more relaxed view of the risk from airborne spiders. She still kept a parasol over Rebecca's pushchair though.

Another nice place to spend a Sunday afternoon was the park. Nowra had a well tended and extensive park with acres of short grass and cool corners shaded by groups of gum and other trees. That afternoon we decided to leave the river bank for another day and we opted for the park.

Before setting off we attached the carrycot to its wheels which turned it into a classic English pram. We had strolled around the edge of the park in a light cooling afternoon breeze for about an hour when our attention was drawn towards a large black dog trotting along on a parallel course with ours and apparently maintaining a distance of fifty yards or so from us. Seeing a dog wandering around on its own was not unusual in Australia but for some reason this one seemed interested in us. Aimlessly we reversed course. So did the dog. We did it again. So did the dog. We continued on our way around the park and gradually our canine companion drew closer until he was behaving like the most perfect carriage trained pet, keeping station alongside the pram and looking as though he was part of our little group. We were concerned lest an anxious owner should turn up and assume we were trying to entice his dog away.

We continued our afternoon around the many paths criss-crossing the park and the dog stayed dutifully with us. Irene picked up a stick and threw it. The dog trotted off at a relatively unhurried gait and returned with the stick which was placed carefully at Irene's feet. The baby slept on under a pram mounted sunshade. Irene threw the stick again with the same result. We continued our walk assuming that the dog would drift away but he stayed dutifully by our sides, out through the park entrance, along the pavement, ignoring pedestrians and the occasional passing car. We reached the junction with Berry Street and stopped before crossing the road. The dog sat beside us and then maintained his precise station as we crossed the road. Off we went down Berry Street, into our open driveway and around to the back of the house still accompanied by the black dog, which we had now identified as a sturdy black Labrador with a trace of cross indicated by a white blaze on his chest.

By this stage we were really concerned about being accused of 'dog-napping'. We climbed the wooden steps up to the rear balcony followed by the dog. We opened the back screen door and he sat on the balcony looking expectantly inside. After a hurried conference we decided that we should not let him into the house but that it would be civilised to put a bowl of water out for him. In the event a bowl of water was placed on the balcony floor accompanied by a bowl containing a few biscuits – human type, not dog biscuits.

We thought no more about the strange incident of the 'dog in the park' and after a few days into the leave period we decided we might just have enough money, provided we were careful, to be able to travel north to try to see some more of Australia and give Irene the chance to complete her recovery.

As it turned out we had a wonderful carefree holiday. We loaded up the car taking care to add a few extras such as a tent (just in case), several collapsible gallon water containers, a hessian water bag to hang from the front bumper and be cooled by air flow causing a slow evaporation, and a case of 24 cans of beer stowed under the floor by the spare wheel.

We drove north through the gentle pastoral lands up to Kiama, stopping to watch the famous blow hole, past the steel town of Wollongong, up through the southern suburbs of Sydney, then known in part as 'Little Greece', on across the famous bridge and out into the lush sub-tropical region of Northern New South Wales. We intended to reach Queensland which would be a one way journey of at least 700 miles, achieving about 200 miles per day and generally stopping in small motels of which there were hundreds, or in caravan parks where we could book an overnight stay in a static caravan for only about three dollars. We passed through the long coastal strip of Surfer's Paradise with its tinselly image and finally found, by accident, the Golden Moon motel in the little hamlet of Currumbin, an oasis sandwiched between the highly commercialised Surfer's Paradise to the south and its Queensland equivalent to the north. We stayed in this beachside haven of peace and tranquillity for a week before returning south again.

The Golden Moon was set against an unfettered yellow sandy beach stretching as far as the eye could see. It was a single storey building formed around three sides of a square with the fifteen or so rooms opening out to a central grass area with a swimming pool and comprehensive barbecue arrangement. On the end of the complex was a communal kitchen with a small fridge and storage cupboard for each guest room, so the residents could buy their food locally and cook it and eat it either in the kitchen or around the barbecue.

Situated across the road from the motel was a bird sanctuary. This had originally been a private house with a large garden where for years the owner had been plagued by visiting lorikeets attacking the flowers he was trying to nurture. Eventually he decided to give up the losing struggle with the garden and try to use the visiting birds to his advantage. He put out trays of bread and honey to attract the birds and when he had sufficient of them arriving he opened the gardens to paying visitors to see the display. His scheme was an enormous success. The word spread rapidly through the bird community and soon, literally thousands of the colourful and noisy lorikeets were flying in twice daily to the delight of the paying customers. The birds often came from thirty or more miles away for their twice daily feast and they became very tame. They would perch on arms, hands, heads or anywhere else in order to get at the honey mixture. For us, on the final stage of the bird's flight path, we were treated to the same daily, often startling display as the birds paused in the motel garden to gather their strength before putting on the big show.

Sadly, the Golden Moon is no more. It remains, however, fixed in our memories as one of the most enjoyable holidays we have ever had. It was luxury, Australian style, with each day starting with the delivery of breakfast – superb grilled steaks, chops, bacon, eggs and other delights – followed by a leisurely swim, then the lunchtime bird display, before an afternoon of sightseeing, swimming or just lazing. It was a wonderful way to re-energise and prepare to face the world. It seemed, all too soon that we had to pack up and return home. We did come back again though.

****

We arrived back in Nowra in the middle of a warm afternoon, following a long and dusty drive from our last overnight stop at Coffs Harbour, some way to the north of Sydney. We turned into the gateless driveway and crunched slowly down past the side of the house. As we came to a stop in front of the garage, I looked out to my right and there, sitting contentedly on our balcony, was a large black Labrador, staring down at us with a gently swishing tale. "Welcome home" was plain on the grinning, tongue lolling doggy face.

Chapter 12
A Lodger

All too soon the holiday came to an end and our freewheeling lifestyle reverted to the more disciplined structure of returning to work each day.

Although I had yet to complete the conversion course to the Wessex 31B, I was surprised on the last Sunday afternoon of the leave period by a knock on our front door. This in itself was unusual because most visitors came to the back.

I opened the door to be confronted with the Squadron Boss. "Bullfrog" peered up at me, and in something of a rush declared that there had been a general recall of helicopter aircrew because of an airliner with an in-flight emergency over Sydney. I took in most of what was being said to me but I could not help being somewhat distracted by the appearance of Bullfrog. This was the first time I had ever seen him in a suit of flying overalls and what drew most of my attention was the fact that the overalls were clearly brand new and had just been taken out of the box.

We rushed off to the station in Bullfrog's car and arrived as a couple of aircraft were being wheeled out of the hangar and 'prepped' for flight. I headed off to the locker room, climbed into my flying overalls, grabbed my 'bone dome' and 'Mae West' lifejacket and headed for the hangar. The first aircraft was ready, rotor blades spread and locked with a starter trolley alongside. At the boss's indication I climbed up to the right hand, First Pilot's seat while Bullfrog levered his bulky frame into the left hand seat. He said we would be briefed on the way so I ran through the checks, started up, engaged rotors on the ground crew clearance signal and called the Tower for take-off. The Tower responded immediately, I taxied forward and lifted into a low hover. Bullfrog sat well back in his seat and kept his hands and feet clear of the controls. I thought he might concentrate on the incoming radio instructions but here again he left this to me, merely responding to questions relayed by me and nodding approval to necessary actions as we climbed to fifteen hundred feet and headed north. The radio confirmed that we were being followed at some distance by two other squadron aircraft.

Eventually we were briefed by Kingsford Smith Air Traffic Control that an airliner was circling Sydney with a suspicious package onboard and a semi-coherent passenger who had claimed that the package was a bomb which would be triggered by the increase in atmospheric pressure experienced as the aircraft descended. As I listened the plot seemed vaguely familiar, either from a film or a book I had read. I ventured to ask Bullfrog what we were supposed to do. "Pick up the bodies," he said. The sun was sinking over the Blue Mountains to the west of Sydney as he said this so I had considerable doubts as to our ability to do anything, particularly with a co-pilot who seemed even less familiar with the aircraft than I was.

As we flew north over the southern suburbs of the great city, the radio burst into life to announce that the emergency was over. The airliner had landed and was taxiing in. The relief in the controller's voice was palpable. Almost immediately the air was full of chatter of all kinds. Previously diverted aircraft wished to return, emergency services were standing down and the 725 squadron helicopters were aborting the operation. Inside our aircraft the atmosphere became lighter. Bullfrog visibly relaxed and started chatting to me about all sorts of things other than the operation of the aircraft. We turned through 180 degrees and headed south, changing to the quieter

Nowra Area Frequency and descended gradually until the airfield came in sight. We chopped across to the Tower Frequency, ran straight in to land and then hover taxied across to the squadron hard standing. I shut down the engine, stopped the rotors and switched off.

"Well done," said Bullfrog as he came around the nose of the aircraft. "You were a great help!" Since he appeared to have contributed nothing at all to the flight, this compliment left me a little underwhelmed. He wandered off in the direction of the squadron offices with his unsullied flying suit still showing the creases of the box it came in and his gleaming white kid leather flying gloves shining in the advancing twilight.

As we drove home I was still pondering the experience of my first – and what was to prove to be my only – flight with my new C.O.

It was dark as Bullfrog stopped his car at the top of the drive. I wished him goodnight and climbed out. As I was walking around to the back of the house I heard a thumping noise behind me and turned to see the large black Labrador sitting at the top of the steps to the balcony. The tail was rhythmically thumping on the wooden floor, a very long tongue was hanging happily over a lop-sided grin and it was clear that I was being welcomed home!

I crossed the balcony with my canine escort, opened the screen door into the kitchen and we both entered, meeting Irene as she came from the living room.

"What's he doing here?" she said.

"He seems to think he lives here," I replied. The dog was sitting comfortably on his haunches surveying his surroundings. He looked very much at home.

"Perhaps he lived here once," I mused weakly.

"I don't think so, there's no sign of anything doggy in or around the house," said Irene thoughtfully. "Perhaps we should give him a drink." She headed towards the low level cupboard containing the bowl we had used previously, closely followed by the dog.

The bowl was filled, emptied noisily, leaving a puddle of water on the floor, and the dog sat back, looking up at me expectantly. I fished in a cupboard and offered a couple of digestive biscuits. They were gratefully received and our visitor headed for the door. I opened it and out he went into the warm night.

Chapter 13
Identification

Monday morning dawned bright and clear. The air was crisp but not cold, with a china blue sky, unbroken from the roof tops of the town to the gum tree horizon. I picked up my briefcase, boarded the Holden, wound open the windows and responded to the waving send off from Irene and Rebecca. I turned left into Berry Street, cruised slowly past the repeated cross roads to the edge of the town and joined the procession of cars heading southeast along the dead straight road carved out of the bush towards the air station.

My uniform and the pass on the window enabled me to be waved through the main gate without pause. Security in Australia in those days was not oppressive. The cars spread out around the station heading for their various destinations. In a few minutes I was pulling up alongside the row of vehicles facing the squadron offices. I hailed the few faces I knew and joined the movement towards the hut containing the briefing room. We sat on loose rows of tubular upright chairs facing a makeshift lectern, a projection screen and a blackboard. The Senior Pilot, Senior Observer, and Air Engineer Officer sat in the front row. A bigger, more comfortable chair in the centre remained empty.

A few minutes after eight thirty, the Senior Pilot stood up, the conversation died down, and the familiar squat figure of the C.O. lumbered through the door. Everyone stood respectfully until Bullfrog was seated in the front row. He nodded to the officer standing behind the lectern, signalling the start of the briefing. To my surprise, an aircraft silhouette was projected onto the screen. "Lieutenant Kinross," said the briefing officer. The aircraft – a Russian – was correctly identified and the process was repeated a few more times with various officers being called to identify ships and aircraft. They all appeared to be quick and accurate and I wondered whether they were skilled at recognition or had been supplied with the answers in advance.

The briefing continued with a 'met' forecast – 'blue throughout' followed by wind speed and direction and the time of sunset – then a run through the flying programme chalked on the blackboard, before the briefing officer turned expectantly towards the figure of the Boss reclining in the centre of the front row. He climbed ponderously to his feet and passed a few remarks about forthcoming events and then said, memorably from my point of view…

"… and I want you all to meet Tom Holmes, fresh out from U.K." I looked around for Tom before realizing that the Boss had not only forgotten that I had been announced some weeks previously but he had also forgotten my name and he was actually referring to me. Clearly I hadn't made much of an impression when driving him around the sky the previous evening! At least he got the initials right and I supposed I should be thankful for that much. Most of the faces surrounding me were now adorned with knowing grins.

Bullfrog turned abruptly about and headed for the door. The briefing was over and we all trailed out after him. There were no aircraft serviceable so some pilots and observers formed little groups to chat and smoke in the sunshine while others headed for the crew room to settle down to coffee, cigarettes and bridge foursomes. Clearly this situation was not unusual. Bullfrog had disappeared into his office with the door shut behind him. He was not seen by me for the rest of the day.

I wandered out into the rapidly warming morning and found myself meeting a few more of my squadron colleagues, as well as recounting my holiday experiences to older acquaintances.

By and by, accompanied by the second coffee of the morning, I found myself chatting to one of the more experienced observers. Gordon Edgecombe was an engaging character with bright blue eyes peering over a luxuriant black beard. He told me he lived near us in Nowra, and he was scheduled to leave the squadron soon to take up a posting on exchange to the Royal Navy. He expected to end up at the naval air station on Portland, which I knew well and he was quizzing me about the operation of the station, the local area and in particular the availability of family accommodation. As the conversation went on he told me that he had already arranged to let out his house in Nowra but he was concerned that his arrangements for boarding out the family dog for the duration of his absence were in the process of falling through.

At the time I didn't register the possible significance of this piece of information but I did mention it to Irene when I returned home that evening. She thought about it for a while and then said, "I wonder...?"

****

The following days passed in a style similar to the first one. I never saw Bullfrog in an aircraft again and I discovered that no one else had either. The social life surrounding the squadron and the wardroom meant that we were meeting lots of new people and making new friends. Life was gentle, the weather, although regarded as the onset of winter by the locals, was balmy. We received a few more visits from our friendly black Labrador, usually of short duration and usually involving a drink and a biscuit before his taking leave of us. The evenings were still warm enough for the occasional barbecue and we learnt the real meaning of 'wear something casual' when one couple turned up with the short bullet headed husband in a string vest accompanied by his wife in a once white but now slightly grey bra. These were, it is true, slight exceptions to the norm – but we learnt that casual often meant very casual indeed.

About a month after first meeting him, I received an invitation from Gordon Edgecombe, who was holding a 'leaving party' prior to his departure for England.

The early evening was cool so the party was to be held indoors. We sauntered across the road towards the Edgecombe house, which we had discovered was almost visible from our front garden. As we approached we both noticed a familiar black shape sitting proprietorially on the front porch. As we drew closer we were in turn recognised and then greeted by our 'mystery' dog, who accompanied us up to the side door. As the door was opened, the dog attempted to lead the way inside, only to be ordered peremptorily "Out!" by our hostess.

"Out, Spoofy," she repeated and reluctantly he obeyed.

Thus, we learnt his name.

The evening was a great success, the wine flowed and tray after tray of food kept everyone happy. Several hours later with the party still in full swing we found ourselves chatting with our hosts about their expectations for the next two years on exchange in England. The house, as Gordon had already told me, was let for the duration and most other arrangements were set but Sip, Gordon's delightful Finnish wife, began to look sad.

"We don't know what we are going to do about Spoofy," she said sadly.

"We think he has already decided," said Irene.

Chapter 14
Arrival

Once the decision was made the details were worked out quite quickly. The Edgecombes were due to leave in about three weeks and their tenants were due in a further three weeks beyond that. We met several times to sort out the details and agreed that Spoofy should move in with us straight away so that if there were any problems arising we all had time to sort them out.

We had one difficulty to resolve straight away – and that was with our landlady. At the first opportunity Irene went to see the agents acting for the landlady. She explained the situation and asked for our rental agreement to be modified to reflect the fact that we would have a dog living with us – type unspecified. They said they would consult the owners and after a few days our landlady's husband dropped by and signified approval. "No probs, no worries mate!" We sealed it with a beer in traditional 'Oz' fashion. A nice easy going bloke.

Spoofy's belongings were transferred across to us and he began to take his meals with us. He still wandered back to his former home from time to time and occasionally in those first few weeks when Spoofy was out in the early evening our peace of mind would be shattered as a long and mournful howl would rise from beside the back door of the Edgecombes' now vacant and dark home. Eventually, quite quickly actually, Spoofy got the message and decided to accept the situation.

He seemed to come to a decision and started to spend most of his time in or close by our house. Once this happened, as far as I know, he never went back to his old home. Certainly we never heard the chilling dog howl again.

When he settled in with us he set up his base, which was dominated by an old blanket, in the spacious laundry and utility room off the kitchen. We also learned something of his history. From various directions we picked up snippets of stories of his early days wandering through the bush with his companion 'Cathy', who also enjoyed the wandering life. Spoofy brought with him a few on-going problems. First of all he was a wanderer and shortly after his arrival we noticed how he would spend his days patrolling his various routes around the town. We were not used to this and at first we became very anxious as to his whereabouts. We need not have worried. Spoofy always returned to base for mealtimes, when he was tired or when it was either too hot or raining heavily. We also had to come to terms with the fact that Spoofy suffered from eczema and tinea. The eczema affected his back and was at its worst during very hot and humid weather. From time to time it was necessary to take him to the vet to have all the hair shaved off his back. He also needed a special weekly shampoo to control his condition, and cream when shaved. The tinea occurrences were less frequent. This was a form of aggressive fungus which would affect the area between the pads on his feet. If he suffered an attack another medicinal cream had to be applied following which his feet needed to be bound with bandages.

We decided that our new status required more transport. Public transport, apart from the railway to Sydney, was almost non-existent in rural New South Wales and I needed to get to work each day, while Irene needed to get into town for shopping and all the other requirements of a young family – with a dog! Our financial situation had improved somewhat, although with various British governments lurching from one economic crisis to the next, Service officers were never going to be rich.

We made a double decision. We would trade in the 'nearly new' white Holden station wagon we had purchased soon after arrival and replace it with a much smarter, brand new, Holden station wagon – this one in metallic gold but modified with a white roof to reflect the intense sunshine we would encounter. We were able to do this only by taking advantage of the arrangement whereby we temporary immigrants were allowed to purchase one car in Australia free of taxes and duties. We were to spend a great deal of time in this car and travel thousands of miles across Australia so we became quite attached to it.

The 'other car' was a different experience entirely. After poring through the classified ads in the local paper, incidentally the only newspaper we ever came across which was able to get both the day of the week and the date wrong, we investigated some likely prospects and finally invested fifty dollars in a 1950s vintage two tone Holden station wagon. It started and ran fairly reliably but the steering was more like a ship than a car and it had other charming little quirks such as a persistent refusal to slot into the selected gear, or occasionally, into any gear. Nevertheless it was a second set of wheels and was never likely to be asked to go further than the air station so it seemed ideal.

The battered old Holden was to prove useful in another, unexpected direction. Shortly after the transfer of Spoofy's base of operations from the Edgecombes' house to ours, when the mild South Eastern Australian winter had begun to set in, he began to spend a lot more time hanging around our kitchen, or dozing in front of the sitting room electric fire. He still followed his regular routine of daily patrols through the town occasionally supplemented by evening or nocturnal patrols. He had also developed a rather protective instinct towards his new home. It so happened that one chilly and dull Saturday afternoon he was hanging around in the kitchen hoping for post lunch scraps and anything that fell from Rebecca's tiny fingers when we were all disturbed by the unfamiliar sound of a car crunching down the gravel and dirt driveway beside the house.

Spoofy reacted instantly. He was not about to have his comfortable new home desecrated by unexpected and unwelcome interlopers. He shot out of the back door, across the balcony and down the steps like an eighty pound guided missile.

I rushed to the sitting room window which looked out over the driveway. To my considerable surprise a brightly painted Sydney taxi was coming to a stop alongside the house. It is fair to say that the driver didn't have a lot of choice other than to come to a stop. The car appeared to be surrounded by a huge black dog with the ability to appear simultaneously on all sides, whilst aiming such a barrage of furious barking at the vehicle that I expected to see dents appearing in the bodywork caused by the sonic onslaught. It looked rather like a large wagon train under siege from a single Indian.

The driver was a small slightly built lady in her fifties. Our previously unseen landlady! From the thunderous look on her face she did not appreciate the humour of the situation. I ran through the house, out the back door, down the steps and grabbed the, by now, definitely unguided canine missile by the collar. The driver's window wound slowly down. "What the hell is that?" she yelled above the continuing barrage of noise. I pasted on my most engaging smile while I sensed Irene arriving behind me. With both of us present Spoofy began to quieten down while I strained on the end of his collar. We both started to explain the situation leaning heavily on the 'Good Samaritan' aspect of taking Spoofy on as well as mentioning in every second sentence that we had already received approval from the lady's husband and from the agent to keep the dog.

I was acutely aware that we were entitled to receive notice of visits from the landlady or her representatives but I didn't think this was the time or place to mention it.

Our visitor was eventually coaxed out of her car and we all tramped indoors to the hospitality of tea and cakes. All, that is, except Spoofy!

We introduced our lovely, but slightly food encrusted, little daughter who had by now graduated to the mobility of a baby walker, mentioning how nice it was for her to have a dog about. We endeavoured to demonstrate how nicely the house was being looked after but clearly the mind of our landlady was on a single track. She kept going on about the size of the dog, its aggressive nature (good for protecting the property when we were away, we said) and the fact that she would never have given her approval for 'an inside dog'. From this we quickly gathered that an 'outside dog', a category with which we were not familiar, might be approved and so the potentially disastrous situation might yet be recovered.

As if working by telepathy, we both began to explain that of course Spoofy really was an 'outside dog' and he just happened to be having a drink of water when her car had arrived – unexpectedly. Usually, we asserted, he lived outside all the time, spending the night inside the garage. Tea, cakes, little sandwiches, blatant obsequious crawling and a modicum of charm gradually dissipated the frost in the room. After an hour or so we seemed to have her approval for Spoofy's continued residence but in the new found capacity of 'outside dog'. This probably wasn't going to bother Spoofy all that much but we were concerned that we had an obligation to Spoofy's owners and we felt that his continuing welfare and safety remained an important responsibility for us.

Eventually, as we trudged back into the house, wiping the very fixed smiles from our faces, we settled down to a council of war. Irene discussed with me the ways of dealing with the new situation while Spoofy – now temporarily re-promoted to 'inside dog' – and Rebecca looked on.

We decided that we would not be browbeaten into changing our outlook on life and that the way to resolve the difficulty with our landlady was by proper preparation and planning. Firstly Spoofy needed an alternative home and this was to be provided by our aged second Holden. When not in use it would be parked beside the house with a window opened. Spoofy soon got the message and habitually hopped into the car for a quiet doze whenever the mood took him. A down side of this was that he became rather obsessive about what he now clearly viewed as his car. This meant that on occasions when we were driving about town in the old car with Spoofy occupying the whole back section we would be suddenly subjected to a torrent of barking and the car would vibrate and shake. Spoofy had spotted a passing stranger of whom he disapproved, or, even worse, a local dog which he wished to dominate or challenge.

Whenever we were in the house, Spoofy would come and go as the mood took him; he would sleep overnight – when not on nocturnal patrol – in the kitchen and he would take his meals on the back balcony, or inside in poor weather. We would remain particularly alert to the noise of a car coming down the drive, which was likely to be our landlady because everyone else parked politely on the road outside the front gate. We would check through the nearest window to confirm that it was the landlady. It was then necessary to ensure that if Spoofy was inside he would be kept inside until our visitor left the car and moved towards the house. If she headed for the back door, Spoofy would be shoved out of the front door and in the unlikely event of her coming to the front door, he would leave by the back door. The timing needed to be such that by the time he had raced round the outside of the house the landlady was being welcomed in through the appropriate door. Spoofy soon cottoned on to this new game and the sound of a car entering the drive would find him posted, like a coiled spring, behind the front door waiting the opportunity to leap out and race around to the drive to welcome – sometimes interpreted as 'to terrorise' – the visiting driver.

Of course, if Spoofy happened to be dozing in the old Holden he would leap out to defend his realm, thus proving that he was an 'outside' dog and delaying the approach of our unwelcome visitor. It worked a treat. We also discovered that the very presence of Spoofy running noisily around the car would deter the driver from alighting, thus giving us a little more warning of the 'inspection'.

Later on in our tenancy there was one visit that caused me something of a sense of humour failure. Late one quiet Saturday afternoon we were alerted to the dreaded tyre crunching noise down the drive. We looked at each other, mutually puzzled, noting that Spoofy was already in position just inside the front door. I opened the door and a black thunderbolt shot out. Part two of the standard plan was developing as Irene left by the back door giving an earnest impression of trying to catch and contain the 'outside dog'. Once Spoofy was under control I left by the front door and strolled towards the car. Our landlady emerged from the driver's seat looking diminutive alongside the huge green taxi. Before I could say anything a very large overweight gentleman dressed like a Hollywood extra from 'Hank Hayseed Comes to Town' climbed laboriously from the front passenger seat. While I was mesmerised by the outsize Stetson which had now appeared to complement the bootlace tie, jeans and pointy-toed boots, I dimly heard our landlady introducing her passenger as Mr someone or other from America who wanted to see a typical Australian home. She had therefore brought him all the way from Sydney – on the meter, I imagined. I was flabbergasted. My mind was doing handstands, alternating between the sheer cheek of the woman, her surprisingly honeyed demeanour which contrasted sharply with her usual rough and blunt style, and the extraordinary vision from America which was smiling at me. I recovered my senses, moved around the side of the taxi, shook Mr America by the hand and pasted a hurt and worried expression over my face – or at least I hoped that I had. "What a shame," I lied, "you've come all this way, and we are just going out." I rambled on. "Can't get out of it I'm afraid, still you wanted to see a typical Australian household – and this is now very English."

"And Irish," I heard Irene mutter quietly. She wasn't looking at all happy and so I burbled on, building on my fabricated important appointment. Spoofy methodically walked to each corner of the taxi, cocked his leg and piddled copiously on each wheel. Deftly, Irene moved between him and the open car door, frustrating Spoofy's next aim which was becoming increasingly apparent. Like any good tactician he was about to take command of the situation by entering the car, and preventing anyone else from doing so. I saw our landlady glance towards her pride and joy, becoming temporarily distracted as Spoofy, thwarted in his grand plan, ambled up to the front bumper and sprayed it liberally, matching the four wheels. This was the *coup de grâce* and our landlady decided that enough was enough. She was still going to get a 200 mile round trip meter fare so failing to force hospitality out of us was not such a loss.

She quickly flopped in behind the steering wheel as Irene manoeuvred Spoofy away from aiming a jet towards the other open door. This wasn't much of a threat actually because his reservoir was clearly running dry. Mrs Landlady didn't know this and from her look of alarm was evidently becoming concerned that her shiny Sydney taxi was about to be totally immersed in dog pee. Hank the Yank stood looking amazed by the unfolding scene and the trend of the disjointed conversation. Within minutes it seemed, we were waving farewell, as if to old friends, while the big six cylinders grumbled the taxi backwards up the drive on to the road. Our landlady concentrated on the road and was unable to return our waves but her passenger gave a brief salute, with his puzzled expression still dominating his big meaty face.

I looked down to see Spoofy with a lengthy pink tongue hanging out, dripping, and his tail wagging steadily. As he looked up I interpreted his expression as "How did I do Boss? O.K. huh?"

We went straight inside and treated ourselves to large slugs of local 'claret' from a half gallon plastic bottle, and a liver flavoured biscuit slab for Spoofy.

It was some time before we had the next visit from our landlady.

"The old Holden –
the mobile kennel"

"Spoofy and Irene at the coast"

"Rebecca bonds with Spoofy"

"Spoofy"

Chapter 15
Getting Acquainted

As time passed we started to notice that Spoofy was a creature of habit. He liked to take a stroll in the early morning, before the heat of the day, and again, in the late afternoon. At first we had no idea where he went on these expeditions but we did notice that trophies would appear on the lawn in the back garden. These trophies were mostly, but not exclusively in the form of large knuckle bones. In the heat of the day, these could not be allowed to remain and fester in the garden but as fast as we removed discarded items, so new ones arrived.

We decided that some detective work was required in order to solve the mystery and deal with the problem. This needed to be carefully managed because if Spoofy got wind that he was being followed by a member of what he regarded as his extended family, he would merely double back, fall in alongside his 'shadow' and turn the exercise into a pleasant and unremarkable walk. After several attempts had ended in failure I left the house one Saturday morning before he did, drove the car some distance in the direction which he usually followed into town, hid it off the main road and lurked among the hedges of the residential side streets waiting for him to pass by. I felt furtive and from the attention I was getting from people passing, I obviously looked furtive.

Eventually, ambling along the west side pavement of Berry Street appeared a familiar shape. He was in no hurry, stopping for a sniff here, a pee there and a routine stop for a scratch as he passed each block. Suddenly my quarry had disappeared. He had turned left into a residential side street. I slunk along the pavement as quietly as I could, keeping close to the hedge and trying to work out whether I was upwind or downwind of Spoofy. I need not have worried because as soon as Spoofy turned off the main street his pace had quickened and he had become focussed on the task ahead. When I turned the corner there was at first no sign of a dog. I stood transfixed and waited; after a few minutes the lower part of a garden hedge about one hundred yards ahead of me began to quiver and a big black head emerged, peered left and right and then pulled the rest of himself out of the hedge and trotted off, fortunately heading away from me. I kept my distance and followed discreetly. I had the distinct impression that I was witnessing a well worn routine – rather like a postman doing his rounds. We worked our way down to the end of the road, turned the corner and continued the routine. After Spoofy had disappeared into the third garden the routine changed. He did not reappear. I waited; still no Spoofy, so I eased along the pavement, still keeping quiet, hoping not to be arrested, and peered carefully over the hedge.

The sight before me was remarkable. Spoofy was standing facing away from me in the centre of a neatly trimmed lawn. In front of him and facing him was a smallish dog of indeterminate breed. Between the two of them was a fairly fresh and quite large knuckle bone. Spoofy was standing with his front legs splayed apart, absolutely still, looking for all the world like a slightly worn statue of a Crufts winner. A low, steady and distinctly ominous growl was emanating from him, accompanied by faint steamy condensation as his warm breath met the cool early morning air. The smaller dog opposite him was standing his ground but giving little nervous "yips". The bone clearly belonged to him and he was aware that he might lose it. The pageant continued. Spoofy stood stock still and every twenty seconds or so the other dog ventured a paw or a nose towards the bone. The steady growl increased in volume and Spoofy moved not a muscle. After nearly ten minutes the bone owner made a mistake. He took a small step backwards and immediately, like a skilled chess player, Spoofy advanced by the same amount. This resulted in another backward step and another advance until Spoofy's snout was poised immediately above the bone. At this, he nonchalantly bent down, gathered up the still meaty bone and turned with a flourish of his tail heading back towards his point of entry. I threw caution to the winds and turned in through the gate of the adjacent garden. I need not have worried because Spoofy was now intent on his prize and was hurrying back home. The former bone owner wandered disconsolately away, tail down, dejected. I realised at once that the mystery of the source of the bones in the garden was solved and that I had been treated to a remarkable demonstration of the local canine Al Capone going about his daily business of threats and extortion.

I carried out my covert surveillance on Spoofy's early morning patrol on two further occasions with much the same result. On the third attempt I was rumbled. I saw Spoofy disappear into a likely garden one street further on from the first incident and after about thirty seconds I moved up to peer over the hedge. There was nothing in sight. I assumed Spoofy had ventured round the back of the house when the familiar black shape emerged from the hedge behind me and gave a doggy whoop of welcome. He was so pleased to see me – and he was not actually carrying any contraband – that I felt quite ashamed as we traipsed home.

On the Sunday following my first covert investigation of Spoofy's habits around the town we decided to go to the morning service at the little Anglican church further along Berry Street. We set off in our lightweight Sunday best, walked down the road with Irene still tending to avoid passing under the bigger trees, parked Rebecca's pram outside and joined the congregation inside. Several almost familiar faces nodded and smiled as we took our places in the back half of the nave, near the aisle and convenient for slipping out, if it proved necessary to remove temporarily a noisy child. We need not have bothered. The service was well underway and the vicar had just climbed into the wooden pulpit to begin his sermon when through the main door came two little figures, one clutching some sort of toy and the other stark naked. Ignoring the assembled congregation on either side, the toddlers, about two or three years old, marched purposefully towards the pulpit. As they approached, the one with the toy addressed the vicar in his pulpit. He didn't get much further than "Daddy, we want…" before they were both whisked into the arms of a lady rising from a pew near the front. The speed, smoothness and skill with which she disappeared through the side door all suggested that this was not the first time she had assisted in this way.

The incident may have distracted us somewhat from the rest of the service and, noticing that nothing was said by the congregation we remained silent on the subject as we left the church. Irene was still shaking the vicar's hand and listening to his words of welcome when my eye was caught by a familiar shape. Spoofy was sitting on the grass verge outside the gate, patiently waiting for us. As we emerged onto the pavement and turned for home he fell into place alongside the pram and accompanied us all the way back, just as he had when we first met him in the park. Waiting for us outside the church was a trick that he repeated from time to time, but I never saw him actually following us towards the church.

Chapter 16
A Problem at Sea

The attitude of the Squadron Senior Pilot towards me was still somewhat cool and I couldn't understand why until I discovered that his seniority as a Lieutenant was below mine. He was junior to me! He had worked this out quite quickly and although nothing was said he clearly saw me as a threat to his position in the squadron hierarchy.

Looking back on that time I realised much later that he had pulled a little trick to embarrass me and damage my reputation in the eyes of my aviating superiors. This occurred one morning when things within the squadron were fairly quiet. The inevitable bridge game was droning on in the crew room with a side team of observers hotly debating which card should actually have been played. Outside, others were enjoying the sunshine, wandering about, smoking and discussing the merits of various cars and women. The born storytellers who are found in every squadron were recounting their anecdotes. Most of the aircraft were in the big hangar, or just outside, with the duty watch toiling away on routine maintenance.

I wandered back into the hut and down the narrow corridor, ducking to avoid the redback spider's nest and settled into one of the ancient armchairs, picking up an aviation magazine and idly turning the pages. The doorway filled with the figure of the Senior Pilot, looking even more scrawny in his green flying overalls. "I've got a job for you," he said, "briefing in my office in five minutes."

I went to my locker to collect the rest of my gear and then clutching my knee pad I went back to the front office for the briefing. I noted that I was to be aircraft captain and the rest of my crew had already assembled. The observer was Robert, one of the British loan team and my co-pilot was to be Andrew, an unusual Australian aviator in that he was always impeccably turned out, eloquent and knowledgeable, rather formal and a thoroughly reliable man who did things by the book. For some reason we were to fly without an aircrewman.

Our task was to fly out to the local sea exercise areas, locate the frigate *HMAS Queenborough*, pick up a compassionate case and return to base. *Queenborough* was not fitted with a flight deck, being a fairly old frigate converted from a Second World War destroyer. The crew member to be collected therefore would have to be winched up into the aircraft. That seemed to be the end of the briefing but I wanted to know more so I asked where on the ship should the winch transfer take place.

"Could be for'ard, could be aft," said Jack, the Senior Pilot, as he started to walk away.

I pressed him. "What about clearances, obstructions and so on?"

"Look," he said, "plenty of transfers have been done before. Just go where they set up."

"Have you got a picture or drawing?" I persisted.

"No. Now are you going to get going or what?" He turned away.

I walked out to the 'A700' desk, signed the aircraft acceptance certificate and headed for the single aircraft out on the hard standing, followed by my crew.

We started up, got Tower clearance, and climbed away to the east. As we crossed the coast we set the Tacan on to the ship's beacon and headed out to sea. I explained my intentions as we flew out towards the ship. Despite the scanty information we had been given it all seemed relatively straightforward and everybody seemed happy. This was an experienced crew who had completed dozens of winching exercises in all sorts of conditions so this task seemed fairly routine.

After twenty minutes or so the ship appeared out of the heat haze, heading towards us. As they turned on to a suitable transfer course with the wind set just off the port bow I could see that a flat piece of deck aft of the main superstructure, which had once housed a gun mounting, was being prepared for the transfer. Our passenger was standing beside an officer wearing a radio headset. Another individual beside the officer was holding direction wands at the front of the transfer space. It all looked straightforward. I moved the aircraft slowly sideways over the deck, following the conning instructions from the back of the aircraft as the observer, Robert, paid out the winch wire. As we moved further over the deck the conning became broken and difficult to hear because Robert needed to stick his head out of the door into the wind and the rotor down draught to see the end of the winch wire. Still, I was quite happy because my position looked good and there was no sign of anyone sticking up a red flag – the signal to break off. A rating rushed forward with an earthing pole, touching the winch hook to discharge any build up of static electricity while another advanced with the passenger's kit. While trying to concentrate on the situation on deck and at the same time straining to hear the instructions from the cabin which had now become very distorted, as the observer stuck his head further out of the door to see the winch and its load, my attention was caught by a group of about eight other officers who had appeared on the deck. They seemed to be moving about as though they were at a party. Several started gesticulating towards the aircraft and something was thrown towards it.

The passenger's kit was onboard and the man was being helped into the winching strop. The group surrounding the unmoving Directing Officer appeared to have adopted a carnival atmosphere and were enjoying themselves immensely. Suddenly I saw fleetingly an object falling down to the right of the aircraft. Simultaneously I heard Andrew say, "I think we've just chopped off one of their whip aerials."

The disjointed instructions coming from the cabin suggested that the passenger was half way between the ship and the aircraft so I held the hover for a few moments more and then eased gently to the left as he was brought into the cabin. A quick three way discussion between the crew confirmed that we had indeed struck one of the ship's radio whip aerials with a rotor blade and chopped a chunk off. These aerials were situated clear ahead of the transfer platform but the combined movement of the ship into wind and the effect of the helicopter's rotor downwash had made all of the aerials flex dramatically back and forth.

There was no doubt that one aerial had been chopped off by the rotor blades but I had felt nothing through the controls and the aircraft was still flying normally in every respect. There was nowhere to land on the ship and so the choice facing me was either to ditch the aircraft or head for the shore. I have never believed in putting an apparently serviceable aircraft in the water so after a few gentle manoeuvres to check the controls we headed for the shore. The trip to the 'beach' was uneventful, so, with the agreement of the crew I continued towards the airfield flying gently and carefully at a reduced speed. I told the Tower we had experienced a rotor strike and that I would like a straight in approach. They agreed and I eased in to a slow running landing on the main runway before ground taxiing in to the squadron dispersal. I shut down the engine and slowed the rotor with the brake while Andrew switched everything off. I climbed out and walked around the aircraft and it was quickly apparent which blade had hit the aerial. Three of the rotor blades had slight nicks in their leading edges but the fourth one had a huge dent taking out about half of the diameter of the main spar which provides all the strength in the blade. I offered up a silent prayer as I headed off to write up the incident report and sign the aircraft in.

I believed that I had done as well as I could, given the circumstances of the almost non-existent briefing and the performance of the various individuals on the *Queenborough's* transfer deck. I had in fact been seduced into an inappropriate transfer position but I had contained the situation, completed the mission and brought the aircraft back with easily recoverable damage.

During the course of the rest of that day I could not help noticing that the usual dour mood of the Senior Pilot had been replaced by an almost jaunty air. I was soon to discover why.

Every accident in aviation requires the completion of an accident report form. This is called an A25 and runs to about five pages of A4. While I was engaged in filling out my A25, in came the Senior Pilot and cheerfully told me that a Board of Enquiry was to be commissioned and my whole crew would be flown off to HMAS Watson, the big naval base in Sydney.

When I arrived home that evening I was in a somewhat sombre mood.

I drove into the driveway, climbed out of the car and immediately noted that the place seemed unusually quiet. The other car was missing, the house was unlocked, but then it often was; more worryingly there was absolutely no sign of wife, dog or daughter.

Chapter 17
Spoofy Goes Walkabout

The missing car suggested that Irene was probably out visiting friends or perhaps returning from a late shopping trip. However this was the time that Spoofy was usually hanging around looking hungry – and it was fast approaching Rebecca's bedtime. Something was wrong, I could feel it. I was miserable and I wanted to talk to Irene about the predicament I had been lured into. I could feel myself becoming frustrated and irritated and I paced the house as though by doing so I would suddenly discover my family hidden away.

Mobile phones had yet to be invented so all I could do was telephone the few friends we had made locally and sit and wait. Eventually with dusk creeping on I decided that I had to do something. I turned the car round and drove out onto Berry Street. I turned right and right again until I was on the Princes Highway heading south. I cruised slowly along the nearside, glancing left and right into each side street I passed. After passing about eight of these and nearing the point where the Highway leaves the town to carve off through the bush heading for Bateman's Bay I caught a glimpse of our familiar old banger off to my right. I stopped, backed up and turned down the neat residential street stopping in front of the other car. My wife was not given to emotional outbursts but she was clearly upset. So was the baby, secured in the carrycot in the usual place in the back seat.

I climbed out and went to the other car. Almost before I had the door open I was hit with the full story. Spoofy had disappeared. He had not been seen all day. He was well known around the town but no one had seen him. He always came back for his food and this time he hadn't done so. His usual arrival time was set around being able to catch food falling from Rebecca's high chair and in this routine he was absolute. He must have been hit by a car we thought and crawled away to die; or been caught in a trap or fallen into a river.

We had a problem but we could do nothing about it agonising inside an ancient car while the baby howled in the back. I said that all we could do was go back to the house and hope Spoofy would turn up.

We cruised in slow convoy back through the town, past our neighbour's large tree covered garden and into the driveway. We looked anxiously towards the back porch but it was empty and the big black dog with the oversized pink tongue was nowhere to be seen.

We were both distraught. What were we going to say to Spoofy's owners?

The evening drew on, we fed the baby, quietened her and put her to bed. We switched on the television and then switched it off again. I suggested a beer but Irene said no. I had one anyway and so the evening drawled on until we went silently to bed ourselves.

****

I was awoken with a strange, distant scraping noise. It was completely dark, without any overspill from the street light, and I couldn't see what time it was. I was alone in the bed.

I hauled myself out of bed and wandered uncertainly, translating from sleep to wakefulness, towards the sound; into the hall, which was empty and then, still rubbing sleep from my eyes, towards the kitchen. There, arrayed before me was a scene of domestic bliss. Spoofy was ploughing through a dog dish piled high with tinned dog meat garnished with the remains of our supper. Irene was crouched alongside him, fondling his ears and cooing towards him. The prodigal dog had returned.

My assessment of the situation boiled down to the immediacy of being able to get back to bed and sleep for what remained of the night with the attractive prospect of the rest of my family returning to normal, at least for the immediate future.

This was to be our first experience of a number of nocturnal adventures in the months to follow, but for now, sleep, blissful sleep was all I craved.

Chapter 18
Board of Enquiry

The coastal strip rolled steadily past my window, alternating between yellow sand, vivid white surf and the light green of the pastureland. The aircraft was full but conversation was impossible above the mind numbing noise inside the cabin of the old DC3 Dakota. Everyone was dressed in their best uniforms; blue suits because we had now eased into what passed for winter in Southern New South Wales.

Kiama dropped away astern as the busy port area of Wollongong passed under the starboard wing. The aircraft gave another lurch which pressed me against my seat strap and I began to wonder just how old it was and what adventures it must have survived over the last thirty years or so. It had certainly gained a few scars and dents but it was still serving as a communications aircraft for the Royal Australian Navy – alternating with two other aviating geriatrics, all based at Nowra. As I sat there in silence I felt it was rather like the wagons of the French Revolution dragging the innocent to the guillotine. I believed I had been set up, advantage having been taken of a situation which was accident prone, so that when the accident (waiting to happen, one might say) had occurred I had been pushed forward as the fall guy. My crew members were also on the aircraft heading for the enquiry but we had been forbidden to communicate. I had no friends.

As we lost height in the approach to Kingsford Smith Airport I found myself going over and over the events in my head. Could I have done something different? I didn't think so. Should I have refused to accept the winching area prepared by the ship? I had no reason to. I had been told that "dozens of transfers had taken place with this ship and the operation was routine". I had seen the whip aerials well in front of me as I moved the aircraft forward and to the right to take up a position over the deck. I had followed the conning instructions of my observer and I had watched to see if there was any form of 'wave-off' signal from the deck. There had been none, and since I was concentrating on looking down at the deck I didn't see either of the whip aerials until I saw a shadow of something falling to the right of the aircraft and Andrew had murmured something like "*Queenborough* could do with a new aerial!"

There was a familiar thud and deceleration as the wheels touched the runway. I was still going over the events above *HMAS Queenborough* in my head. Why were there so many people on the deck below the aircraft? Why did they seem to be having a party? Then – a flash of recollection – someone had thrown something towards the aircraft. And in another clear vision of the scene before me that day – the officer in charge, known as the Flight Deck Officer, had not even been holding his signal flags (green for O.K. carry on and red for Danger, Stop). Additionally, if I had allowed the aircraft to creep too far forward, the Flight Deck Officer should have waved me back with flags or bats. But he didn't. He couldn't. There were no bats and the rating behind him was holding his flags. I brightened up a bit – but only slightly.

As we taxied along the interminable taxi tracks leading to the hidden corner of the airfield where battered old warriors, such as the one I was riding in, were parked, my thoughts moved on to what had happened after my aircraft's rotor blades had chopped off the whip aerial. The answer was nothing. Did I do the right thing? What could I have done? Dropped the aircraft in the water alongside the ship? Taken the passenger back and winched him back down? Ditched on the way home? I didn't think so. The aircraft had shown no sign at all of any aerodynamic damage and had performed normally. I still believed that I had done everything I could and should have done but if I was guilty, I was guilty of taking too much on trust and allowing myself to be pushed into a risky situation. As we climbed out and walked in the direction of the navy bus my backbone stiffened.

****

The enquiry, I began to think, could have been crafted by Gilbert and Sullivan. Witnesses were assembled in a large room, silence being maintained by a couple of grim Naval Police. My crew was present, as well as about half the ship's company of *HMAS Queenborough* – and a whole lot of important looking people whom I did not recognise.

A commander who did not wear wings on his sleeve occupied the chair in the centre of the table with two officers on each side of him. An attractive young woman in a neat grey suit was recording proceedings as a stenographer. I had sat for a day and a half in the uncomfortable waiting room watching as a seemingly endless trail of witnesses trooped into the enquiry room. I had no idea who they were or what, if anything, they could contribute.

Now it was my turn. "We would like you to tell us in your own words exactly what happened," drawled the Chairman of the enquiry in his Western Australian twang. I did. At the same time I found myself wondering whether I should be thinking of him as the President of the Court. Certainly that seemed to be the way he was acting.

After about twenty-five minutes or so the interruptions began and the feeling of hostility increased. I was the 'pommie' who had not only wantonly damaged their ship but had also hazarded their aircraft, or so they had obviously already judged. It was evident that my crew had borne out my version of events but it was equally evident that this had been dismissed on the basis of 'well, they would say that, wouldn't they'. One point they could not easily dismiss was that I was a skilled and experienced pilot, holding a commendation for my part in winching to safety over a hundred people from a Fijian ferry stranded on a reef in a storm. I could also establish that I had the helicopter in the right position.

As well as the raft of engineers, supply officers and others who had been lined up to confirm the rather obvious notion that the ship's whip aerial had been cut in two and several rotor blades damaged, it seemed that practically every member of the *Queenborough* ship's company had produced some sort of statement suggesting that a gung ho Brit pilot had deliberately and with malice aforethought hazarded their ship. Or so it seemed from the questions and challenges directed at me, and from the inevitable scuttlebutt which floated around for a while after the enquiry had ended.

I stuck to my guns throughout the second day but it was with a sense of angry frustration that I sat in the old Dakota while it rattled and bounced towards the runway. By the time I arrived home that evening, hot and tired from my grilling and from having spent the warm winter day in my 'number 4s' – meaning best formal uniform – I was in a despondent mood.

I parked my car beside the old Holden, which had the window still open for Spoofy to hop in, climbed the steps to the back porch and there was my little girl charging out to meet me with the new mobility of her toddler walking frame, followed by Spoofy, leaping at me with the huge enthusiasm that only a dog can produce and slobbering all over my best serge uniform. Irene was already grilling steaks so I fetched myself a large cold Toohey's Dinner Ale and proceeded to wipe away the effects of a foul two days.

Chapter 19
A Change for the Better

Although now winter, the days remained generally warm and sunny except in the evening when the temperature would drop dramatically as the sun went down. It didn't get really cold but the difference between the high point of the day and evening made it feel pretty chilly. In the squadron, life droned on at its usual unhurried pace while at home Spoofy had taken to spending more evenings with us in the house. He had become a useful companion to Rebecca who was becoming more mobile and adventurous daily. When unsupported by the wheeled toddler mobile her movements were reduced to crawling, rolling and pulling herself upright using convenient handholds. Spoofy would assist this by allowing himself to be used as a step enabling Rebecca to reach higher and sometimes forbidden things.

One curious aspect of my temporary employment with the Australian Navy was that, as I was on loan to the Australians (as opposed to being on 'exchange service') I was paid in Australian dollars by the Australian Navy. However the amount to be paid was the Royal Navy salary I was due but converted from pounds sterling to Australian dollars at the current rate of exchange. At home the Labour government was not doing well and the value of sterling was taking a battering. This meant that through no fault of my own, every time I was paid I was actually receiving less money. Additionally I had lost the security of knowing what I was going to be paid next fortnight. Things were tight and getting tighter.

About a week after the completion of the 'enquiry' three things happened almost simultaneously. At a morning briefing it was announced that Jack, the Senior Pilot, had been selected for General Service training and was to be appointed to an available training slot at sea – in *HMAS Queenborough*! He was to leave to start his course of training in just under three weeks. The squadron gossip turned immediately to who the new Senior Pilot would be. The appointment of Jack had created a problem for the Navy Appointers in that some years back the Australian Fleet Air Arm had been almost closed down. Appointments had been allowed to lapse and the result had been a gap in the seniority lists of aviators so that there was almost no one between six years seniority as Lieutenant and four years seniority as a Lieutenant Commander. This empty band was exactly where they would need to look for Squadron Senior Pilots.

The second thing to happen was the arrival of an official Navy Office letter addressed to me declaring starkly that I was to be re-appointed with immediate effect as the Senior Pilot of 725 Naval Air Squadron. The brief letter went on to announce that as the Squadron was complemented for a Lieutenant Commander in this role I was to receive the pay and allowances of a Royal Australian Navy Lieutenant Commander.

I was shocked. It seemed that this announcement, coming out of the blue, was the answer to all our financial worries. Rates of pay were higher for Australian officers than for British so my own salary would rise from that of a Lieutenant to something above a Lieutenant Commander in the Royal Navy. At a stroke, by courtesy of the Royal Australian Navy, we were to be enabled to enjoy the finer things that Australia had to offer once again.

Hot on the heels of this letter, another letter arrived, this time a rather unwelcome one. This declared that the conclusion of the Board of Enquiry was that I was guilty of unnecessarily hazarding my aircraft and that I was to be given seven days in which to provide reasons why I should not receive the Severe Displeasure of the Australian Navy Board. As I suspected, the 'enquiry' had conveniently converted itself into a court martial and convicted me without bothering to inform me that I faced any charges. I resolved there and then that I would respond robustly to this travesty of justice. I said nothing immediately about my appointment as Senior Pilot, concentrating on my rebuttal of the unstated charge.

The flying programme was light because most of the aircraft were unserviceable and the greatest level of activity was around the Bridge table. I took the opportunity to slope off early, heading home to concentrate on my most important letter.

As usual at this time of year, Spoofy was very much in evidence, having become less of a wanderer as the weather had grown colder. He came lolloping up the drive as I turned in from the road, having correctly identified the particular noise of my car before he could see it. As I climbed out he climbed in, then he sat hanging half in and half out of the driver's seat. I took my briefcase and strolled indoors to tell Irene my news and form a plan of battle. As I was earnestly explaining what had happened my attention was dragged away to a little domestic scene whereby my tiny daughter was sitting on the floor beside the dog bowl and selecting little morsels of tinned dog meat, examining them and placing them in Spoofy's mouth. Spoofy was happily enjoying this new and interesting way of being fed, which contrasted dramatically with his usual process of an untrammelled attack on the contents of the bowl clearing it entirely in about fifty seconds. Both Irene and I had now tailed off into silence and we watched, fascinated, as the spectacle concluded by Rebecca upending the bowl, tipping the contents on to the kitchen floor, where Spoofy happily licked it up, tail waving in a lazy, contented fashion.

Spoofy and Rebecca provided the inspiration I needed. Neither one ever seemed to be deterred by whatever obstacle was placed before them. Spoofy had survived itinerant travel through the bush, avoided snake bites and spider bites, despite his adventurous patrols wherever his nose or his curiosity led him. He had happily accommodated to several changes of ownership and he was quick to identify what should belong to him or his 'family' and protect it accordingly.

Rebecca, although not yet a year old was adept at seeking out what she wanted within the house and was increasingly skilled at moving rapidly around the rooms utilizing whatever came to hand to do so. She had also formed a firm and co-operative bond with Spoofy, of which the hand feeding episode was but a minor example. It was intriguing to watch her using a recumbent Spoofy as a step to climb up to an otherwise unreachable kitchen work surface. Occasionally she would chase after Spoofy, travelling rapidly and erratically in her baby walker. He seemed to react by happily wandering around assuming the role of very slow moving fugitive. If finally cornered his tactic was to lean forward and breath heavily towards Rebecca. Rebecca would recoil dramatically, and accept that this marked the end of the game.

As I watched the conclusion of Spoofy's assisted dinner and the removal of Rebecca to be cleaned up prior to bedtime, I resolved that I too should stand up and be counted. I moved to the dining room, dug out the offending letter from the Navy Board, found some notepaper and started writing.

I concentrated at first on my response to the invitation to provide reasons why I should not receive the 'Severe Displeasure of the Australian Navy Board'. I described the circumstances in which I had been instructed to carry out the transfer from the frigate, my request for proper briefing details and the refusal to provide them. I also described in some detail the arrangements around the transfer point in the ship. In the enquiry the 'Flight Deck Officer' had claimed to have raised a red flag which would have been the signal to break off the transfer. He also said he had used bats to wave the aircraft back. He had said nothing about the group of other officers cavorting around the forward end of the flight deck, nor the object – which I discovered to be a beer can that had been thrown towards the aircraft. I pointed out in forthright terms that not only were no flags or bats waved by anybody, but the Flight Deck Officer didn't even have any. I criticised the manner in which the enquiry had been conducted including the biased nature of the questioning to me, the failure to inform me of possible charges and the failure to offer me representation.

I concluded by asserting that I had not hazarded my aircraft but that after the accident had occurred I had done everything within my power to assess the damage and return that aircraft safely to base. The alternative, I said, would have been to ditch the aircraft with resultant risk to the lives of the crew and passenger, as well as the loss of an expensive aircraft which the Australians would not be able to replace. Was this what they wanted?

It was late when I finished the rough draft of my letter; the rest of the house was in darkness, the street outside was quiet and Irene had gone to bed. I put down my biro, looked up from the table and found I was staring into a pair of liquid brown eyes, fixed on me and seeming to emanate sympathy. The message coming from dog to master was, it seemed, "Don't worry, Boss. I'll stick with you".

I leaned down and ruffled Spoofy's head and his tail thumped three or four times in reply. I read the letter quietly aloud to see how it flowed and my one dog audience appeared both enraptured and approving. With that kind of support, where could I go wrong?

I made a couple of minor amendments to the letter, burned a bit more midnight oil by writing a fair copy, and stuffed the pages into my briefcase, ready for the morning. It was almost three o'clock when I opened the back door into the garden for Spoofy. For once, he didn't disappear into the night but merely sprayed the fence post (for an impressive length of time) and ambled back into the kitchen and his basket.

****

The aircraft was flying through dense black clouds. I tried again to transmit an emergency call on the radio but I couldn't even hear my own voice. The instruments in front of me had become a blur. There was something wrong with the cockpit lighting and I had become confused about the array of switches in front of me. The wind was whistling through the aircraft now, drowning out all other sounds and I knew we must have descended close to the ground but the aircraft wouldn't respond. I could now feel blasts of hot air searing the side of my face and I couldn't get my helmet off. I was going to abandon the aircraft but I had to get the crew out first. I still couldn't speak so I pushed my right arm out and shoved the co-pilot but he didn't move. "Go, go," I shouted but it came out as a whisper. The co-pilot moved closer – which was all wrong. "Go," I at last managed to shout out loud. "Woof!" he replied, then spoiled it all by licking my ear. I opened my eyes, turned my head and found myself staring beyond a black nose, two inches from mine, and into two limpid brown eyes, which were staring fixedly back at me.

I shot bolt upright. What the hell was Spoofy doing in my bed? More to the point, where was my wife? I was confused, with the dream still vivid in my head and finding myself in odd and inexplicable circumstances. I had gone to bed a few hours ago with my wife fast asleep beside me, still clutching the book she had been reading. Now she had been replaced by a big black dog, comfortably stretched out in the bed beside me, filling the air with the faint aroma of stale dog dinner.

In a state of considerable alarm, and running through all sorts of dreadful possibilities, I left the bedroom and crossed the hall to peep into Rebecca's bedroom. My tension reduced and I breathed out. She was where she should be and sleeping soundly. I turned and almost ran through the sitting room to peer out at the drive way. Only one car! Had I been deserted? Had she left me? Was I that bad? Then I realised that she would have taken the baby. I breathed out heavily for the second time. I turned to find some clothes and fell flat on my face as I tripped over Spoofy, who had been following me from the bedroom.

As I threw on clothes over my pyjama trousers and looked about for my keys I saw that the front door and the fly screen door were both open. Adding this to the crazy things that seemed to be happening to me was no help at all. I stopped, sat, and thought. There must be a rational explanation. It was just after three a.m. I felt I had to do something but I had no idea what. Had my wife been abducted? Was she sleepwalking? Both propositions seemed bizarre. All I could do was to go and look – but what about the baby? I settled on a compromise. I would switch lights on, leave Spoofy in the house, make sure it was firmly locked up and then take the remaining car and search the immediate vicinity, returning in no more than fifteen minutes. If there was no result from this I would call the police.

I opened all the car windows and set off on a motoring version of a square search. The roads in that part of Nowra were set out on a grid pattern so all I had to do was turn left at appropriate times and I soon covered the immediate area around the house. In fact I had only been out for six or seven minutes when I heard, distantly, a woman's voice. I tried to pinpoint the sound without success but as I turned the next corner I saw the headlights of a car either stationary or moving slowly. I accelerated towards it and with enormous relief, I recognised it. As I approached I could now clearly hear Irene's voice, "Spoo-feee, Spooo- fee."

I choked back my initial response and simply said that Spoofy was home, and in slow convoy we drove back to the house. As we came quietly into the sitting room, there was the cause of the drama, illegally curled up on the sofa.

We sat and drank coffee and the story came out. Irene had woken with a terrible feeling of something being wrong. She couldn't get back to sleep, and not wanting to wake me, she got up and tiptoed around the house, first checking on Rebecca and then looking outside for Spoofy, who, if returning late from a night patrol would usually curl up on the front porch. There was no sign of him so she went outside to call him. There was still no sign so she expanded the search just a bit, by now convinced that he must be lying terribly injured somewhere or trapped and unable to return home. By this time, of course, he already was home and had nosed his way past the screen door and the front door, neither of which were locked.

Irene promised she wouldn't do it again. Spoofy was ejected from the sofa and secured behind the door of the utility room, not without protest. We went back to bed.

****

Next morning I was up early, feeling fresh despite my lack of sleep. Rebecca was rounded up and encouraged into her high chair to spread her breakfast over and around the table and Spoofy was in his station placed to ensure that nothing dropping from Rebecca's efforts actually reached the floor. As I ploughed quickly through my breakfast I explained as best I could to Irene what I had crafted during the night. She sensibly found the letter and read it herself. By the time I drove out of the driveway, not only was the sun shining and warming me through the open window but I was going into battle with the support and approval of my wife, my daughter and my dog. My tail was up. I couldn't lose.

The activity in the squadron was light. There were no operational demands and six of our eight aircraft were in the hangar undergoing maintenance. I was Senior Pilot now and I had changes in mind but they would need to be introduced incrementally if I was to carry the aircrew with me. The squadron assembled for morning briefing and when everyone was present I walked to the other hut and fetched the C.O. As Bullfrog ambled in I called the room to attention and they all stood. We went through the routine of Flying Programme, Met, 'Question of the Day' to one of the younger officers and a few words on various activities from me. The Boss declined the offer of addressing the assembly, got up and scurried off to his office, shutting the door behind him. I walked across to my office which I shared with Gerry, the Senior Observer.

I dealt with one or two routine questions from pilots, told Gerry that I would be in the Flight Planning Room in the other hut, gathered up a bundle of paper, took my briefcase and headed off that way.

Several hours later, approaching lunchtime, I had converted my late night copy to the final, immaculate version of my letter. I had taken great care but I had no typewriter and so every mistake or correction meant starting that page again and the letter was inevitably quite long and detailed. It ran to several handwritten pages.

I went back to the office, walked across to the wardroom where I had a sandwich lunch in an annex set aside for aircrew in flying clothing, returned alone to the squadron and telephoned the office of 'Commander Air' asking for an appointment that afternoon. Strictly speaking I should have taken the letter first to my C.O. but I didn't want to run the risk of it sitting for days in his in-tray while the cloud over my head gathered substance.

The phone rang and the young WRAN Air Staff Officer – another name for Wing's secretary – told me that he would see me in his office, this said with emphasis (where else? I thought) at 1500 that afternoon. That gave me a couple more hours to make a copy of my letter for myself and change back into my uniform before the meeting.

In every naval air station, the man in charge of the flying operations is always formally called 'Commander Air' but invariably referred to as 'Wings', the American Navy being an exception in calling their equivalent 'Air Boss' which I sometimes thought was a more representative title.

At a quarter to three, smartly dressed in uniform, I arrived at Commander Air's office just below the glasshouse top of the control tower. Despite being recently elevated to the minor peerage within the air station and being a foreign officer on loan I had seen, but never met, the great man. I waited in the visitors' chair in the empty Air Staff Officer's office. After ten minutes or so, a small, pretty girl in WRAN's uniform came out from the inner sanctum, smiled and said, "He'll only be a few minutes." I sat and waited, clutching my letter in its addressed but unsealed envelope.

Three or four more minutes passed. The inner office door opened and Wings appeared in the doorway. "G'day Tony," he said, in the time honoured Australian manner. I found this surprising and assumed he had checked my name on the personnel records. "Come on in. Alva, coffee for two please."

We both went into the small office, he sat behind the desk and I sat opposite, facing the picture window which looked out over the main runway.

"I just came to give you this, sir," I said. "It's my response to the enquiry letter."

He opened the envelope, spread the five pages on his desk and glanced quickly through them. Then he examined sections in more detail. Four or five minutes passed, the coffee arrived, he looked up and said, "O.K. I see. I'll pass this on straight away." He swept the pages back into a single pile and then, leaning forward over his desk, looked quizzically at me. I assumed this meant the interview was over and for the moment at least, I remained tainted.

"Well, thank you sir," I said. "I'd better be getting back to the squadron." He nodded. I got up and left. I passed Alva, busy, head down, at her typewriter. The coffee remained untouched.

I walked back across the air station to the squadron and got on with my life.

The Golden Holden –
our carriage around Australia."

"The Author relaxing in the sun."

"Rebecca ready to travel."

"By courtesy of the RAN Fleet
Air Arm Museum".

Chapter 20
Spoofy goes AWOL

I arrived home that evening feeling reasonably comfortable with what I had done. As I drove into the drive I looked for the familiar black shape leaping and cavorting around the car as it entered his terrain.

There was no black shape. This was unusual but not unheard of, so I called out to Irene as I climbed the steps to the back porch, "Where's Spoofy?"

Irene appeared, with the tiny face of Rebecca behind her knees and called back, "Out – he's been out all day."

I wandered inside, kissed my wife, got a wet, snotty kiss from my daughter and flopped down on one of the kitchen stools. Dinner was already in the course of preparation so I opened a can of Tooheys, poured Irene a glass of really rather good local wine, which came out of a half gallon plastic flagon marked 'Claret' and relaxed.

By the time Rebecca had gone to bed there was still no sign of Spoofy. This was now becoming mildly alarming because our custom was for Spoofy to attend Rebecca's evening meal as a 'gatherer' and then to eat his own dinner.

We had dinner ourselves and there was still no sign of Spoofy. At Irene's insistence, I got the car out and drove slowly around the nearby streets. There were several dogs around but definitely no Spoofy. I thought it a pity that I couldn't ask his street colleagues if they had seen him.

The next day was Friday and by breakfast there was still no sign of our dog. Things were advancing towards crisis in the Holt family. Irene didn't say anything but as I left for work I knew that she would get the old Holden out as soon as she could, strap Rebecca in the back and systematically tour the town until she found Spoofy.

As soon as I arrived at work the inevitable routine took over and after Morning Briefing I had a flying programme to run and at least two sorties to do myself so the disappearance of Spoofy was pushed inevitably to the back of my mind as the trivia of the day crowded in on me.

I was also somewhat preoccupied with the task of taking the reins as Senior Pilot and establishing my position and authority among the other aircrew. I had never held a real and lasting position of authority before but I had sufficient experience to recognise that much of the complex and delicate process of flying operational helicopters was accomplished in a rather different manner from that which I had experienced in Britain.

Australians, by and large, are charming, easy going and likeable people but they are fiercely independent and have inherited a stubborn streak which their ancestors had deployed to great effect to carve the country out of an unforgiving wilderness. One of the best ways to light up and activate that stubbornness was to criticise the way in which they went about their business. Telling them that almost anything was done better in the UK was the equivalent of pouring a lot of petrol on the fire, so I had to tread very carefully indeed. Additionally, of course, I knew that I was being closely compared with my predecessor, who, although a reasonable manager, had, in my view, presided over a rather slack organization where the expression "She'll be right", (meaning "let's do nothing and see what happens") and "We'll give it a go – tomorrow", (meaning "Hopefully we'll forget all about it"), had been commonplace.

I also had the burden of the threatened 'Severe Displeasure' hanging over me and, although nobody raised the subject or discussed it, I knew that this was a point of intense interest among the pilots working for me. At least a third of the older hands believed that I was a nine day wonder who had been merely drafted in to fill the gap while the powers searched for a proper Australian to take over the key role and wave good bye to me as I was packed off home to Pommie-land with my tail between my legs. The Boss, as usual, took little interest in the day to day running of the squadron and continued to spend much of his time behind the closed door of his office. Certainly I never saw him step into an aircraft again.

The one source of support for me within the squadron at this time was Gerry, the Senior Observer. We shared an office and while I was responsible for flying operations and the general administration, Gerry was responsible for the squadron's capability as an anti-submarine force. The pilots flew the aircraft but the observers operated the systems that made them useful. Gerry and his observers fought the fight at sea but we, the pilots, were responsible for taking them there and getting them home safely. An easy going, unflappable man, a bit older than the rest of us, Gerry never once changed his attitude towards me and always dealt with me in a professional and respectful manner. I was grateful.

****

At the end of that afternoon, as I cruised in convoy with the other home going vehicles down the long, straight, tree lined road from the air station to the town my mind focussed once again on the absence of Spoofy. I reviewed the amount of time he had been away and came to the conclusion that since he had so far given the distinct impression of being indestructible, in all probability he would now be at home sleeping off his extended adventure.

It was hot and dusty in the car and the weather promised to become even hotter over the coming weekend, so as I drove along with the front windows wide open I began to contemplate a refreshing cool shower, a cold beer on the back porch with my wife and daughter and a relaxing weekend. Spoofy slipped once more to the back of my mind, having partially convinced myself that I would soon be greeted by the big black cavorting animal with the whirling tail and wet tongue, putting on his special 'welcome home, Boss' display.

My easy mood was quickly shattered. There had been no sign of Spoofy throughout the day, despite Irene's motorised searches, covering wider and wider areas around the town. People on his usual routes, and those who would recognise him were questioned, even the owners of the dogs that we knew he bullied, but without result. The evening was horrible. Irene was distraught and Rebecca had caught the mood and so had become inconsolably fractious.

After she had been put to bed and finally gone to sleep we had supper almost in silence and punctuated only by guesses as to where else we might look, what might have happened to him and how were we going to break the news of his disappearance – or even death – to his distant owners.

****

All through Saturday we continued in much the same vein. My circumstances at work were completely forgotten. We trudged through the day, fetched the newspaper, went shopping – where I found myself actually peering down between the aisles in the supermarket in the hope of seeing a dog – but I knew that dogs were not allowed into shops so I must have been tainted with near paranoia. Later in the day, we went out again in the car and continued and repeated the search, even rumbling down the dirt roads into the bush in the hope of seeing Spoofy coming back from some remote homestead. We discussed over and over, the possibilities of what might have happened to him. Had he been hit by an interstate truck on the highway and was even now lying dead at the roadside? Had he been bitten by a snake? Was he locked in somewhere? Had he just upped and left us? Our neighbour old Mr Booth was also asked to look out for Spoofy when he was out on his routine wood collecting trips into the bush.

By evening we had both decided that we should make one more round of our friends and acquaintances in Nowra, by phone or by visiting them. We knew that none of them had seen Spoofy or by now we would have been told but, in our desperation, we were seeking ideas for any possibility that we had not yet considered.

It was about six o'clock when the phone rang. Irene's friend Sue, the wife of another British pilot who had transferred to the Australians to fly Skyhawks, had been visited several times in the past couple of days and had discussed our plight at length.

"I just thought, have you tried the pound?" said Sue.

"What pound?" said Irene, not quite understanding the question.

"You know – the dog pound."

"I didn't know there was one." Irene had hope in her voice at last.

The phone conversation went on while I stood next to Irene, becoming increasingly impatient and frustrated by the snippets I was picking up from one half of the conversation.

It turned out that Nowra had a dog catcher – generally rather under employed because of the habit of allowing dogs to roam around the town. However, there were a few waifs and strays and even some dogs that had run away from owners passing through, or perhaps who had been dumped. Others had been injured on the highway or lost in the bush.

Sue didn't know exactly where the dog catcher operated from or where the pound was situated but she had given us the first hope in several days.

We searched for and found the telephone directory. A quick scan revealed plenty of 'pounds' but they were all people, or in two cases shops. A more detailed and slightly more frantic search was no more successful. "It must be under some other name," I said.

We looked through the 'Ds' for dog and district, 'Ns' for Nowra, 'Ls' for local authority, and we were on the 'Ss' for Shoalhaven when the front door bell rang. We stopped, rooted to the spot, staring at each other as if suddenly quick-frozen. Nobody came to the front door. Everybody we knew would know that we were more likely to be in the kitchen or on the porch, both at the back.

The frozen moment ended and we both headed for the front door. I reached it first, wrenched it open, pushed open the fly-screen door and there facing me was a man who could have been the advertisement for outback Australia. He removed his slouch hat, shifted his feet and stuck a hand in one of his military style shirt pockets, bringing it out with a small scrap of paper.

"G'day," he drawled. "Is this where Spoofy lives?"

"I've been across at the Edgecombe's, but there's nobody there," he continued.

"They've gone away," murmured Irene.

"To England," I said.

"Well blow me," said our visitor. "That explains it."

We were both agonising about what he might have to tell us.

"Well, yer going to have a bit of a bill. Ya see, I've had him three days now, and Jeez, can that feller eat!"

I couldn't stand it any more. "Come in," I said.

Spoofy, we learnt, had been a guest of the District of Shoalhaven, in the area dog pound for about three days now. The pound was situated about four miles along the road towards Jervis Bay and Huskisson, but set well back from the road and well clear of the nearest habitation so that people would not be disturbed. It was signposted but the advancing bush had obscured the sign. We had been looking for a lost, dead or injured dog, not a dog pound and our passing car had not disturbed the dozen or so inhabitants of the pound sufficiently for us to notice them.

Charlie, the dog warden, was very apologetic. He knew Spoofy quite well and on his rounds they usually simply nodded to each other – or so he said. On this occasion Charlie had been summoned to a house adjacent to the highway where it entered the town on the south side. The lady occupant had a rather nice retriever bitch, heavily in season, and besieged with about twenty of the more randy local dogs. They were in her garden, on her lawn, in the road, scratching at her door and intermittently brawling with each other. Spoofy had assumed a magisterial position right in the centre of the road where he could survey the competition as they gathered and remain aloof to the traffic thundering past on either side of him. The

135

besieging dogs were rounded up in ones and twos and secured in the large cages on the back of Charlie's truck, while Spoofy calmly remained in his strange but dominant position waiting until there should no longer be any competition to frustrate his lust.

Charlie had attempted to shoo Spoofy away unsuccessfully and since by then his truck was pretty well full he started climbing aboard hoping that hunger for food would shortly lure Spoofy back onto his patrol, heading for home.

"What about that one – the black one?" shrieked the anguished and harassed woman.

"That's Spoofy, everybody knows him," Charlie attempted to explain.

"You take him. I demand it."

"Ah – go on, he ain't no harm," Charlie continued in the defence of his friend.

"Take him! Take him!" shouted the now enraged woman.

A crowd had gathered and Charlie decided he had no choice. Throwing the dog catching kit in the back of the truck he had nudged Spoofy out of his road blocking position, holding a piece of liver about a foot in front of the shiny black nose. Spoofy got up, ambled after Charlie and stopped by the cab door. "C'mon Spoof, hup," said Charlie. Obediently, Spoofy hopped up into the front of the truck and sat on the left hand seat as Charlie climbed in behind the wheel. Together, they trundled off towards the animal pound (we had not looked under A!) looking for all the world like a team of custodians shepherding their noisy cargo into temporary captivity.

Spoofy had not been incarcerated during daylight, only when Charlie went home. Most of the time, he had followed Charlie around on his daily duties, acting rather in the manner of the new assistant warder.

Charlie stayed for a while, and over a cold beer – several cold beers in fact – we swapped our various experiences of Spoofy. An hour later, immensely relieved, we agreed to follow Charlie's direction the following morning and pick up Spoofy ourselves from the pound.

Sunday dawned predictably bright and clear, and as soon as we had breakfasted we strapped Rebecca into her chair, in the back seat of the better Holden, put Spoofy's blanket in the station wagon area behind the rear seat and set off for the reunion. Charlie's directions were accurate and half an hour later the car was slowly negotiating the narrow, potholed track that led to the pound. Emerging from the trees we came across a clear area big enough to turn a truck around without reversing, behind which was a high chain link fence with a path running around the inside of it and a series of spacious cages on the other side of the path.

We stopped, Irene lifted Rebecca from her seat and walked over to the gate as Charlie appeared, bucket in hand and opened it for us. At that moment we spotted Spoofy wandering along behind Charlie. He was sniffing along the lower edge of the cages and occasionally pausing to lift his leg and direct a generous spray into the cage, occasionally spattering the unfortunate animal inside.

Then Spoofy spotted us and with a sort of low pitched grumble – demonstrating recognition tinged with recrimination, I thought – he bounded across the intervening space, leapt up and placed a pair of grubby front paws on my white trousers before moving immediately to greet the ladies of the household. Spoofy, clearly, was ready to come home.

Irene was hiding a tear and Rebecca was reaching to grab handfuls of short black fur while I handed over a bundle of dollars to a still apologetic Charlie and received the official animal (dog) pound receipt. We still have that piece of paper today.

Before we left, Charlie showed us quickly around his small kingdom. As well as about fifteen dogs, he had some cats, two ponies and, curiously, a small wallaby – almost tame and living in a big grassy paddock on its own.

We took our leave, waved farewell to our new friend and headed for home, with Spoofy standing stiff legged in the back compartment of the station wagon, protecting us all by barking furiously and noisily at everything and anything or anyone who happened by. The only family member who seemed to enjoy this fusillade of barking was Rebecca, strapped into her seat just in front of our canine protector. We could hear her gurgling and making her little sing song noises, frequently drowned by furious barking so it was with amazement that on arrival back at the house we found she was happily and blissfully, fast asleep.

Chapter 21
Changes

I still felt somewhat shattered and mentally strained from the after effects of the great Spoofy hunt as I motored down Berry Street and turned into the traffic flow heading to the air station. It was Monday morning, a new week and I had things to think about other than our adventures with a lost dog.

I was worried about the possible outcome from the enquiry and not a little angry at the unfair way I had been scapegoated. The more I thought about what had happened that day during the transfer with *Queenborough* the more angry and frustrated I became. On the other hand, chance had dealt me a compensatory hand by providing me with the opportunity to prove myself in my new elevated position.

By the time I passed through the gates and returned the salute of the naval sentry I had reached a decision. There was nothing more I could do to defend my position and reputation at the moment. I had written my letter of response to the Navy Board and I was sure that anyone reading that letter would begin to harbour serious doubts about the conduct not only of the transfer operation but also of the handling of the Board of Enquiry. My best foot forward now lay in showing what I could do to bring a rather tired and somnolent squadron up to a reasonable peak of efficiency. I knew I could do it but I knew also that I needed to introduce my ideas carefully in order to carry the opinion formers with me.

I parked the car and walked briskly into my office, then quickly across to the flying locker room to change into flying overalls. A few minutes later the squadron briefing was underway, with, somewhat unusually these days, the C.O. present. We went through the usual procedure under the direction of the Duty Officer and as I started to rise to my feet to emphasize some important points I was waved down by the Boss. Bullfrog stood up and without much ceremony told us that he would be leaving shortly to go on to another appointment and he was going to be replaced by Lieutenant Commander Eddie Bell.

There was an immediate low buzz of reaction in the room. Bullfrog said nothing more, and strode from the room. To fail to inform his senior officers before making such an announcement was a major breach of protocol but all that had passed cleanly over the top of my head. We were about to get a new C.O. who would actually lead the squadron. Eddie Bell had a reputation within the Australian Fleet Air Arm for being a bit of a firebrand and a difficult man to work for. I had already served with him when I was completing my flying training where he had been a flying instructor on exchange service. He was a man who set very high and exacting standards but he could also play hard and he was always fair and even handed. I thought that he was exactly what I needed to back me and support me in my as yet unannounced campaign to raise the standards and status of the squadron. I was delighted. I was cock-a-hoop. I couldn't wait for him to join.

Before the end of that Monday both Gerry and I had been made aware of the meaning of 'shortly' in relation to Bullfrog's departure. Eddie Bell would arrive next Monday and he would assume command on Tuesday. There were some pale faces in the crew room and the bridge table was surprisingly empty throughout the day. Things were looking up.

****

By mid week the atmosphere within the squadron had begun to change. I decided that I should seize the opportunity presented by introducing the first of my improvements. I started by insisting on a proper daily serviceability statement from the maintainers. Each day we were told how many aircraft were serviceable but it never seemed to be more than two or three and coincidentally just enough to meet the stated flying programme. I wanted to know not just how many were available to fly but what was wrong with the remainder and when they were expected to become serviceable. I also wanted the pilots to be interested in this, particularly the Duty Officer. Of course the serviceability would change during the course of the day so I insisted that the Duty Officer knew when this happened and kept me informed.

Next, I demanded the removal of all the neat little pockets designed to hold a packet of cigarettes or a lighter which had been sewn onto the shoulders of flying overalls. There would be no more smoking in the aircraft despite the fact that several of them were fitted with ashtrays. Once this message had been received and the various gripes had come and gone I started to look at how the aircrew were spending their time when not flying. I made it clear that I didn't want to see groups of aircrew clasping cups of coffee and hanging about taking in the morning sunshine unless they could convince me that they were already masters of their trade. I am not ashamed to say that I presented our soon to arrive replacement C.O. as someone to be respected and feared, in equal proportions; a man, as I frequently said, who would accept nothing short of the best, stand no nonsense, and "take no prisoners".

By the end of the week, our present C.O. had left. I have tried to recall but I cannot remember seeing much of him after Monday's announcement and I never actually saw him leave. On Friday, Gerry looked across from his desk and mentioned, almost as an aside, that he was temporarily in charge. I just said O.K. and we carried on with our separate tasks.

Later that day, while all the 'boys' were beavering away tidying up our premises, cleaning the 'Coffee Boat' and generally making the squadron look a bit more ship shape, Gerry came in and said, "Oh, message for you. Wings rang at lunchtime and wants to see you."

A shiver ran down my spine. This could be the answer to my letter although if it was, it was quick. I knew that the wheels of the corridors of power turned slowly so I thought I must be required for something else. The shiver returned. But what if it was not? Suppose my response had been rejected? Would I still be Senior Pilot on Monday? There was only one way to find out and I wanted to get this over with quickly so instead of walking, I climbed into my car, drove out onto the perimeter road and round to the station offices in the Control Tower.

I parked in one of the marked Air Traffic Control slots, jammed my cap on my head and walked smartly towards the tower, up the stairs and into the outer office. Alva actually smiled. Could this be an omen? Before I had a chance to consider that thought any further Wings called from inside his office. "Hi, Tony. Come on in." I went in.

"Good afternoon, sir."

"Have a seat," he threw over his shoulder as he stared out of the window. I sat facing the cluttered desk, idly wondering why his bone dome and an oxygen mask assembly were sitting on it.

He finished watching whatever was holding his attention and turned as Alva placed a mug of coffee in front of me and magically disappeared carefully shutting the door behind her. I waited. "You know Eddie Bell, I believe." He sat, smiled and leaned towards me placing his coffee mug, which I had only just noticed, among the litter on the desk.

"Yes, I do," I said, "he was one of the instructors at Culdrose when I was going through."

"He's a good man, just what we need." He sipped his coffee, peering at me over the rim of the mug.

"I liked him," I said, "I think he stands no nonsense and goes by the book."

"Yeah, just what we need," he repeated, thoughtfully. Then, "How are you enjoying being Senior Pilot? I see you've already made a few changes."

"Yes." I couldn't immediately think of what else to say. Was this the prelude to saying well done and goodbye?

We carried on chatting inconsequentially for the next twenty minutes or so until I said, "Well, I had better get back to the squadron, sir, before the boys all slide off on early weekend."

"Yes, sure, fine," he said as I slid the chair back and stood up to leave. As I turned to go, he reached into the heap on his desk and pulled out an official looking envelope.

"Oh, by the way, this is for you."

As I reached out and took it my stomach had started doing aerobatics. Could this be the Black Spot? The kiss of death? My face must have betrayed the turmoil of my thoughts and as he climbed to his feet he peered down towards me and the ghost of a smile touched the corners of his eyes. He said, "No further action. It's over, done, the matter is closed."

It was almost an anti-climax. I could feel the cloud lifting from above my head as I clattered down the stairs.

I sat for several minutes in the car breathing deeply, before starting the engine and cruising smoothly across to the squadron dispersal. I parked the car, and strolled across to my office. As I arrived I got my second shock that day. Jack, the former Senior Pilot was coming back to the squadron.

****

The traffic was particularly heavy, with the air station emptying out its people for the weekend. My euphoric mood had not exactly evaporated but I was confused and frankly irritated by the news that Jack was coming back. Did this mean that I was about to say goodbye to my new position and – more important – the money that went with it. The extra income certainly had been very handy and had enabled us to plan holidays so we could see more of the country but, in reality I knew we could get by without my additional pay if we had to.

I was so distracted by my confusion of thoughts that I didn't really notice the journey until the familiar pine trees in Mr Booth's front garden identified my destination. I crept forward in the queue of walking pace traffic, indicated the turn and then crunched down the driveway to stop just in front of the door-less garage. I was anxious to discuss developments with Irene who I knew would apply sufficient logic to enable me to concentrate on the good news and ignore the other. I was right. Her view was to celebrate the lifting of my unfairly imposed professional cloud and simply ignore the rest while getting on with life. Not for the first time I thanked providence for being blessed with a practical, sensible, problem solving wife.

But before all this, there was something else of interest. I climbed the stairs to the back porch and there, on the kitchen floor was my wife, my daughter and my foster-dog, all staring at a horrible little object in the centre of the tiled floor.

Spoofy had preceded my arrival by only a few minutes. He had trotted happily down the driveway, stopped for a brief scratch on the lawn and then climbed the stairs, passing the already opened screen door and shouldering his way through the kitchen door before depositing, with some ceremony, a chicken head at the feet (or rather just in front of the wheeled baby walker) of his very best friend – my little daughter Rebecca. Irene had turned to see the expression of delight and hear the happy gurgle from Rebecca as Spoofy sat back on his haunches and then lowered himself to the floor to put him on a level with the child, with a look of such pride on his grinning, tongue lolling face that he looked rather like a canine version of a favourite indulgent uncle.

The chicken head was not new. The dry crusted blood around it and one or two little white maggots suggested that Spoofy must have salvaged it from some untended un-emptied bin. Clearly he had put a lot of effort into the selection and recovery of this present and Rebecca, who was thankfully restricted by the baby walker from picking up the chicken head – which in those days would have found its way quickly into her mouth – was delighted to receive such a thoughtful and unusual present. She clapped her little hands, cooed and trundled the baby walker forward, passing right over the pungent morsel causing Spoofy to lurch back to avoid a collision and giving Irene the opportunity to scoop up the chicken head and swiftly drop it into the kitchen bin. Spoofy and Rebecca both looked puzzled and then sad. At that moment I appeared at the door and both child and dog went into high gear greeting mode.

Usually, when Spoofy went foraging, his technique was to dispossess some other dog, by sheer weight of character rather than any direct aggression, I could readily understand why he had been unsuccessful in obtaining a bigger prize on this occasion. Considering the huge number of knuckle bones and marrow bones which had appeared in the back garden, in the garage or even in the old car, it was quite possible that Spoofy had used up the entire supply of bones in the town. Alternatively, the owners of the dogs he habitually robbed might just have become wise to him.

The evening ended merrily, with Rebecca tucked up in bed and asleep, for once without protest, and the two of us recounting the events of the day, sated with some good Australian steak and mellowed with some equally good Australian wine.

Chapter 22
Mr Booth

Our neighbour was a character. Small, wiry, sunburned, wrinkled and tough as old leather, Mr Booth kept a protective eye on us, making sure that we didn't fall victim to any of the natural or unnatural risks that Australia had to offer. He typified the original, totally self sufficient cobber who had opened up and developed Australia. His store of energy belied his ninety-six years. He had arrived in Nowra some seventy-five years before we did, when it was nothing but a potential settlement. Mr Booth, we never knew his given name, had staked out his claim, planted his crops and fruit trees, headed off into the bush and cut his timber to make fence posts, a barn and a large, practical but rambling house. At first he had grazed a few cows and sheep, kept a pig or two and plenty of poultry. He had shot dingoes, kangaroos and wallabies, primitively tanned their hides and fed the meat to his dogs.

As the town had developed and grown up around him his little self made kingdom had been pressed in on all sides. The road, Berry Street, had replaced the track and the newly inaugurated Shoalhaven Council had taken his land for that. Other streets had been built, water mains had been laid, land was needed for shops and offices and so Mr Booth's smallholding had become smaller.

Nevertheless, he was still pretty well self sufficient and he demonstrated this by his twice weekly trips, now in a very battered old Land Rover, into the bush to cut timber for fencing, heating and repairs. He stored the results in his large barn, with all sorts of wood immaculately sorted by size and length and stored accordingly. I wondered, in conversation with him one day, why he needed so much. He quickly retorted to me that he also collected wood for his seventy-year-old son who only had one arm.

Mr Booth's domestic needs were catered for by two spinster daughters in their late sixties, who were rarely seen outside of his property. However I did notice that occasionally, on his return from his expeditions into the bush, he would have bunches of wild flowers in the cab of his Land Rover.

Mr Booth was in many ways the perfect neighbour. He kept himself to himself, as they say, but he also ensured that we were provided with abundant supplies of nuts, apples, pears, oranges, plums and other fruit as each came into season. He would stand peering over the top of his fence and shout in his high reedy voice, "Missis 'Olt, Missis 'Olt!", continuing until Irene and Spoofy came out to acknowledge his call. Then, with much greater expenditure of effort than if they had been carried up his drive and back down ours, a sack or two of nuts or fruit would be manoeuvred over the fence.

The nuts supplied by Mr Booth bear special mention. They were almost impenetrable. If you did manage to get at the kernel it was delicious but getting there was a problem. I devised all sorts of techniques, mostly, unless we found a particularly weak nut, to no avail. Ordinary nut crackers were not worth considering at all. Then I bought a set of nut crackers where the nut was held in a miniature vice which was progressively tightened. One of two things happened: either the thread on the screw stripped or the nut suddenly pinged away into the distance, never to be seen again. I bought a small engineer's bench vice. I realised quite quickly that I should have bought a bigger one.

On another occasion, I had acquired a seven pound hammer. I placed a small pile of nuts on the concrete path behind the house, and observed closely, very closely in fact, by

Spoofy I selected a nut, picked up the hammer and took careful aim. The nut spun away into the lower lawn. I tried again, this time wedging the nut between two flat stones. As I did this I noticed that my earnest helpmate was also selecting nuts, one at a time and taking them away to some other part of the garden. My pile of undamaged nuts was growing smaller. I took the hammer, aimed carefully and struck the nut a mighty blow – dead centre. I looked at my handiwork and noticed that the nut appeared completely undamaged. When I picked it up I saw a small nut shaped indentation in the concrete, with stress cracks radiating out from it. I gave up.

Not all of Mr Booth's generosity was as difficult to deal with as the nuts. As the various fruits ripened, the familiar call came from the other side of the fence and sacks or large paper bags were handed over. We were never short of fruit.

Another example of Mr Booth's generosity could have landed us in deep trouble with the law. The national flower of New South Wales is the waratah. A large single bloom on a tallish stem, the waratah is not unlike the South African proteas. It is a protected species and it is forbidden to remove them from their natural habitat – usually deep in the bush – or damage them in any way. These striking and very noticeable flowers are quite rare and are revered by authority.

Imagine the reaction of, first Irene, and then later, me, when Mr Booth arrived unexpectedly at our front door with a large bunch of waratahs. Irene had the presence of mind to thank him profusely, while keeping the incriminating bouquet as far out of the view of any passers-by as she could. When I arrived home, there they were in all their glory, in a large vase in our sitting room – with a special space in a cupboard having been cleared to hide them in the event of any visitors. I was acutely aware that being discovered in possession of just one waratah was enough to bring down the full majesty of the law so I could not imagine what penalty a whole bunch of them might incur. Maybe 'transportation' back to England, I wondered.

Unfortunately both Spoofy and Rebecca seemed to have taken an interest in the recently emptied cupboard – which was worrying. The flowers were indeed beautiful and lasted about eight days, after which we crept down the garden to the barbecue and burnt the stalks late one night.

Mr Booth was a kindly neighbour and everyone loved him, particularly Spoofy who was given to standing up on his back legs and trying to peer through the horizontal gaps in the fence whenever Mr Booth's voice was heard on the other side, heralding yet another parcel.

One other advantage of living next to Mr Booth was that the tall trees he had planted liberally around his front garden shielded us from northerly and westerly winds and provided some shade over our driveway, which encouraged Spoofy to take up a position where he could laze in the shade provided by the trees but also keep watch on anyone who might have the temerity to enter his territory uninvited.

Also, more importantly, the trees encouraged all sorts of exotic birds, some of whom stayed and others who were just passing through. The semi-residents included a group of about a dozen large black cockatoos. These were huge birds who cackled and squawked noisily as they hopped and flapped from branch to branch high in the pines adjacent to our fence. We had acquired an eight millimetre cine camera and I determined to commit the antics of these interesting birds to film.

It was Saturday morning and the birds had arrived. There was not much wind so the trees were fairly still and the sun was in the right position. I went out into the front garden accompanied by Irene, Rebecca and Spoofy. I started filming which went well for about two minutes and then everything went black. The film ends to the sound of Irene's laughter and a soft single "woof". I turned the camera round and looked at it in horror. I had been bombed. The camera had almost disappeared under a huge dripping running blob of multi coloured guano. This matched the stripe of bird shit which ran from the top of my head to the bottom of my jeans. That was the last attempt at filming black cockatoos.

Chapter 23
A New Regime

I made an early start on Monday morning. Breakfast moved at its usual hectic and slightly chaotic pace with Spoofy making a point of remaining at the required distance from the breakfast table whilst planning to take the advantage offered by our discussion of the day ahead and the distraction of meeting the feeding needs of a lively toddler. The bond he had formed with Rebecca enabled him to become aware of cascading food while apparently deep in disinterested sleep and to ensure that a covert patrol seemingly taking him from one reclining position to another would follow a course understood by his tiny benefactor and rewarded accordingly.

Mild recriminations were directed towards both guilty parties but priority had to be given to my imminent departure, the avoidance of tiny sticky hands marking my clean white uniform shirt and the gathering of the various necessary bits and pieces I would need to take with me. A scene no doubt replicated in one way or another in thousands of households all over the world.

But today was different. I had a new Boss and I wanted to make sure all was well prior to his arrival.

I was an hour ahead of the normal start time and the traffic along the tree lined road to the air station was light to the point of being almost non-existent. There was no wind and the morning was clear and already warm, promising a very hot day to come. I was still rehearsing my John the Baptist role as I drove easily around the perimeter road towards the squadron. My preparations were working, I had given myself plenty of time to check around and through our buildings as well as to go across to the hangars to pick up the serviceability state and touch base with the engineers. On the previous Friday I had organized a blitz of the offices and crew rooms as well as a litter patrol to make sure there were no offending items to sully the pristine appearance of our squadron dispersal. Everything looked good and I felt good – until I turned off the perimeter road into our car parking space. There in solitary splendour, stood a car instantly recognisable to me. It was a burnished bronze coloured Mark 9 Jaguar Saloon last seen sitting in the car park of 705 Flying Training Squadron at the Royal Navy's huge helicopter base at Culdrose in Cornwall. The car was the pride and joy of Lieutenant Commander Eddie Bell, who had purchased it free of income tax while on exchange duty to the Royal Navy and was so enamoured of it that when the time had come for him to return to Australia he had arranged for the car to be shipped out to join him.

I parked, smoothed the travel creases out of my uniform and headed resolutely for the squadron offices. I was halfway there when I was intercepted by the Duty Officer, a young sub-lieutenant who lived in accommodation on the base. He blurted out, rather unnecessarily, "The new Boss is here, sir."

"I know," I said without breaking my stride. "Where is he?"

"In his office," I was told.

"I gave him some coffee and he's just settling into his office," he continued. At least something was going right.

I took a deep breath, scurried through my own office, noting on the way that it still looked efficient and tidy, dropped my briefcase and kit, and headed for the closed door marked 'C.O.'. I knocked and was invited in.

My new C.O. already dressed in a lightweight green flying suit, was standing to one side of the modest desk shoving something into a grey steel locker. He turned, smiled and thrust out a hand towards me. "Nice to see one of my own protégées," he said.

"Welcome to 725, sir," I responded. "Briefing is in about forty five minutes."

"Siddown," he said, then, roaring over my shoulder, "Sub."

"Sir?" came the immediate response from the Duty Officer who must have been lurking outside the door.

"Two coffees, please." This, in a disconcertingly quiet and polite voice.

The coffees arrived and after the usual polite enquiries of each other we got down to a rapid fire discussion on the squadron and its people. Our new Boss had lost none of the sparkle nor the dry humour and colourful wit that I recalled from our previous acquaintance. He had lost some hair but balanced this with a neat grey beard – and the light blue eyes were as piercing as ever. He was quick to take in what I had to say and had already made himself aware of the successes and failures of his new command. He retained his 'no-nonsense' attitude and called a spade a spade, or rather, in his terms, "nothing but a bloody shovel!" He was going to lead a tough and sharp routine but one which would improve the squadron and make us proud to be part of it. Most importantly for me, before we left together to walk across the few yards to the briefing room, he put my mind at rest on the two subjects of concern to me. My job as Senior Pilot was safe, and his several descriptions of the *Queenborough* incident and the ensuing Board of Enquiry as "garbage", as "Shit defeating logic", as "crap" and as "bloody nonsense" left me with no doubt at all as to where he stood on the issue – which he finally described as "dead and forgotten". As I stood in the doorway of the briefing room calling the assembled aircrew to attention I felt I had grown at least two inches in height.

The briefing followed its normal course but with the complete absence of any of the usual occasional banter from the floor. I stood up at the end, asked the 'question of the day' an easy one to avoid undue embarrassment and subsequent debate, talked through a synopsis of the flying programme, gleefully corrected a small error in the Duty Officer's serviceability report, asked if there were any questions and then asked the Boss if he would like to say anything.

He stepped out from his front row seat turned to face the assembled squadron, paused as he deliberately ran his eye over the five rows of chairs, nodded towards the venerable Chief Aircrewman sitting in the back row and said, "Nice to see you, Tansy." Chief Aircrewman Lee, unusually lost for words, nodded back.

"There are a couple of things I want to get straight, right up front." The Boss spoke slowly and distinctly, letting the import of each phrase sink in. His eyes continued to move around the completely silent assembly as he spoke. No one coughed. No chairs moved. No one yawned. Facial expressions remained neutral and fixed.

"First, this is a good squadron, but for some reason you don't seem to have serviceable aircraft. That's gonna change. Aircraft come back because some tin pot piece of cockpit rubbish goes tits up, when you could, and should – make that 'must' from now on – complete the sortie." He continued in much the same vein for four or five minutes more, then, "We are going to get more and more 'heroes' from South East Asia, with six months' experience and thousands of flying hours – and habits that can kill. It'll be our job to turn them back into proper aircrew and that means we have to look to our own standards – and I'll be around to help SOBs and Splot to help *you* to get it right." He placed heavy emphasis on the "you" and allowed his gaze to move methodically along each row as he spaced out these last words.

He turned as though to leave the rostrum and the room and then paused as if struck by another thought. He moved back and stood squarely in front of his audience.

"One more thing," he said. "There have been several instances of spurious engine fire warning lights." He paused. "And aircraft have been ditched, only to discover that there was nothing wrong with the engine – only the bloody warning light." He shifted his feet and leaned forward slightly, dominating the front row and continued, speaking even more slowly than before. "I know that SOP says that you shut down the engine if the light comes on but I don't want anybody losing a three million dollar aircraft because a ten cent light comes on." He paused again, longer this time and then, quietly, said, "If anybody ignores that very good advice and we lose another aircraft for no good reason, he'll be taking his balls home in a jar." With that he turned and strode from the room.

I watched the boys file out with a mixture of expressions on their faces. The older hands seemed to be generally unaffected but some of the younger pilots looked worried, puzzled, and in one case furious. As the morning wore on I thought more of what the new Boss had to say and I began to wonder whether a parallel could be drawn between my recent experience and his comments on fire warning lights leading to catastrophic but unnecessary losses of aircraft. The situation which I had faced as I hovered over the deck of *Queenborough* was not dissimilar. I could have chosen to minimise the risk of a main rotor blade failure but only at the cost of the loss of the aircraft and the more certain and immediate risk to the occupants. The Board of Enquiry had concluded that my decision was wrong but the decision I had taken had saved the aircraft, crew and passenger. I had made my decision with the knowledge of rotor blade construction and I believed that as it had not failed immediately when struck, it was not likely to. Did I make the right decision? I think I did. Was Eddie Bell giving me a coded approval of my actions? I think he was.

The day fulfilled its early promise to be hot and even with all the windows open the effect of the uninterrupted sun shining on the corrugated tin roofs, the inside of the squadron huts became very uncomfortable. When this had happened in the recent past, most of the squadron had sought to ease their discomfort by taking their coffee or cigarettes outside to the shade of the overhanging roofs or onto the car park to take advantage of the breeze. Conversations would turn into ill informed debates. Anecdotes which many listeners already knew by heart were recited again. Time keeping had become a casualty of this, resulting in planned ground training being delayed or even abandoned while out on the dispersal area in front of the hangar, frustrated pilots sat sweating in the cockpits of returned aircraft with rotors still turning while they waited to be relieved by the next crew. Not so today.

There was already a change within the squadron, people seemed sharper, events happened on time and, to my surprise the day ended with the same number of serviceable aircraft it had started with.

Having completed three sorties including one with the new Boss I was still at my desk as most of the aircrew were packing up and heading for their cars. I was working on the next day's flying programme but even as this reached completion and was pasted onto the Gestetner machine for the necessary copies to be produced, I found myself looking for other things to do. Having been beaten to the morning arrival by the new Boss I was determined that I should still be at my desk when he went home. I succeeded but it meant that it was an hour and a half later than normal when my Holden rolled slowly down the drive.

I realised that Irene would be concerned by my unscheduled late return because in those days such an event could herald a flying accident and wives did worry. This time, as I was greeted on the back steps I could see that there was a greater and more pressing reason for worry. Spoofy was not well and was still in the care of the vet, who, helpfully, worked from his home immediately across the road from us.

****

The heat and humidity had increased dramatically during the day and, when he returned from his morning patrol it had become apparent that Spoofy was not well. His eczema had flared up along his back which must have been itching badly and causing him a lot of distress. He had been scratching but couldn't reach the affected area resulting in him scratching his sides until they had started bleeding. When Irene had taken him across the road to the vet he had looked unhappy, forlorn and dejected. His normally glistening coat had been dull, dirty and streaked with blood. He was still in the vet's consulting room when I arrived home.

Chapter 24
A Difficult Patient

Half an hour later, as I looked after Rebecca who was demonstrating her limited vocabulary to me by repeating "Poo-feee", Irene went across the road to collect Spoofy from the vet. She returned quite quickly with a much revived Spoofy, tail wagging and ears cocked, as well as any Labrador can. Fortunately, Spoofy was unaware of his now rather unusual appearance. Along the centre of his back the fur had been shaved off and the bare patch was covered fairly liberally with a white cream. Irene was carrying a bag full of jars, bottles and toothpaste like tubes.

We could both see that this was going to provide us with several ongoing problems. How were we going to keep the cream in place on Spoofy's otherwise raw back while he carried on his perambulations around the town? How were we going to prevent the transfer of the cream to Rebecca, our furniture, us and anything else he came into contact with?

We considered bandages, not practicable, or locking him in the house, but we had designated him as an 'outside' dog and trouble would ensue if we were caught out. We enticed him into the laundry room for the remainder of the night and Irene consulted the vet in the morning. He said that the cream would have already been very effective in damping down the inflammation and it was possible that we could continue the process by washing Spoofy with a special shampoo which was contained in one of the bottles already provided. A soothing powder would continue the healing process by easing the urge to scratch, and these treatments, if applied regularly would obviate the need for the rather messy cream.

The powder was no problem at all but the medicinal shampoo was a different deal entirely. Irene complained that Spoofy was uncooperative and this made it difficult to get him shampooed properly. To complete the task she was required to dust him with an anti-bacterial antiseptic powder and this also presented a problem. It was not until the end of the week that I was able to see just how difficult the job was.

Spoofy could be pretty well guaranteed to be present for breakfast because there were always benefits to be had, usually supplied by Rebecca, and so it was determined that the best time to carry out his treatment would be immediately after breakfast. He had worked this out by about day two and had decided to make himself scarce when the meal was finished. Precautions needed to be taken to counter this and Irene had worked out a system of going into a state of lockdown prior to the application of the shampoo.

In fact, Spoofy wasn't too unhappy about having the shampoo rubbed into his back, but after a short period it had to be washed off and this was where he applied his real rebellion.

Pieces of raw steak were produced as bribes and as a means of distracting his attention as well as retaining his presence. The bucket of shampoo was prepared away from Spoofy's sight and hopefully out of range of his sensitive nose. The steak was shown to him and some of it placed on the wooden floor of the porch. Hanging on to his collar as he wolfed down the morsels of steak, the shampoo was quickly applied and rubbed in vigorously. So far so good. This took about two minutes while the steak was also being consumed, at which point Spoofy became 'zoom-dog' and charged towards the steps down to the garden, wrenching away from my grip on his collar and knocking Irene to one side while sending the bucket of shampoo spinning and crashing down the steps behind him.

Irene recovered very quickly and was off down the steps almost as fast as the bucket. She grabbed the garden hose which was placed conveniently ready and charged so that a simple twist of the end fitting produced a strong jet of water. I looked over the edge of the balcony. Spoofy was charging around the garden diving onto his side while still running at full pelt. He was being accurately pursued by the hose jet held by Irene who was proving her aptitude for the Fire Department. It became a competition. Spoofy headed for the washing line which had a set of sheets and pillow cases hanging from it. He hit the first sheet at a height of about three feet above the ground. The sheet was ripped from the line and immediately folded itself around the speeding dog. Surprisingly, he continued, speed only marginally reduced, around the garden, still flinging himself sideways left and right. The sheet was suffering damage and taking a real pounding. No holes had appeared in it but it was partially soaked, and turning a mixture of green and brown from contact with the wet earth and the fairly luxuriant grass. Doggedly, Irene continued to follow him with the hose until he parted company with the sheet.

He sat on the grass panting with the wreckage of the sheet beside him, actually allowing Irene to make an attempt to dab his back dry. Finally there was an application of the powder whereupon Spoofy immediately trotted off in the direction of the front gate, leaving a little cloud of medicinal powder hanging in the air behind him. We retired exhausted.

Next morning I was treated to a variation in the performance. As soon as the bucket had been knocked over, Spoofy hurled himself down the steps and with two athletic bounds and an impressive leap he shot through the open front window of the old Holden station wagon. Unabashed, Irene advanced rapidly behind him and directed the hose through the same window. There was a yelp, a brief baring of teeth and then a scramble into the back seats. Irene had the back door open instantly with the hose redirected towards the miscreant patient. After a few seconds it was all over and the soaking wet dog slunk out of the back door of the car, followed by a stream of water flowing from various points inside the car. Fortunately, because of the climate and the bug and animal life, carpets were not usually fitted in Australian cars at that time and the heat of the day meant that the vehicle would quickly dry out without any damage. Nevertheless it was an alarming performance.

This pantomime continued, with variations thrown in, for another ten days, by which time the Holden had suffered a number of internal washes and Spoofy's condition was sufficiently improved to allow the frequency of the shampoo and wash routine to be reduced to once a week. We were all pleased, but Irene most of all.

****

The weekend drama with Spoofy at its centre was still uppermost in my mind on Monday morning as I eased the station wagon out of the drive and pointed in the direction of the air station. The treatment had been effective and the raw appearance of parts of his back had disappeared. His unfazed, easy going demeanour had returned as had his daily routine. The vet's bill had arrived and we were shocked to see that in all likelihood treatment by an eminent surgeon would have been cheaper. However the bill would be the concern of his owners, who were still enjoying the delights of a southern English winter.

I fell in with the usual column of cars, vans and campervans trailing up the long road to the air station and my thoughts began to move towards the day, and the week, ahead.

Already, after only a fortnight under the 'tough love' command of Eddie Bell, significant changes were evident. There was a new air of professionalism about the squadron. The small improvements that I had been introducing were now standard procedure. Heads were held high, the daily flying programme was achieved without ending the day with a lot of unserviceable aircraft and our flying rate had increased markedly.

I arrived half an hour before the daily briefing and was pleased to note that I was ahead of the Boss as the Duty Officer greeted me and reassured me that all was well, six of the eight aircraft were ready to go and the briefing room was set up.

Forty-five minutes later, as we filed out of the briefing room, the Boss called me into his office. We sat on tubular chairs either side of his desk, and peering at me gimlet eyed as though he expected some sort of challenge, he said, "I want us to fly our arses off this month. I want us to beat 817 and see just how many hours we can get out of these aircraft."

I thought that I might have to employ some gentle persuasion with the engineers but if the higher serviceability held up and the flying programmes were followed diligently we should be able to do what was required. I talked it over with Gerry who raised no objections, indeed he thought that more flying, dedicated to proper exercises would be good for his observers.

As I returned to my office and before I had the chance to talk to Gerry I saw a familiar figure standing near my desk. Jack, the former Senior Pilot, was back.

"Hello," I said. We shook hands formally. I suggested he would need to complete a joining routine even though he had only recently left. He collected the requisite forms and headed off in the direction of the crew room and I amended the outline programme for the following day to get him airborne as soon as possible. It turned out that the reason for his sudden reappointment to Nowra had been brought about by his young child having contracted a very serious illness. The child's deteriorating condition had necessitated an admission to the local hospital followed shortly afterwards by an emergency transfer by ambulance to one of the big hospitals in Sydney. This had added to his problems because in Australia at that time ambulance journeys were not free. Most people took out insurance to cover the cost of emergency medical transport but Jack had not done this. The uninsured cost of the journey was very expensive and to add to his other worries, his pocket had been hit hard.

I thought the best way ahead would be to draw a line under what had previously passed between us, ignore it and establish a professional relationship. Obviously, I commiserated with Jack over the misfortune which had overtaken his family, and I welcomed him back to the squadron, explaining briefly, the C.O.'s optimistic plans. He seemed to want to just get on with his job, with the unstated message that he had no intention of getting in my hair.

****

When I arrived home that evening I felt more at peace with myself than I had for some weeks. There were no longer any threats to my position, I had achieved the change of professional direction that I had sought for the squadron – or at least I had started the process which, with the outspoken support of the Boss, was unlikely to encounter road blocks.

Most heartening of all, Spoofy was back to his old self. Indeed he was making up for lost time and our back lawn was already littered with little 'presents' and other evidence of his skill at extracting 'donations' from the lesser canine orders.

Spoofy's weekly medical 'bath' would still produce occasional drama for us as well as great entertainment for Rebecca, who was now able to peer around the edge of the balcony steps and add to the general chaos by cooing "Poo-feee" as loudly as she could.

Nevertheless, Spoofy was getting better and that was important.

Chapter 25
The Pace Quickens

It was about three weeks after Jack had rejoined the squadron that the accident happened. It was another gloriously sunny afternoon without the extreme heat we had been used to, but with a pleasant fifteen knot wind exactly in line with the standby runway. We had no offshore exercise commitments and so we had the perfect opportunity to go through some basic but necessary pilot training. I had three aircraft airborne. One was away to the north doing a tactical navigation exercise, another was deployed to the far side of the airfield practising low level precision work and the third, under the captaincy of Jack, was taking a series of experienced pilots through their 'engine-off landing drills'.

These drills took place at least once a year and were designed to give each pilot the opportunity to experience the effects of an engine failure and to teach him how to bring the helicopter down and land it safely without engine assistance. Contrary to some views, if a helicopter suffers an engine failure it does not immediately fall out of the sky like a wingless brick. Instead, the initial forward speed together with the air flowing upward through the rotors will keep the rotors turning and enable the aircraft to maintain control and to descend to a safe, unpowered landing. The procedure is called autorotation and might be likened in some respect to a sycamore seed fluttering gently to earth.

When practising 'engine-off landings', the helicopter would first be used to conduct a couple of 'power on' autorotations, to familiarise the pilot with the rapid rate of descent, each of which would end in a powered hover. For the actual practice engine failure the helicopter would be flown initially at about a thousand feet above a clear runway surface and then the throttle would be closed hard against the stop so that the helicopter would be committed to descend and land without any further input of power from the engine. Once the throttle is closed, the pilot must immediately lower the Collective Pitch lever which reduces the angle of pitch applied to the rotor blades. The helicopter will need to maintain about sixty or seventy knots of forward speed until it has descended to a hundred feet or so above the landing point, when the pilot must pull up the nose, flaring the aircraft and killing the rate of descent. Using the last of the momentum in the rotor head the helicopter should be able to sink gently towards the runway and run on at about thirty knots or so.

Once the basic technique has been practised successfully, further attempts are tried from different positions and from various heights, including adjusting the speed on arrival at the ground to almost nothing – a technique known as the 'zero zero' approach which would need to be used if landing on rough ground or in a restricted space.

Because it is a critical exercise with some increase in risk, engine-off landing exercises are always practised under the supervision of a Qualified Helicopter Instructor, a QHI. Jack was such a QHI and he had been tasked that afternoon to take four pilots in sequence through the exercise.

About halfway through the afternoon, one of the engineers telephoned me and tersely and rather cryptically invited me across to the hangar. "There was something I should see," he said, before putting down the phone rather abruptly. I pushed the next day's outline flying programme to one side, left the office and strolled across in the warm sunshine to the hangar. As I neared the hangar I could see a big Wessex 31B standing just outside the Air Engineers' offices. A group of half a dozen or so men seemed intent on examining the front of the aircraft.

They were talking in low earnest tones, pointing repeatedly under the nose of the helicopter. Joe, our Canadian deputy Air Engineer Officer straightened up, saw me and called out, "Look what your people have done." I think he intended to finish the remark with "...to my aircraft", but he didn't. Instead, the entire group straightened up and in one case scrambled out from underneath the bulbous nose, and everyone looked at me in silence. I took the last few steps and squatted down to peer under the nose section. What I saw shocked me. The whole underside of the usually curved nose section was ground flat and the array of aerials and lights mounted under the nose was completely missing. "What in God's name happened here," I said. This was greeted at first with silence until Joe said quietly, "I suggest you ask the pilot."

This I intended to do and, seeing from the number painted on the side of the aircraft that it had been programmed as the 'engine-off lander', I motioned Joe towards his office. As he closed the door behind me I said, "700?" Wordlessly, Joe scooped the Aircraft Flying Log and Maintenance Record – called the form A700 – off his desk and handed it to me. I glanced at it and noted that there did not seem to be any report of the damage I had just witnessed. The helicopter had been returned apparently in a normal, serviceable condition. I returned to my office as quickly as I could. I shut the door and told Gerry what I had seen. "You better talk to him," he said, then after some thought, "alone I think."

I walked out of the office, down the narrow corridor and into the crew room. Jack was there, drinking coffee and chatting with a couple of pilots, who, I recollected, were his 'students' for the afternoon. Keeping my voice as even as possible, I asked Jack to come across to one of the briefing rooms in the other hut. "Bring your coffee," I said. "I'll get one myself."

Coffee always seemed to be the lubricant that would ease stresses and problems and today was no exception. I started by casually asking how Jack had got on with his afternoon's flying. He seemed nonplussed and said it went O.K., "No problems." He looked at me quizzically, waiting for more from me. I took a deep breath. "Did you notice anything unusual about the aircraft when you came back?" I said.

He peered steadily back at me. "No-o," he replied hesitantly. I decided to stop the verbal fencing and get straight to the point.

"You hit something with the nose of your aircraft, probably the ground."

He bristled, jerking back from me as though he had been struck. Clearly I had shocked him and he was unaware that he had returned the aircraft in a state of significant damage.

He obviously didn't believe me so I said, "Let's go and look at it."

We set off in silence and remained that way until we were standing alongside the damaged helicopter. When he saw the state of it, the colour drained from Jack's face. He just stood there, saying nothing, not moving.

"I think we should talk," I said, indicating with a nod of my head that I expected to go back to the squadron.

When we were alone in the briefing room, the story was gradually eased out piece by piece. On the first sortie of the afternoon, with Jack, as the instructor, sitting in the co-pilot's seat, the 'student', flying the aircraft from the right hand seat had rattled through the 'engine-off landing checks' and Jack, recognising that his companion was an experienced pilot, had not monitored all the 'check' actions. Specifically, he had not checked that the wheel brakes were off. The aircraft had been taken down through two autorotations before climbing up to one thousand feet over the runway, requesting clearance and then committing to an engine-off landing. As the aircraft wheels touched down it had become dramatically apparent that the wheel brakes were locked on. The aircraft had tipped violently forward, Jack had grabbed the controls and using the remaining inertia in the rotor disc, had hauled back on the cyclic stick and slammed the tail down. The main wheel brakes actually gave way slightly and the aircraft trundled to a stop. There was no indication of anything structurally wrong and so the brakes were released, a 'discussion' took place between the two pilots and it was reckoned that lessons had been learned. Neither believed there was much advantage in making an issue of the incident, and so they put it to one side until the de-brief, and moved on.

Jack had remained in the aircraft, with the engine running and rotors turning as each successive 'student' came out to climb into the pilot's seat. It happens that when advancing towards a grounded helicopter with the rotor blades whirling round, the roar of the engine and the wind caused by the downwash, few pilots stop to inspect the airframe. In particular they would be most unlikely to crawl about under the nose of the aircraft, which in a Wessex, contains the engine air intake and is not a comfortable place to be.

None of the replacement pilots noticed anything amiss as they approached the aircraft. In the aircraft, despite the flattened nose, the missing aerials and fittings, there were no indications of the damage. All of the aerials mounted underneath the nose are replicated by aerials mounted on top of the nose section, so all the radios and navigation systems continued to work.

As I listened to Jack I could sense his mounting embarrassment, but I was also thinking of the similarities of this incident with my own experience some months beforehand. In each case, the pilot knew that the aircraft had suffered an unusual occurrence – but of course Jack was unaware that part of the airframe had actually hit the ground – and in each case the aircraft gave no indication to the crew of being damaged. In each instance, the damage could be fairly quickly repaired, but the big difference was that in this latest incident there would be no Board of Enquiry, no threat of an official reprimand, no witch hunt.

I told Jack to fill out an A25 incident form and left him to do this while I went across to break the news to the Boss. In fact the Senior Air Engineer had already stolen my thunder. The Boss knew what had happened but he didn't know how or why it had happened. When I entered his office I was carrying two mugs of coffee, partly to ease the tension and partly in the recognition that it is very difficult to get your hands round somebody's throat if you are holding a mug of hot coffee. Jack was safe for the moment.

Eddie Bell, who was a QHI himself, was at first unimpressed with my reconstruction of events, particularly the failure to check that the brakes had not been released on entering the engine-off landing configuration. I kept talking and we got hold of a model Wessex helicopter, holding it at the angle that would allow the underside of the nose to touch the ground. The tail would have been canted up in the air at a frightening angle and I convinced the Boss that we were lucky the rotor blades had not hit the ground as well which would have turned this recoverable incident into a major accident with multiple casualties.

The Boss calmed down somewhat but he told me to send someone to fetch Jack, who a few minutes later, disappeared behind the closed door of the Boss's office. I knew that although essentially a fair man, Eddie Bell could work himself up to an irascible tongue-lashing and I really did not envy Jack his half hour of exclusive interview with the Boss.

A quiet afternoon had gone badly awry and it was late by the time I heaved myself into the Holden and drove slowly off around the perimeter track towards the gate. As I drove past the wardroom a figure hailed me from the roadside. I pulled over. The Boss leaned into the open window and suggested we should put this day away with a quiet drink.

It was even later when I arrived home. Rebecca was in bed and asleep, Irene, as always was patient and kind but Spoofy spent the rest of the evening following me around and staring at me with a look that said "How could you?"

He was a creature of habit and obviously expected me to be one as well!

Chapter 26
Horticulture

We had a long weekend holiday coming up so we decided to take the opportunity to see a bit more of Australia. Including the weekend, we had six days altogether and this was just enough time to travel down to Canberra, have a quick look around and then venture into the Snowy Mountains. Spoofy was boarded out with our helpful near neighbours once again. We had discovered that the way to get the message through to Spoofy about his temporary residence was to take his food dish and his blanket and walk up the road with him carefully following his belongings. We knew also, that Spoofy was in the habit of returning to our garden and spending a bit of time there, perhaps in the hope of welcoming us on return. In view of this we left the old Holden in the garage with the front windows open, providing a recognisable haven in which Spoofy could wait, clear of the hot sun.

We packed a few belongings into the car, added the essential emergency tent. The case of beer, two collapsible four gallon water containers, a three litre plastic wine bottle, a toolkit and finally Rebecca, strapped into her tiny seat, with her mobile cot alongside her, before heading off down the highway.

Canberra is a fairly new city, designed and built as the new capital of Australia, on land which is not part of the five states and in the 1970s it still had the air of a newly built housing estate, yet to mature. We stopped long enough to have a look around the surprisingly compact parliament building and a few other parts of the city before driving off again in the direction of the Snowy Mountains. The area is Australia's winter playground but we were in high summer so there were few tourists around, little snow other than on the high peaks and easy driving through the magical lakeland and mountain scenery. We drove up past the man-made lakes of Eucumbene and Jindabyne, with the air becoming beautifully cool and fresh as we climbed higher.

We took pot luck and checked in to a nearly empty but very comfortable skiing lodge at the ski village of Thredbo before taking the car on up the mountain road aiming for the summit of Mount Kosciuszko – the roof of Australia.

The narrow dirt road was carved out of the side of the mountain with a rock wall on one side and a steep grass covered slope dropping away several hundred feet on the other. At the top, there was a cleared area where we parked the car. I picked Rebecca out of the car and put her on my shoulders as we set off on the final climb through crisp snow to the summit. We took photographs, threw snowballs, peered down at the headwaters of the Snowy River and as the shadows lengthened and the temperature dropped we boarded the car and set off at a leisurely pace back down the mountain.

For some reason I decided that I needed to look in my wallet so I eased the car to the side of the road and dug into my hip pocket. Panic! No wallet. It must have fallen out of my pocket while I was carrying Rebecca up to the summit. I piled back into the car, turned it round on the narrow mountain road with immense care and drove as quickly as I could back up the mountain. I was sweating as I launched myself up through the snow on the final trudge towards the summit for the second time in half an hour. Not only would this loss set back our holiday but it would put a serious and damaging dent in our finances for the immediate future. We didn't have a lot of spare money in the first place, credit card economics had yet to be born and our Australian bank wasn't keen on offering overdrafts to temporary residents from overseas.

Variations of these concerns and the possible versions of disaster which awaited me were going round and round in my head as I trudged mournfully upward. About halfway to the top I thought I heard a cry above the wind. I turned and looked down. There was Irene, hopping about beside the open door of the car waving furiously at me – and she was holding something in her hand. A surge of hope shot through me. It had to be my wallet. I turned and, as quickly as the snow and rocky ground would allow, I trotted, slid and scampered down the slope. It was my wallet. Irene had been cleverer and less panicky than me and had searched around under and behind the driver's seat of the car. She had found the wallet wedged behind the seat adjustment mechanism and was triumphantly brandishing our immediate financial future in her right hand.

We treated ourselves to a gourmet evening based around thick steaks and fine Australian wine when we arrived back at Thredbo.

We left a bit later than intended and weaved our way around the amazing river diversions of the Snowy River engineering scheme, the trout filled streams and the huge scenic lakes before turning south through the mountains towards Victoria. We stopped among grass and tree covered hills and camped overnight by the side of a fast flowing river. As we packed up our camp next morning we were seduced into trying out the river. With Rebecca watching from the safety of her pram we plunged in and swam furiously against the current, managing to remain almost stationary. The ice cold water, contrasting with the warm morning air was superbly invigorating. Later we were joined by a girl riding her bay horse into the deeper, colder water, and then by Rebecca, playing in the shallows.

We planned to go home by following the coast from southern Victoria, calling briefly on my aunt in Melbourne, see the fairy penguins of Philip Island, and then press on to Nowra.

Just to the west of Melbourne and Geelong lies the tiny coastal settlement of Port Fairy and it was here that we stopped to fill up with fuel for the final run to Melbourne and beyond. The petrol station was complemented by a small café set under a big sign inviting drivers to 'fill up while we fill the car up'. Another sign, almost as big declared that there would be no obligation to pay for the fuel if the attendant didn't clean the windscreen, and check the oil and tyres. This service was fairly common in the country districts but has now been almost certainly killed off by the 'self service' culture.

Irene took Rebecca into the café and I stood chatting to the attendant while he busied himself around the car. He asked me if I had seen their aquarium. I hadn't, and I looked around, wondering what he was talking about. Most of his customers must have been similarly confused, so he launched into a quick explanation of where it was, and that, although small, his aquarium was worth visiting because it contained unusual specimens – "all caught locally", he said. Pointing towards a large corrugated iron shed behind a patch of ground offering half a dozen used cars for sale, he finished by saying "since you're a customer it's only fifty cents each – and the kiddie goes free". As I fished for my wallet he added "pay me when you've had your coffee – I'll park the car in the shade when she's right".

I joined Irene in the café had a coffee accompanied by a delicious steak sandwich while we both watched Rebecca push bits of food around her plate. We tried her with more success – and greater mess – with a small ice cream and then we strolled over to the aquarium, paid the required dollar and stepped into the gloomy interior.

We both stood mesmerised and shocked, while Rebecca squeaked and pointed a tiny index finger. The building was circular and apart from the combined entrance and exit, all the outer walls were formed by large glass tanks, each about the dimensions of a good sized sitting room. Most of the tanks had only one occupant – indeed they only provided space sufficient for one occupant. The occupants were giant crabs. I tried to estimate their size while simultaneously peering closely at the tanks to detect any magnification or other trickery. There was none. All of the crabs measured at least four feet across the shell and the bigger ones seemed about eight or nine feet across, with pincer claws more at home on the front of a JCB digger. The whole scene was overpowering and we found ourselves involuntarily moving back away from the glass cages. Even our chatterbox daughter was silent.

As we stood back from the tanks I felt cold metal behind me and turned towards the big circular water tank that occupied the middle of the building. I placed my hands on the edge of the tank and quickly withdrew them as I felt them being nuzzled by wet noses. Looking down I saw that the tank was home to a group of rays of various colours and sizes. They all seemed fascinated by us visitors and had gathered around like an expectant congregation waiting for the sermon. As we became bolder we all dabbled our hands in the water which the rays seemed to enjoy – behaving like playful dogs.

We circled around the building, peering again at the formidable beasts contained within the glass tanks, before wandering out, silent in thought, into the hot sunshine. As we drove away in our spruced up car we both realised we had just witnessed something extraordinary.

****

We rumbled back through Nowra, with the car covered in dust inside and out, tired but content, joined Berry Street from the highway and prepared to turn into our driveway, marked out by Mr Booth's tall pines. As we entered the open gateway I stopped the car and peered ahead. Something had changed. It took only seconds to see what. Spaced out like a line of soldiers, paralleling the drive, was a line of newly planted trees. Rubber trees. They were each about six feet high and, to our eyes looked inappropriate, out of place and horrible.

Clearly our landlady had taken it upon herself to call while we were away.

We unloaded the sleeping Rebecca and took her into the house, and as we were finishing unpacking our travel kit from the car, Spoofy trotted into the drive from the pavement. He dashed towards Irene, then me, and, tail wagging so much that his whole back end was in motion, he gave his very best 'faithful dog welcomes masters home' routine. He cavorted around the car, jumped, squeaked, growled and rolled in exultation. As soon as the car was empty, Irene disappeared inside the house with Spoofy, and with the aim of transferring Rebecca into her cot. I hopped in the car and drove quickly down the road to recover Spoofy's dish and blanket. Our friends reported nothing untoward except that Spoofy had spent some time hanging around our house, mostly inside the old car, or so they thought.

As I drove the few hundred yards back to the house I couldn't get the rubber trees out of my mind. Rubber trees are not native to New South Wales which suggested a probability that they had been smuggled over the border from Queensland. The Australian states took that kind of thing very seriously indeed and if such plants could be established as having been brought into the state illegally, mere ownership of them could result in a heavy fine.

Irene and Spoofy were standing beside the house surveying the new plantation as I arrived back. "They are totally out of place," said Irene.

"In more ways than one."

"What are we going to do about them?" Irene stood back as Spoofy moved from one plant to another, spraying each one with an impressive jet of dog pee.

"He's got the right idea," I said.

"But we're supposed to be living here," muttered Irene, then, more firmly, "she has no right!"

Well, you're right there," I said, "but the best thing we can do is to go inside, get a cup of coffee and think it through."

"I'd prefer a brandy," said Irene. We went inside and I poured two generous glasses of Bundaberg brandy. No solution occurred to us so we went to bed.

Next morning, as I strode out to the car in the usual morning rush, I couldn't help looking across to the rubber trees. Interestingly, at least three of them were surrounded by fallen leaves and as I stood looking another fat glossy dark green leaf fell into the dust. "There's hope yet!" I shouted as I backed the car up the drive.

When I returned home that evening it looked as if there were a few more leaves on the ground and a few less on the trees.

This process continued for just over three weeks. Spoofy would trot out in the morning, pause and sniff at each tree in turn, then retrace his steps back to the first one in line and then move back along the line, peeing copiously on each one until his tank was dry. Each day we would clear a few more of the still thick and glossy leaves from the ground and out of a sense of misplaced guilt Irene would take the hose and water them but the plants were not used to the harsh parching sun occasionally accompanied by what the locals called 'the hot wind', and each evening there would be a few more leaves on the ground, until eventually we were left with a row of ugly leafless poles.

We held a family conference, that is Irene and I discussed the situation closely observed by Spoofy and Rebecca. Should we pull out the dead stalks and return the aspect of our garden to normal? If we did, we surmised, our unhelpful landlady would probably assume that we had deliberately sabotaged her illicit smuggled Queensland rubber trees, or worse, that we had ripped them out and thrown them away.

We compromised. We decided to photograph the now leafless poles and then send a sad little note to the letting agent to tell him of our surprise at finding such a nice selection of tropical trees planted while we were away and then to say how sorry we were that they had not survived despite all our efforts to look after them. Then, we would pull them out.

"Bush fire near Vincentia."

"Irene and Rebecca visit the
Blue Lake at Mt Gambier."

"Spoofy goes maritime."

"Spoofy on the rocks."

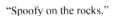

Chapter 27
The Captain's Solo

The short midsummer break seemed to invigorate the whole air station. With a complex all arms exercise taking place offshore, all the squadrons were busy. A task force comprised of the carrier *HMAS Melbourne* accompanied by a group of Australian escorts, a single New Zealand frigate, four ships of a visiting British deployment group and a couple of landing ships, were to make their way north up the coast from Sydney, then turn south to head down towards Jervis Bay where they were to carry out an opposed landing by an Australian army Battle Group. All of this was to be subject to simulated attack by Australian and British submarines, and Skyhawk fighter bombers from the naval air station at Nowra.

Melbourne was fresh out of a minor refit and not worked up for carrier operations so her air group was not embarked. However, as she moved south into the local area there was a certain amount of scurrying back and forth from ship to shore by helicopters from the front line squadron. VIPs, exercise observers and other hangers-on were carted about together with large quantities of stores and baggage. Inevitably many of these people were quite senior and important.

Back at Nowra, the Skyhawk squadrons were busy practising landings on the dummy deck, getting in some general flying practice and, in between, they were acting as the 'enemy' air force, simulating raids on the advancing naval force. The army units were to be landed in Jervis Bay on the beautiful sandy beach near to the Naval Officers' Academy.

Exercises such as this took place all over the world and were usually designed to show off the capability of the host nation in addition to increasing understanding between the participants, but also to provide a satisfying warm glow to the admirals and generals in charge, and of course to those who had slaved away late into the Sydney night to set the whole thing up and write the numerous and lengthy Operation Orders.

Our squadron was to be deployed in providing a day and night helicopter anti-submarine screen for the fleet, supported in turn by the Navy's S2F Tracker aircraft who would also provide anti-submarine defence – flying four hundred feet above our helicopters. The exercise was split into phases with nice breaks in between – which many of us thought of as 'Gin and Scran breaks'.

Despite the extensive and no doubt excellent planning work involved, things don't always go according to plan.

The first noticeable problem occurred as the force headed into Jervis Bay before the landing phase. A conference had been arranged at Nowra for the key senior officers and this was conveniently set for late afternoon so those attending could stay for dinner and return to the flagship after breakfast the following morning. The captains, colonels, generals and admirals had been assembled complete with their overnight kit onboard *Melbourne*. Three helicopters came out from Nowra, a Wessex and two smaller Iroquois, to pick up the conference delegates – about twelve officers in all. The passengers were split into two groups and packed into the Iroquois while the Wessex picked up their overnight bags as an underslung load in a large cargo net. In fact, when all three got airborne from the *Melbourne's* deck, the Wessex, with the underslung cargo net left first but was quickly being overtaken by the two Iroquois flying in a neat formation.

The system for carrying loads slung beneath helicopters has a double level of operating controls. In order to operate the load lifting hook, an 'armament master switch' must be switched on. When the hook is connected to the load and clipped shut, the weight is lifted from the deck and then the armament master switch is set to off. There remains only one way then of jettisoning the load which is for the pilot to lift a spring cover on the top of the 'cyclic' stick and depress the red button underneath. This is exactly what happened as the formation of departing Iroquois drew abreast of the Wessex. There is a pretty good view from the back of an Iroquois – which enabled the shocked senior officers to watch the spectacle of their goods and chattels tumbling gracefully into the sea.

The personal effects of the senior officers had barely sunk below the surface when the next interesting event occurred. Jervis Bay is shaped like a letter C with a narrow east facing entrance giving access to the huge body of water in the bay. The plan for the landing included a preliminary landing on the two facing promontories, presumably to allow unfettered entrance to the bay for the main landing force. A small group had been already landed on the north headland to check that all was well and the plan was feasible. A few hours after the soldiers had landed on this remote piece of rock an emergency call was made by UHF radio to *HMAS Melbourne* – one of the soldiers had been bitten by a spider. This could have been serious and the emergency was immediately relayed to the medical centre at the air station, which was well set up to deal with such problems.

Medics rushed towards the S.A.R. helicopter. Radio calls went out to the ship and on to the troops. What kind of spider was it?

"Big," came the answer.

Could they identify it?

"No."

Had the spider been caught?

"Yes."

The helicopter sped through the late afternoon sunshine as the doctor inside climbed into his protective clothing. They arrived by the soldier's temporary encampment with an impressive flair to reduce speed and landed with a thump. The doctor, followed by his team of two medics, ran towards the group of soldiers.

First priority was to find the spider – essential to determine the treatment.

"Where's the spider?" called the doc.

"Over here," a sergeant was waving his arm.

The doctor walked quickly across the dozen or so yards, where the sergeant was pointing triumphantly towards a flat piece of rock. In the middle of the rock was a small squashed mess – unrecognisable and unidentifiable as anything other than perhaps an over enthusiastic ink blot.

Disappointed but undeterred, the doctor was escorted across to the man who had been bitten – who looked remarkably sanguine as he squatted on his haunches brewing tea over a small fire. "When were you bitten?" asked the doctor.

"Early this morning – 'bout six hours ago," came the reply.

Wordlessly, the doctor, followed by his still laden entourage, walked back to the helicopter and climbed in. He shouted one word in the ear of the Aircrewman: "Home!"

Back at Nowra the third incident which was to mark that afternoon was building. The station Commanding Officer, a distinguished senior Captain, was approaching the completion of his refresher training in a Macchi jet trainer. A man who had first qualified as a pilot around the time of the Korean War, he had not been actively employed in the role for a number of years, as he had progressed up the promotion ladder. When he had been appointed to take command of Australia's only naval air station he had formed the reasonable view that he should obtain a closer understanding of flying modern jets by embarking on a refresher course, fitting in sorties over a protracted period between his other duties.

Today, the course was to be completed and the captain was to fly the Macchi jet trainer solo for the first time. He taxied out, lined up and roared down the runway without incident. His briefing had been to make a couple of dummy approaches, overshooting the runway at the late 'finals' position.

It was a nice clear day, with a light wind blowing exactly down the centreline of the main runway. Everything looked so good that someone in the Control Tower was moved to make an announcement over the station broadcast. The voice boomed out, "D'ye hear there. The Captain is about to make his first solo landing in the Macchi Trainer."

Now, was that testing fate, or what?

The small bright red and silver aircraft lined up perfectly on the approach to the runway and started down the 'slope'. The station C.O. called 'finals'.

"Continue," replied the Tower. The aircraft continued lower and lower, crossed the threshold a little high, missed the late launch of the red flare from the runway 'caravan' and landed perfectly on the centre line – with the wheels still up!

As the aircraft skidded along the tarmac in a cloud of sparks, the duty fire engine roared after it and a disembodied voice with the deep accent of Queensland was heard over the Tower radio frequency. "I thought youse was goin' to do that."

Fortunately no one was hurt, but it would be a long time before that aircraft flew again – as it was for the Captain.

The final punctuation mark for that day came from the fire crew. Having sprayed sufficient foam over the wreck to prevent any possibility of fire, the fire crew took the opportunity of the short enforced break in flying operations to nip back to the canteen for a quick 'wet' – a procedure officially frowned upon.

Because they had limited time, the driver put his foot down as he drove off round the perimeter track, with the recent excitement causing him to forget that the fire engine had a defect. Its brakes only operated on the front and rear near side wheels. There were no brakes on the other side. The time to remember this was when cornering, and even more so when cornering at speed. The driver didn't. Neither did the crew leader.

As they negotiated the last bend of the narrow road, in sight of their destination and in some cases, already savouring the tea, the whole fire engine toppled majestically outward like a rolling whale, completing the final few yards on its side, trailing hoses, extinguishers and bits of 'fearnaught' suit.

Chapter 28
Bong Bong Races

Australians love to gamble. They also love horse races and in the summer both these affinities come together in the country race meetings. Traditionally the Wardroom Mess at the air station would lease a horse and enter it in the local country race meeting – Bong Bong Races. Equally traditionally, despite the application of considerable amateur expertise, the engagement of a training stable – usually the same stable that provided the horse – and enormous supporting enthusiasm, the horse would come last in every race for which it had been entered.

The process would go something like this. About three months before the race meeting the Mess Committee would meet and someone, normally one of the older but still junior officers, would mention that Bong Bong should be included in the social calendar. This would be agreed fairly quickly because it was recognised as a good day out and there was already a well worked up routine for setting up a temporary wardroom at the event. This would be discussed in increasingly complex detail and the meeting would set up a sub-committee to arrange a marquee, transport, tickets, food, wine and volunteer staff, before adjourning to the bar.

By the end of the second round of drinks a previously undiscovered expert in horseflesh would emerge from within the group. The discussion would move on to the opportunity presented by Bong Bong to any competent horse backers. Before the bar closed for the evening a second ad hoc sub-committee would have been established consisting of the aforementioned expert and perhaps three others who had drifted into the bar. Some sceptic would raise the fact that the wardroom's leased horse had never won anything in living memory. The debate would roll on with each side becoming more entrenched as cold beer followed cold beer. Within a matter of days, notice board announcements would appear indicating that not only was the wardroom once again going to provide a really entertaining day out for officers and their families, but this time the local horse flesh experts had already identified a horse that was not only available for lease but that was known throughout the racing rumour factory as having the finest country racing talent yet known to man, which had been carefully disguised and hidden to keep the odds favourable and enable everyone who had been let into the secret (that is everyone who had read the notices) to make a financial killing.

In all the married quarters and officers' homes in Nowra, ladies would be digging out fine summer dresses and extravagant hats. Needles would fly back and forth as adjustments were made and heed was duly paid to the most recent changes in fashion. Conversation during coffee mornings and other social gatherings would hinge around who was going to the races, who would wear what, and how to avoid the more common race-going gaffs.

Despite the fact that every officer on the base knew the dismal record of all the previous attempts to get rich by means of the turf, a wave of enthusiasm would sweep through the whole station. "This time it would be different" was the phrase on everyone's lips. As time moved on, daily reports were furtively issued announcing the result of training gallops and translating the information to the circumstances of Bong Bong, gradually leading up to and then handsomely by-passing course records. This ignored the inconvenient fact that records were never kept for country races, all that was of interest on the day was, who came first, second and third, who fell off and who had to get the next round in.

As race day approached, the original self proclaimed expert would be excused from his normal duties, assuming he actually had any, and he would become the NAS Nowra Honorary Training Manager. It had long ago been decided not to include the station's proper name in anything to do with the wonder-horse because 'Albatross' had unfortunate connotations with elderly mariners. Visits to the stables became frequent and protracted and on return, the tap of optimism and enthusiasm would be turned up to full bore. People would set up as amateur bookmakers and illicit money would change hands.

The afternoon before Race Day, a convoy of trucks would trundle out of the air station, preceded and followed by smart cars containing the organisers, and head off in the direction of the country town of Bowral and the pasture land beyond. On arrival, tents, tables, chairs and a bar would be set up ready for the arrival, early next morning, of the pre-prepared food, wines and cans of beer in forty gallon ice filled drums. Racing would usually start at midday and the runners and riders would assemble up to three hours beforehand, mostly in horse boxes but with a sturdy few trotting in from nearby farms. From ten o'clock, betting would be heavy and continuous.

The Nowra horse would run in the third or fourth race around the middle of the afternoon, allowing plenty of time for an elegant lunch to be completed in the officers' enclosure, a stroll around the hundreds of stalls set up, essential comfort visits, a bit of playtime for the children, a final check on the bookmakers, perhaps yet another bet on *the* horse, before assembling along the rail within sight of the finish.

The loudspeakers would continue to boom out inconsequential rubbish as they generally tend to do on such occasions among the background cacophony around the race track.

Eventually, with everyone listening intently, the runners and riders would be announced for the race. A great cheer would go up when the Nowra horse and rider's name was heard. Another cheer, even louder would accompany our equestrian hero as the horse cantered past, the jockey's garish silks billowing in the rising afternoon wind. A tension would settle across the naval pack as the starter struggled to get the horses into some semblance of order. Then after an agonising wait – of perhaps only four minutes – "they're off!" would echo along the rail. The race would be round the circular track twice so hopes were raised as the packed horses galloped past in a shower of divots and thudding hooves – with Nowra well placed behind the leaders.

Sadly, on some occasions this might be the last the Nowra supporters would see of their horse.

On the race meeting we attended, we did see our horse again, but quite some time after the others had finished. The main field had all just galloped past the winning post when our nag came into view at an easy trot, looking quite bright and chipper, having shed itself of the irritating burden of a jockey.

The ground outside the rail was littered with the torn remains of hundreds of betting slips. The smiles on the faces of the bookies would be enough to light up the race course after the sun had set. A despondent trail of smartly dressed punters descended on the bar to drown some sorrows and create others. There was no sign of any members of the racing sub-committee and the owners of our leased horse had already spirited it away, possibly for a new career in Bowral, pulling a milk cart. The remaining beer cans disappeared from the oil drums as fast as the melting ice surrounding them.

I gathered together my little family and resolved to head off home before the bulk of the boozers reached their cars. The breathalyser had yet to be invented and police were rarely seen either in cars or on foot in the Australian countryside so a certain amount of defensive driving was necessary.

We made it back home without further incident and with our modest loss on the Nowra horse nicely offset by a six to one win in the fourth race and a place in the fifth. We were tired but happy.

As we pulled into the drive in the early gloaming we both noticed something different. A neat row of eighteen inch high pau-pau plants filled the places formally occupied by the rubber trees. Our landlady had made another clandestine horticultural visit and as I looked at her handiwork it occurred to me that although pau-pau trees could sometimes be found in the very north of New South Wales, in all probability these had originated, like the rubber trees, over the border in Queensland. However I didn't think anyone could prove where they came from so I was fairly sanguine about them.

"They won't last," opined Irene. The climate's far too dry for them, I thought. Did Mr Booth have pau-paus? No, he didn't, I answered my own thought.

I had no idea at that point just how prophetic Irene's words were to be. I stood looking at the unhappy and scrawny looking trees as Spoofy wandered down the drive, tail wagging easily. He leaned hard up against my legs, looked up at me again and then wandered across to the nearest plant and cocked his leg to send a steamy jet over it.

****

All through that early summer we had enjoyed the services of an enterprising local teenage lad who spent his Saturdays mowing lawns. He came complete with his own petrol engine powered mower and would mow the front, side, and back lawns for two dollars. We had no set arrangement as to when he should mow the lawns. He just looked at them and when they needed mowing he would do them, calling later for his pay if we were not around.

Still suffering from a misplaced sense of guilt over the recently demised rubber plantation, one or other of us did actually attempt to go out each day and water the pau-pau plants. It didn't seem to help them all that much and I was fairly convinced that they were also being watered regularly by Spoofy.

Two weekends after Bong Bong, we decided to take advantage of the slightly cooler but still sunny weather to take Spoofy for a walk along Callala Beach. We set off after an early and light lunch down the tarmac road towards the settlement of Huskisson and the miles of yellow sand beach beyond. Callala Beach stretches for over ten miles around the edge of Jervis Bay. After a forty minute drive we arrived at the beach, I hoisted Rebecca onto my shoulder and we set off along the water's edge. Irene had a stick which she routinely threw a few yards for Spoofy, who was enthusiastic at first but soon tired of the game and pointedly dropped the stick along the edge of the dune grass.

We wandered on, beachcombing away the afternoon, stopping to examine cuttle fish bones and other bits and pieces of maritime treasure. Spoofy trotted at our heels, investigating this or that, taking the occasional roll in the sand, and then running ahead, through the small waves breaking on the sand. It was an idyllic afternoon and we seemed to be completely alone on the long crescent of beach stretching away ahead and behind.

Our peaceful reverie was shattered.

"Hey, you, ya bludger, get yer dog out of the water," a raucous voice yelled from somewhere behind the dune line.

I didn't know what a 'bludger' was but it didn't sound like a compliment and I wasn't, anyway, very happy at being thus addressed by the scrawny unshaven, unkempt figure that appeared from among the dune grass.

I thought, I've met a genuine jolly swag man.

"My dog isn't bothering any one, least of all you," I shot back.

"Ignore him," said Irene, attempting to hurry us along.

I stopped and faced the man who looked in even worse shape as he came closer. He was obviously living rough.

"Dogs in the water attract sharks!" he yelled.

"Are you going swimming?" I asked quietly.

"No way, mate," he said as he drew nearer. "I don't invite the sharks into my back garden and I don't go in his swimming pool," he announced triumphantly.

I had heard this before. I said, "Have you got a back garden?"

"Well, er, no."

"Well there's no problem then, is there?" I said.

"Er." He stopped and stood still on the sand.

Spoofy had now left the surf line and was standing close to my legs staring intently at the ragged newcomer, who was looking nervously back. Spoofy's tail was not wagging and I could see the hackles slowly rising on the back of his muscled neck. I put my hand down and took hold of his collar. "Easy boy," I said as a menacing rumble emerged from under my hand.

As he felt my hand on his collar, Spoofy gave a great lunge towards the tramp accompanied by a single booming "Woof". The man clearly had suffered some difficult experiences in the company of big dogs in the past and he equally clearly didn't want another one. With a blood-curdling yell, he spun round and sprinted off at an impressive pace disappearing into the dunes. Spoofy underlined his first comment with about four more great single booming barks.

We carried on for a bit and then realising that the incident with the tramp had taken some time, we turned and headed back down the beach to where we had left the car. We had wandered about half way along the beach so the sun was low in the sky by the time we returned to the car. I was quite pleased to see the car because I had no idea where the ragged man was, or what might be his intention, although I thought he was unlikely to risk a close quarters situation with Spoofy. I had also wondered whether revenge might have been exacted on our car so I was relieved to see that this was not the case.

The drive back to Nowra was uneventful, except for an occasional ear shattering bark from the back of the station wagon as Spoofy practised his recently successful technique while adopting his standard car travelling position of standing stiff legged in the middle of the luggage area swaying to the bends in the road. Traffic was heavier, especially for a Saturday afternoon, and so it was dark by the time we arrived at the house.

We pulled into the drive and in the headlights I could see that all the lawns had been neatly mowed.

So had the pau-paus.

All that was left was a row of little green stumps barely distinguishable from the grass around them. "Perhaps they'll recover," said Irene, without any sign that she really meant it.

"I don't know," I said staring at the carnage and wondering what might come of it.

I did know though. These tiny stumps were never going to grow into anything. They were ex pau-paus.

****

Actually, we heard nothing more about the short-lived pau-pau plantation. And, pleasingly, this was the last attempt at planting the garden in our absence. We were delighted.

Chapter 29
A New Face

Although I was still only a Lieutenant, because I was the Senior Pilot of a squadron, I was dragooned into the Duty Commanding Officers' Roster. Duties only came around about once every three weeks and since the daily duty team also included an Officer of the Day and an Air Officer of the Day, who between them dealt with most of the routine and ceremonial requirements there wasn't a lot left for the Duty Commanding Officer. Each duty effectively started at the end of the working day and went through the night, requiring the incumbent to sleep in a specially designated cabin overnight. With little to do other than walk or drive around the station making a casual check on the general state of things, time tended to drag a little. Like most Duty Commanding Officers I got into the habit of changing into evening dress uniform – known in the Service as 'Mess Undress' having a leisurely dinner and then spending the rest of the evening in the Mess, not far away from the bar, the theory being that this might deter some of the more objectionable behaviour which can arise when spirited young men are placed within easy reach of cheap alcohol which they will not have to pay for until some indeterminate time in the future. Having said this, I knew from my own and others' experience that it was essential to tread carefully when dealing with drunks because even the most normally mild mannered men could exacerbate the situation if handled unsympathetically, occasionally ending up by playing the 'race card' and uttering the words "Pommie Bastard!"

It was a quiet Sunday evening and the time was dragging even more slowly than usual. Most of the officers and men were at home with their wives and children or away living it up sampling the dubious delights of Sydney. These were unlikely to appear before the early hours of the morning by which time the bar would have long since shut.

I was sitting quietly at one end of the hut which housed the wardroom bar, reading a not very interesting novel, and occasionally pretending to read, whilst in reality observing the group gathered around the bar. Everyone was wearing civilian clothes and at first there had been only two or three officers talking in low tones. By ten o'clock, with at least an hour to go before the bar closed, assuming that someone didn't sidle up to me at the last minute and ask me to authorise a bar extension, the casual group had become a party.

Rounds of beers were being ordered with increasing frequency and the noise level was rising. Aviation anecdotes were being recounted with the occasional flailing arms of the jet jockeys explaining some intricate manoeuvre. A jug of water was knocked off the bar, and while the bar steward was still mopping it up someone's beer was spilled. The centre point of the group seemed to be occupied by a small fat man, a lot older than his companions, who I didn't recognise. He was doing a lot of the talking, buying more than his fair share of rounds of beer and becoming noisy – I thought.

I decided that I had a troublemaker here and I would have to deal with him before the situation got out of hand. I reckoned he was a dyed in the wool SD Sub Lieutenant. That is, he was an ex ranker, a rating who had been promoted to the lowest rung on the commissioned officer's ladder – but no further. I had experienced this type before and I formed a plan to wander round the wardroom glancing at one or two of the newspapers lying about as I moved closer to the bar. I would buy myself a soft drink and perhaps pass the time of day with one or two on the edge of the group.

It didn't work out like that.

I got to the bar. "What'll ye have, sir?" said the barman. Before I could answer the voice I was homing in on called, "I'm buying." I was stuck. I took my glass of lemonade and eased across to thank my benefactor. He looked up at me and stuck out a small fat paw. "Nobby's the name, son. What do you call yerself?" I took a deep breath. I wasn't having this from any cocky little subby even if he had bought me a drink and even if he was old enough to be my father.

I was slow. I was still formulating the right words to put this upstart in his place, when one of the others, with whom I had a passing acquaintance said, "Do you know the new Captain?"

Not only did I not know the new Captain, I didn't even know we were getting a new Captain, and I had been within a hair's breadth of bringing my blossoming career to a premature end.

So I was stuck. The party went from strength to strength. It was our new Captain, Captain "Nobby" Clarke who actually asked me – very nicely – to authorise a bar extension, although as the Station Commander he was technically a guest in the wardroom. Eventually, it seemed about three years later – the party broke up, they all staggered away to their beds and I stayed until the Bar Steward closed up and then lurched away to my cabin, awash with lemonade.

****

The next time I saw 'Nobby' was some weeks later when I was hanging around among the officers attending the 'defaulters' hearings at the Captain's 'Table'. I was there as a witness to a charge of technical negligence but the man pleaded guilty so I was not required.

As I was waiting for my case to come up I took an interest in proceedings as run by 'Nobby'. In several instances, after a case had been heard and a guilty verdict pronounced, mitigation had been listed by the man's Divisional Officer and the Captain paused, consulted the Master at Arms by his side, in a whispered conversation, then turned back to the rating and intoned a litany of the punishment to be meted out. This would have been something like three days Number 14s (extra work and drill) or stoppage of leave or pay. Then the Captain would lean forward over his tall desk and say earnestly "or you can take *my* punishment". Usually, the reply was "I'll take your punishment, sir" – all this while standing stiffly to attention with the man holding his cap in his right hand by his side.

The Master at Arms would then march the man away from the desk and he would disappear round the corner. When the last defaulter had disappeared thus, the Captain would follow them, accompanied by a salute from all those present. Rumours were rife as to what '*my* punishment' meant. It could have been anything between nothing and something bizarre. Speculation formed the centre of many crew room discussions but, so far as I was aware, none of the recipients nor the Master at Arms ever divulged the secret. Our Captain was indeed a colourful chap and his unconventional ways endeared him to the sailors. He toddled around the airfield, addressing by name those he knew and throwing a cheery "G'day sailor" or even "G'day Mate" as he responded to salutes from those he passed. He possessed a kind of Napoleonic charm with which he could engage and captivate anyone at any level, yet he maintained the dignity of command and the respect of those he commanded. He was a true, if somewhat unconventional and unsung, leader and I was sure his men would follow him anywhere.

I thanked providence that I had not followed my inclination to 'sort him out' in that first social meeting late on a Sunday night in the bar. Who knows, I might have discovered myself what '*my* punishment' meant.

Chapter 30
A Walk in the Park

Our first encounter with Spoofy had taken place while walking through Nowra's extensive and attractive park. We learned that the park formed an important part of Spoofy's patrol routine. He also enjoyed trotting along beside Rebecca's pushchair so when he saw the pushchair and other accoutrements being assembled for a walk, he would hang around expectantly, waiting patiently but observing the preparations from different locations around the house and garage. He knew that if anything serious, like shopping, was planned it would involve a car and he was not interested in travelling about in cars. He was even less interested in the prospect of being left to wait in cars and was wont to while away the time while waiting by making small adjustments to the interior trim. Consequently his trips in our cars were few and he was never left to his own devices in the back of a car – other than the old rattletrap Holden wagon that did double duty as his kennel.

It was a fine sunny morning with just enough breeze to ease the temperature when Irene had decided to take Rebecca and join up with her friend Sue, and her children, so that all of them could go for a walk in the park.

As the little party made their way out on to the pavement, they were trailed by a big black dog. Spoofy had dispensed with his usual ground covering brisk trot and had matched his pace to the much slower group of women and children. They all headed for the park.

Half an hour later, Irene, Sue and the children, followed more closely by Spoofy, entered the park. They strolled onto the grass and stopped by a bench. The two housewives chatted while the children played around on the grass. Spoofy sank into a sphinx like position, head on front paws while discretely watching the children as they played. After a while they got up, stopped playing, and set off around the park, now following the winding network of paths which led between the clumps of shrubs and trees. Progress around the park became a little faster because the pushchair moved more easily on the tarmac.

As the park sloped upward towards the west, the paths all began to converge on the trotting track. This was a circular track used for trotting races – which were a form of horse racing where spirited single horses towed a small lightweight 'carriage' occupied by a jockey, at furious speeds around a circular track. This sport is peculiar to Australia and every meeting prompts a surge of official and unofficial betting as well as spectacular crashes.

They wandered on past the trotting track and, seeking the shade of the clumps of tall eucalyptus and ornamental trees, made their way down the hill and back towards the main path. As they did so, some way ahead of them strolled a middle-aged man who, as they got closer, could be seen to be walking with a small terrier type of dog on a longish lead. Nobody remarked on this but Irene noticed that Spoofy's constant position trailing the group had now changed and he was walking along just in front of the children – riding 'point' as they say in cowboy films. Considerable experience and some instinct made Irene take more notice of where Spoofy was and what he was up to. Spoofy, for his part, had long since spotted the man, which for him was a point of interest. When he realised that the man was attached by a string to a very small animal, and when, as they closed the distance, Spoofy had identified the small animal as a tiny dog, Spoofy's interest became intense.

In Spoofy's code of living, small dogs were placed upon the earth primarily for the purpose of being chased and terrorised by larger dogs – specifically, he actually thought, by himself. As he gradually opened the distance between himself and Irene, she noticed him moving from a shambling walk to a more stiff legged posture. His nose was pointed unwaveringly towards the man and his small dog, neither of whom appeared to have noticed the drama building inexorably behind them. Irene took a pace beyond the pushchair and called, fairly sharply, "Spoofy! Here." And then again, "Here Spoofy." In reality both she and Spoofy knew that he would only respond to the call if it suited him, and at the moment this did not appear to be the case.

He heard Irene's call, there was no doubt. As each phrase was uttered a close observer would see a perceptible movement of the dog's ears. They were now pointed backwards, giving an impression of being 'stripped for action' and would seemingly close over as the calls for obedience were made. While Spoofy was now single mindedly heading for the small dog on the end of the lead, Irene was showing that she too was not to be trifled with and she could demonstrate just as much determination as a Labrador dog.

Spoofy moved faster, Irene responded by moving ahead of the group, leaving the pushchair being propelled by Sue's oldest daughter. At first she kept the gap between her and the dog unchanged by walking very fast. Spoofy broke into a trot, and Irene, now thoroughly annoyed, broke into a run. The trot became a canter. Irene yelled at Spoofy and ran faster. She could now discern Spoofy's plan of action, as he was heading directly towards the small dog, which had just become aware of Armageddon bearing down on him. He fled towards his master and was swiftly gathered up. Irene had no wish to witness canine slaughter in the park so, now hurtling at Olympic pace after her four legged attack force, she paused to scoop up a large branch from the side of the path. Spoofy was either going to respond or get bashed.

Unfortunately, the gentleman dog walker, who had only just turned to take in the scene developing behind him, misconstrued what was happening but this was possibly understandable in the circumstances.

Seeing his pet desperately at risk from the huge black dog thundering towards him, and there, beyond the dog was an equally enraged woman heading straight for him, brandishing a great tree branch he took the view that he and his dog were under attack and, gripping his pet even more tightly, he let out a strangely high pitched yell and took to his heels across the grass. At first Irene tried to follow, at the same time shouting to the man to explain that she meant no harm while attempting to continue the voice battering of Spoofy. The combined effect did nothing to improve the situation. The poor man was convinced that an unearthly banshee, accompanied by her black-hearted hell hound had inexplicably taken against him and he and his dog were at imminent risk of total destruction. He continued his rapid retreat towards the park gate and beyond.

Spoofy was now losing interest and beginning to turn his attention towards the placation of his angry mistress. He stopped, adjusted his expression to his limpid brown eyed 'I love you' face and looked up at Irene as she arrived, breathless. In the distance the unrestrained laughter of Sue and the children could be heard above the wind soughing through the trees. "You sod," said Irene to the cause of it all. Spoofy gazed back, bewildered.

Chapter 31
The Record

Eddie Bell was in excellent form. As the morning briefing neared completion he positively leapt out of his chair and bounced out in front of the seated aircrew. He turned, planted his feet wide apart in an exaggerated 'at ease' position and clasped his hands behind his back. "We're gonna go for the record," he announced, moving his head slowly from side to side to encompass everyone present. What record? I wondered as he continued.

"The 31B has never achieved its full potential, and we're gonna change that," he continued. "We've had a good flying month so far and we've got ten days to break the record for the number of hours flown in one month." Privately I thought he might have put it better because I saw little point in punching holes through the sky just for the sake of it but then as I reflected I could see that this might be a way of invigorating the squadron and putting a bit of zing back into it. On the other hand the real achievement over recent months had been an overall improvement in the aircraft serviceability rate. No longer did we have half a squadron of 'Hangar Queens' waiting for spares which took forever to arrive and when they did, were frequently found to be wrong. Most of our aircraft were capable of flying every day and the Flying Limitations and Deferred Defects (known as 'Part 2 Entries') in each aircraft's log book had reduced to a pleasantly manageable state and in one or two cases disappeared entirely. It reflected great credit on our Air Engineers and their maintenance teams but if Eddie did mention this, he didn't dwell on it.

We all filed out of the briefing room with the Boss, accompanied by me, in the lead. Snippets overheard from the buzz of conversation behind us suggested that the boys were looking forward to some unusual and interesting flying over the next few days which would create havoc with the card schools. As we strode towards the Boss's office I was thinking hard. Although he had omitted any mention of his new scheme, my Boss was an action man and he would expect a whole lot of ideas to come pouring out of me on arrival in his office. I was not going to disappoint him.

As soon as we were seated either side of his desk, coffee mugs in hand I took the lead. "We've got a fairly busy programme this morning," I said, "but not much on the programme this afternoon. There are seven cabs serviceable so I think we could add in a bit of GFP (General Flying Practice) which will keep the Beefers happy, and then maybe take the opportunity for a three aircraft formation practice." (A 'beefer' is a slightly derogatory expression for a Qualified Helicopter Instructor – alluding to the fact that they always have a moan or 'beef'.)

"Great!" said the Boss. "I like the formation bit; I want every pilot to get in some decent formation flying so we can have a Balbo at the end of the month. A 'Balbo' is a term used to describe a large formation of aircraft in flight and is taken from the name of a pre-Second World War Italian Air Force General who specialised in organizing large formations consisting of dozens of biplanes which flew through the skies of 1930s Italy to impress the locals. For us the term was more frequently used to describe a formation of 'all the aircraft you can get off the ground'.

If we in the squadron could manage to get eight aircraft into the sky together, going the same way, on the same day, we would indeed cut a dash.

We continued discussing possibilities for useful training sorties which would stack up the flying hours for the rest of the month until a head popped around the door to tell me that "I was on". I had to go flying, in other words.

I was programmed for an hour of solo general flying practice over and around the airfield. As I bumbled around, practising autorotations, precision hovering with various systems disabled, simulated heavy weight running take-offs and landings and flying precise circuits as accurately as I could, I worked out my plan of campaign. As soon as I had landed and handed the aircraft over to the next crew, signed it in, and completed the 'Authorisation' form I headed for the office and committed my plan to paper.

I skipped lunch and so, as the Boss arrived back from his, I was able to present my outline plan for the rest of the month, which I pointed out, would achieve his aim with a bit to spare to allow for unpredicted problems. He liked it, gave it his blessing and marched off to lead the briefing for the afternoon's multi aircraft formation practice. I wondered, in view of the stark lack of such practice ever since I had been with the squadron, whether it was really wise for the great man to pitch his expertise in so soon. Well, I thought, too late now.

Back in my office, having changed out of my sweaty flying overalls I copied out a rough version of the plan I had presented to the Boss, and talked it over with Gerry, the Senior Observer. I asked him if he wanted any changes or additions and he asked for some extended navigation sorties, including one or two 'land-aways'. These involved flying to a distant military or civilian airfield, landing, re-fuelling the aircraft, carrying out the turn-around inspection, writing out and filing a full Flight Plan and then returning to base.

My next task was to break the proposed plan as gently as possible to the Air Engineers. As I expected, the meeting, in the Senior A.E.O.'s office started with a whole series of objections from almost everyone present. In fact, the objections came thick and fast from everyone except me.

Within minutes I was wallowing in a sea of thousand hour checks, tie down runs, engine changes, level wind tests, rotor changes, Tacan calibration, radio frequency crystals, oleo charges and a raft of other suffocating technical paraphernalia. I got the message. The engineers did not entirely approve of my proposed intensive flying programme for the remainder of the month. Worse than this, they had not hoisted in the essential fact that I was merely doing my Master's bidding and had not dreamed up the whole thing for my own gratification. I was sure that, in the background, I heard the muttered word "Pommie". This signalled a crisis of confidence that was likely to undermine the whole plan.

I decided to change tack. But as I opened my mouth to speak, a great roar of sound from above us drowned out any attempt at speech as three Wessex helicopters flew low over the squadron dispersal in pretty good echelon formation. I abandoned my ploy and, looking at the row of engineers, said, "Doesn't that make your heart swell? Doesn't that make you proud?" Before anyone could produce a smart-alec retort I was on my feet clapping the engineers collectively on their backs and warmly pumping the hand of the Senior Engineer. A strange piece of human psychology is that if someone suddenly starts shaking you by the hand it interrupts every thought you have and you continue to join in the handshake despite the fact that you really don't know why you are doing it.

I had my chance. Their guard was down. I ploughed ahead as quickly as I could whilst still appearing reasonable and persuasive. I told them that it would be a great idea to improve massively the morale of the troops by demonstrating that their work was appreciated and that we, the aircrew, were proposing to show off to the whole station, and maybe the whole state just what could be achieved by the collective efforts of the supermen of the squadron maintenance teams. Or at least – something like that. I waited. I had found a crack in their resolve and eased my virtual crowbar in far enough to widen it.

I could see my new attempt at persuasion slowly taking root, like a plant which had been struggling for survival and has finally produced signs of growth.

We began to talk sensibly and after another hour we had agreed on what both sides thought a reasonably achievable plan. I walked back towards the squadron huts with a spring in my step – which became progressively less springy as I neared the huts and could hear the angry voice of the squadron C.O. bellowing his de-briefing views at his silent audience. Eddie was cross, there was no doubt about it. I stepped unobtrusively into the back of the room and listened. As I took in what was being said I realised that things were not nearly as bad as had first seemed to be the case. Eddie was really quite pleased with his team but he didn't want anyone to become over-confident so he was concentrating on every little detail of the sortie with the consistent mantra of "it's O.K. as far as we have gone but this is the base from which we will build real excellence". He was a skilled instructor and I was being treated to a demonstration – a class act – of how it should be done.

The next morning, for the first time in my experience in Australia, we had eight serviceable aircraft out on the dispersal ready for the first sorties of the day. Briefing was brisk and workmanlike and we then launched into our ambitious programme of navigation, general flying, instrument training, winching, formation flying, box knocking (accurate hovering over objects in the sea) low level tactical flying and load lifting. Surprisingly, it worked. By the end of the afternoon we had achieved ninety per cent of the day's programme and still had six serviceable aircraft. The two needing work did not have serious snags and would be ready by morning.

Next morning we had seven helicopters available to play with, a situation that continued much the same in the days ahead. It seemed as if by actually using the aircraft fairly intensively, they were growing more accustomed to being used and were enjoying the experience. Anyway, I continued to plan ambitious daily programmes and they continued to succeed. By the middle of the fourth week of the month it was clear that we were going to match the present record for monthly flying hours achieved, and, barring a complete ban on flying, we were going to blast straight through the existing record and establish our own. We were so encouraged that we even embarked on a programme of night flying.

At about eleven o'clock in the morning of the last Friday of the month, a beaming Eddie Bell stalked into my office, rubbing his hands and announced, "That's it! We've done it! We'll do the Balbo, then cancel the afternoon! Then, Squadron to the bar!" I decided to interpret the instruction for the latter part of the day as cancelling the flying programme set for the afternoon as I considered that cancelling the time itself was probably above my pay grade.

At 11.45 that morning eight Wessex 31Bs were lined up on the dispersal, manned and ready to start. Radios were switched on and every aircraft had checked in. Eddie's voice came simultaneously into each helmet receiver. "Start Engines." Eight electric starters were pressed and eight gas turbines whined up to a whoosh of power, with one or two accompanied by brief flames from the exhaust. Next, following the single word 'rotors' over the radio, eight sets of rotor blades began to turn, winding up quickly to the flying speed of 220 revolutions per minute. Chocks were removed and the helicopters turned ponderously into line taxiing towards the auxiliary runway parallel to the main. One by one, they lifted into a low hover and moved across to the main runway forming two box, or diamond formations as they did so. Take off clearance was achieved and Eddie Bell led the first four aircraft steadily skyward. I counted to eight and with a wave from my co-pilot, led the second set away. We climbed at 70 knots to one thousand feet and made a shallow turn towards the north. Once through the turn, still at 70 knots I brought the second formation up behind the first and gave the instruction to merge. I took my wing man out onto the port side of the front 'vic' and the second pair moved to starboard. The fourth man of the front formation dropped back to form the shaft of the arrow head made by the other seven aircraft. Once we were set in the formation the C.O. took us down to three hundred feet, we tightened up and roared down the main runway, past the tower and commenced a big sweeping turn to run in across the main accommodation area of the station. Briefly I saw tiny figures emerging from the buildings to stare up at us. It wasn't often that a big formation of helicopters buzzed this airfield. Finally as we flew away across the virgin bush towards the town, the formation was moved smoothly from 'vic' into a long echelon to port of the leader. A run down the main runway at about two hundred feet and a phased break to starboard allowing each aircraft to land individually, completed the flight. We were all rather chuffed with ourselves and in high spirits as we shut the aircraft down and completed the post flight routine.

****

A 'Make and Mend' was declared for the rest of the day. This tradition dates from the days of sail when sailors were stood down from their work for an afternoon in order to make, mend and wash their clothes. For us it signalled an afternoon off. Maintenance was suspended, and the lads trooped off to their messes or to their homes to begin an extended weekend leave. As the aircraft were towed away, the aircrew, now clad in pristine white uniforms, strolled in small groups in the direction of the bar.

A few signs of friendly rivalry greeted our arrival at the wardroom bar. As the first arrivals were ordering cold beers, our Boss breezed into the bar. "Stop!" he shouted. "Today, 725 Squadron broke all the records for the number of hours achieved in one month on a 31B." I mused that since there were only two such squadrons in the world it was an achievement that had its limits. However the squadron tails were up and Eddie was going to make the most of it. Addressing the barman he boomed, "Twelve bottles of your best champagne for my squadron, barman."

"Right away, sir," said the barman, deftly moving bottles and glasses, all crisply chilled, up from the shelf below the bar. It was a fix of course. The Boss had set it up beforehand. Not to be outdone, I seized the first opportunity and invited the barman to add a further six to the first dozen bottles. Gerry added six more. The engineers arrived and increased the liquid hoard. The Boss added another dozen. The party was *ON.* Other station worthies began to trickle in and quickly took up the challenge to prevent us all expiring from alcohol poisoning by ploughing into our supplies. Within a short time the gathering had turned into one hell of a boozy party.

At about four o'clock, I had reached my capacity and evidently some others had exceeded theirs. Recumbent bodies were slumped in various poses of relaxation in armchairs, with some even sitting on the floor. The senior officers of the station had drifted away but a hard core of pilots and observers was still going strong. Bawdy songs were battered tunelessly until the singers forgot the words and they all reverted to the A25 song – a simple but bawdy series of never ending verses describing dubious and calamitous enterprises in a variety of generally historic aircraft types and each ending with the words "But I still have to render my A25". An A25 is an air accident report!

It was still a hot day and even hotter inside the bar. Somebody had had the presence of mind to open the big sliding picture windows, which, if not actually cooling the place, did at least give some change of air. Like everybody else stumbling out of that bar, I strolled across to my car. After a little difficulty with the key, I settled into the seat. I set off quite slowly, and, shamefully, I have no recollection whatsoever of any part of that journey.

Irene was out when I arrived home. I know that because she told me later. She also told me that she found me fast asleep – sitting on the loo!

She somehow encouraged me out of the bathroom, across the hall and into our bedroom where I re-entered oblivion and where she later discovered me, stretched out on the bed, my hands crossed across my chest, looking for all the world as if I was ready to go into the coffin – as she described to me later.

When eventually I came back into the world, I had a headache but it didn't seem too bad and gradually eased as the evening drew on. I played the part of the repentant sinner so that before we all went to bed both my wife and my daughter had expressed some understanding of my predicament – and I had been forgiven by them. Our dog, however, was not of the same view. In his eyes I was guilty of ignoring him on arrival, behaving in a way he didn't understand, and failure to play ball throwing or tug of war with him. Forgiveness from this quarter was going to take a little longer.

Elsewhere, things were not so calm. Brad, a recently joined but experienced pilot had decided that as the supply of champagne ran low – Australian champagne but just as powerful and easily quaffed as the real stuff – the party should continue back at the married quarter he occupied with his wife. A trail of miscreants in various stages of inebriation followed Brad out of the bar and around to the Married Patch. Most of the houses provided as married quarters in those days were fairly basic and the one Brad enjoyed was no exception. It was in fact the upper section of a two storey building divided into two separate apartments with access to the upper one achieved by an external wooden staircase.

Brad and his diminishing band of followers made it to the foot of the stairs and started to climb. Alarmed by the noise approaching her front door, Mrs Brad had locked and bolted it. Brad led the way up the staircase, failed to gain entry through the locked door, and with surprising lucidity loudly demanded access to his residence. A flat refusal was returned from inside. This started a debate into which those nearest to Brad joined in while others, further down the stairs gave up the struggle to reach the top and slid or tumbled to the bottom. As the size of the party demanding admission diminished and the noise began to subside, Mrs Brad's resolve started to weaken until, assuming that there was just her husband outside the door, and in need of some tender care, she opened the door a fraction, only to slam it again when she saw that there was still a group of sleepy sailors occupying her balcony. Unfortunately she did not slam the door quickly enough to stop Brad from sticking his left leg through the opening. The door was slammed forcefully on Brad's leg. Brad, mercifully, appeared to be sufficiently anaesthetised to avoid feeling any pain at all. He fell down the staircase all the way to the bottom, bouncing off the last of his companions who were also beyond registering pain. It was here that his wife found him, dozing peacefully, all alone, later that night.

****

On Monday morning, everyone was subdued. The usual banter about what people had done or not done over the weekend was absent and it seemed that all that our people wanted to do was get on with the day and put some mental distance between now and Friday's party.

As the flying got underway the atmosphere improved. The impressive serviceability of the previous month had not been maintained so we had fewer aircraft on the line. Nevertheless the 'workhorse' jobs and the training routine continued. Just after lunch I found myself doing an instrument flying trip with Brad as my co-pilot. The way instrument flying was practised in those days was by using what were called 'two stage ambers'. This meant that all of the windows around the cockpit were fitted out with amber screens so that both pilots could look out on the world but see it in a rather different light. The pilot practising instrument flying would wear a pair of blue goggles. The combined effect of looking through both amber and blue meant that the pilot could see nothing outside the aircraft but could still see the instruments inside the cockpit quite clearly. The other pilot, who had a full view of the outside world would act as safety pilot as well as devising a series of manoeuvres for the pilot under test to attempt.

I was wearing the goggles while flying the aircraft and doing all right, meeting all the demands placed on me when I heard Brad say, "Can you push the left pedal a bit. My leg is aching – but it'll be O.K." I thought this was an odd request since, as the pilot flying the aircraft I was also pushing the rudder pedals as necessary to maintain the aircraft in balance. I suggested it was time to swap over, partly so I could look and see what Brad was getting at. I handed over control to Brad and took off the goggles. As I handed them across to him I noticed that his left leg was tucked back under his seat, well clear of the left pedal. This was not in itself a problem because provided the aircraft was in balance and a straight course was being flown it was not necessary to keep feet on the rudder pedals all the time. Brad put the goggles on and started scanning the instruments. When he said he was ready I handed over control to him. He was normally a highly accurate and skilled pilot but not today. After telling me his leg was still giving him a bit of trouble he suggested that I should look after the rudder pedals and he would manage the rest of the flying. We tried this for ten minutes or so but it was not very satisfactory and he was not getting much value out of the flight so I decided to abandon the sortie, and return to base. On the way back, I suggested several times to Brad that he should go to the sick bay and have someone look at his leg. He assured me that it was not really that much of a problem and would go away of its own accord.

I didn't think much more about this until I found myself flying once more with Brad, only to go through the same routine as before. I did most of the flying while Brad checked the engine instruments from time to time and acted as left hand lookout.

Although I was completely ignorant of what had happened on Brad's doorstep after the party, I knew my friend had something wrong with his leg which was clearly not going to resolve itself. I insisted quite forcefully that he should report to the sick bay and in the meantime I would not programme him to fly.

Much later that afternoon Brad hobbled into my office leaning heavily on a crutch, with his left leg swathed in plaster. He looked a bit sheepish and gradually the whole story came tumbling out. I realised that I was hardly in a position to take the moral high ground so we both drew a line under it and moved on – as they say.

Some weeks later, Irene and I found ourselves playing doubles tennis against Brad and Mrs Brad. By this time she was heavily pregnant and he was still hobbling around on his plastered leg. Embarrassingly, they beat us every time!

Chapter 32
Spoofy has a Problem

When Spoofy first came to live with us we had been given a full description of the various medical problems which might afflict him. We had learnt to cope efficiently and successfully with his eczema although his weekly treatment still had to be arranged with subterfuge and a degree of secrecy which would have impressed the C.I.A. – assuming they had a canine division.

Spoofy was a bright dog and he could work out when the next shampoo, or powder application was due so he would place himself on high alert and at the mere sight of the accoutrements being assembled, he would make himself scarce. He even got wise to the type of clothing we would wear to deal with the inevitable soaking in water and dog slobber that an attempt to shampoo him would entail. He could be fooled, but not easily and each ploy could only be relied upon to work once. He could not be corralled because he knew every escape route from the house and garden, and we learned that being bowled over by an eighty pound dog leaving at high speed could be an unpleasant, even painful experience. As time passed we learnt that there was one way. He could be bribed. The bribery had to be subtle and carefully managed. Bones from the butcher had no use in coercing Spoofy, no matter how fresh and meaty they might be. He knew that he could – and did – take his choice from almost any of the other canine residents of the town. Similarly, other doggy tit-bits whilst readily accepted would not serve to detain him long enough to launch into the 'process'. We knew he liked smelly things, the smellier the better, and so Irene concocted a series of bits and pieces made from very old cheese, minced liver made into a sort of pâté and little rolled up balls of slightly aged fish skins. These items would be placed strategically to induce him to thinking there must be more of them about and when distracted by his olfactory search we – or Irene – would pounce. The technique was to get the shampoo mixture applied as quickly as possible, and if the powder was required that could be flourished, magician like, producing a cloud all around him – and us.

We had settled into a routine during the hot months and although no participants looked forward to it, it worked. It was with some surprise therefore that on one occasion in the late summer, the routine seemed suddenly much easier. Spoofy was almost compliant. He didn't try any ducking and weaving, or rolling on his back with feet in the air – and he didn't try to run away. As we finished the shampoo we saw the reason for his apparent forbearance. He was having trouble walking. He hobbled up the steps and inside the kitchen to flop down in a heap beside his feeding bowls. A little later, when his evening meal was put in front of him he just looked at it and turned his head away. Alarm bells were ringing for both of us. We made sure that Rebecca could not interrupt with her baby walker and Irene examined Spoofy. She soon spotted that he had an angry looking inflammation between the pads on his paws. The front paws were worst but all four seemed to be infected in one way or another. By the time we discovered this it was about five o'clock on a Saturday evening. It didn't take us long to decide that we needed to do something about this now, and the fact that the vet's surgery was immediately opposite our house made the decision easier.

Without waiting any longer, Irene dashed out and made an exploratory visit to the vet. The vet was about to close for the day but was prepared to see our patient provided we brought· him straight away. Irene was back within ten minutes but by that time Spoofy was looking really sorry for himself. Time being short we set to work straight away to try to get him on his feet but he was having none of it. I attempted to carry him but he countered this by turning himself into a disjointed floppy lump of dogflesh, moulded to our kitchen floor. We tried to lift him together with much the same result but then an idea struck me. I went into the utility room – Spoofy's bedroom – and took out the old grey blanket that he spread around his bed. We put it on the floor beside him and started to roll him onto it. This loss of dignity was just too much for Spoofy. He refused to be rolled but instead clambered slowly to his feet and took a tentative pace or two – reminiscent of a losing boxer before the final bell. This was progress.

I ran to the driveway and opened the back door of the mobile kennel while Irene coaxed Spoofy towards the steps down from our kitchen balcony. Once at the top of the steps he seemed resigned to whatever awaited him and it was fairly straightforward to get him down the steps and, with our combined efforts, lift him into the back of the car.

I backed the car the twenty yards up our driveway, looked left and right along the road, and continued in reverse across the road and up the twenty yards of the vet's driveway.

The vet and his nurse took over and Spoofy was led away to the treatment room. His problem was quickly diagnosed as tinea, a virulent infection which affects the 'toe' pads around the animal's feet.

In a surprisingly short time Spoofy was back with us. He had been given a sedative to keep him quiet while his feet were examined and after some cleaning up, anti-bacterial ointment had been applied, following which all his feet and lower legs had been bound with bandages. We were given more sedatives with instructions to keep Spoofy indoors and quiet. We also had a supply of the ointment which was to be reapplied at regular intervals. We paid the bill, thankful in the knowledge that we would be reimbursed by Spoofy's owners, eased him into the back of the car and set off on the fifty yard journey to the bottom of our drive – travelling frontwards this time.

Carefully and slowly, we eased Spoofy out of the car and up the steps into the house. By this stage the sedative seemed to be taking effect and Spoofy was obviously feeling less pain, as well as looking rather spaced out. We flopped him down in his bed, propped the intervening door open and retired to the living room to relax. Rebecca, who had also travelled to the vet's, was now playing around on the floor.

We put Rebecca to bed, ate some supper and then, before retiring ourselves, considered the problem of how to deal with Spoofy's necessary comfort break. He would need to spring a leak before settling down for the night.

We eased him up out of his bed and guided him like an elderly drunk, through the house towards the front door, down the step and on to the path. I believed I would need to take Spoofy to a tree, or pole, or lamp post in order to encourage him to go through the routine of relieving himself without thinking too much about it.

Between the two of us we got him up the path and there, on the grass verge, was a small ornamental tree. I steered him deftly towards the tree. He stopped. He leaned against the tree but nothing else happened. After a hurried conference it was agreed that I should lift his back leg which was nearest to the tree while Irene tried to stop him falling over.

I lifted his leg, and after a considerable pause it happened. Spoofy ejected a long pungent jet of dog pee – all over me.

Spoofy stood back on four legs and swayed first against the tree then back towards me. Irene had collapsed onto the grass, trying and failing to suppress her laughter. I climbed to my feet and led my unsteady charge back towards the house, where we gave him a second dose of sedative by the simple expedient of shoving it down his throat and keeping his mouth shut until he swallowed, then left him sleeping contentedly in his bed.

We were both up early next morning. As we opened the door into the utility room we were met with a big black dog that seemed to have been turned into a badly tied Egyptian mummy. He had undone all the bandages on his legs, chewed them and rolled around in them. He seemed to be covered in miles of bandage as well as trailing the tattered remains of many more. The good news was that he was up and although walking gingerly, he was not hobbling around as he had yesterday.

A revised plan was hatched. We gathered as many undamaged bandages as we could and Irene shot off to Rebecca's room, returning with a set of woolly babies bootees. Spoofy's feet were re-bandaged, then covered with the bootees which were finally tied in place with their own silk ties reinforced by short strips of bandage. As instructed by the vet, another sedative was administered though with more difficulty and less success than the previous evening.

We guided our canine invalid once more out towards his tree and propped him there. He was still exhibiting signs of being slightly drunk but this time he seemed to be a happy drunk. He raised his back leg on his own and began to pee enthusiastically against the tree. I kept well back and marvelled at how long he could go on for. As the jet became a dribble, Spoofy toppled slowly over on to his right side. I would swear he looked sheepish as he clambered hesitantly to his feet. Finally he stood upright with all four paws, in their pink and white bootees, planted firmly on the ground. At this point Spoofy's gaze became fixed on some object further down the road. I peered along his line of sight and there, about a hundred and fifty yards away, stood another black Labrador, who by the greyness around his muzzle must have been a generation older than Spoofy. Actually we had seen this dog from time to time and, within the family, we called him "Spoofy's grandfather". We were also aware that there was not much affinity between the two dogs, so as we followed Spoofy's gaze we both felt the first prickling of alarm.

As we stood there watching, a remarkable transformation took place before our eyes. Our happy go lucky spaced out canine drunk became a tough belligerent drunk, who was already taking off in the direction of his enemy. One after another, we tried to catch him but failed, as he reached full gallop along the grass verge, all foot pain forgotten and trailing a wreckage of bandages, cotton wool and bootees behind him. The older dog stood his ground as the renegade patient closed in for the kill – or more likely, for a demonstration of how to collapse into instant slumber. Thankfully, just when we were convinced that we were going to have another visit to the vet to deal with battle scars, the other dog disappeared from view – back into the garden from which he had emerged. Spoofy became confused and slowed to a stop, surrounded by the remains of his bandages and trailing bootees. Irene caught up, grabbed his collar and led him, unprotesting, back down the road. I helped to hustle him inside, we re-dressed his feet with what was left of our medical supplies and endeavoured to keep him quiet for the rest of the day.

Dogs have amazing powers of recovery and by the next morning he was quite bright, had removed the second set of bootees of which only two were ever located, and most of the bandages. He wolfed down his breakfast and devoted his energies towards escaping from the house. He was definitely on the mend.

Chapter 33
A Little Drama

We had a huge aircraft hangar, shaped like a long rectangle with the longest side opening on to the concrete dispersal area. Deep maintenance took place inside the hangar with shorter routine checks being carried out after the helicopters had been pushed or towed out to the dispersal area. A series of sliding doors ran along the side of the hangar so that the whole hangar could be opened to face the aircraft operating area. Aircraft undergoing deep maintenance would be stowed at the back of the hangar with the main rotor blades folded back along the fuselage and the tail rotor section folded forward. In this way they occupied the smallest space but it was a time and manpower consuming exercise to fold the aircraft up in this fashion so it was often the case that serviceable aircraft would be rolled into the hangar with the main and tail rotors still spread and ready for flight.

About fifteen feet behind the wide door of the hangar, a thick white line was painted on the floor parallel with the doorway and running along the whole frontage of the hangar. Every part of a parked helicopter had to be behind this line before any attempt was made to shut the hangar doors and this fact was dinned into the maintenance ratings. It was also announced in bold terms on various notices as well as being painted on the floor at intervals in front of the line.

It was Wednesday afternoon and all flying had ceased within the squadron. Preparations were taking place throughout the air station for the bi-annual inspection by the Flag Officer Commanding Eastern Australian Area and in the squadron the opportunity was being taken to catch up on paper

224

work, clean the place up, paint what needed painting and bring the aircraft planned maintenance schedules up to date.

As the afternoon wore on the Watch Chief stuck his head in the ready room, spotted a young sailor with a mug of coffee in one hand and a dodgy magazine in the other. "Drop that," he said, "Get out here and shut the left hand doors."

The prescribed method, in fact the only method, of carrying out this task was to take a large cranking handle, insert it in a worm drive on each door and wind the handle to move the heavy doors along their tracks until they were closed. This would take some time as well as being hard work.

But there was another way. A forbidden, illegal way. This was to take one of the tractors used to tow aircraft and place the small front wheel of the tractor against an extrusion on the side of the door, engage low gear and drive slowly forward. In doing this, the tractor driver would not be able to see any obstructions, it wouldn't do the tractor's tyre or transmission much good and it could damage the door rollers. Everybody knew this shortcut was forbidden and most of the men knew why – except, that is, the man who had just been detailed off to do the job. He was not very bright, had a poor reliability and discipline record and, most of all, had his mind entirely focussed on finishing his afternoon watch, heading to Sydney and re-establishing himself with a short skirted blonde lady of his recent acquaintance.

He climbed aboard the tractor, started it up, looked around to check whether he could see the Watch Chief or any other sign of authority and hence possible retribution, and then put it into low gear. He drove carefully up to the end door unit, placed the wheel against the door extrusion, eased up the clutch and began to move the heavy door forward. He glanced along the line of helicopters noting that they were all comfortably behind the line. What he didn't do was to glance upward. If he had done so he would have noticed that the nearest helicopter, although placed with the fuselage behind the line, still had its main rotor blades spread with the two front blades sticking out at angles of forty-five degrees from the fuselage and very definitely extending well beyond the line. Inside the cockpit, the rotor brake was set firmly on.

The tractor ground steadily forward and the hangar door began to grumble along its track. The door came into contact with the nearest rotor blade and became more difficult to move. The tractor was shifted down to a lower gear and more power was applied. This had the effect of forcing the door against the blade which translated the force against the locked rotor brake and through the aircraft. The helicopter began to lift on the side nearest the tractor, compressing the main wheel oleo on the other side. By now every bit of power possessed by the tractor was being deployed but the movement of the door had slowed dramatically.

Suddenly, the poor old aircraft could take no more. The main spar of the rotor blade passed through its elastic limit. The blade didn't break, it folded in half, producing a sort of elbow halfway down the blade. This happened in an instant and as the outer part of the blade whistled downward, it caught the tractor driver on the back of his head with sufficient force to fling him out of the driving seat and on to the hangar floor. The tractor, with hand throttle still set and no driver, detached itself from the door and made a stately progress across the hangar, scuffing toolboxes aside until it buried its nose in the side of another aircraft, folded and stored at the back of the building. Helicopters, whilst superficially appearing large and sturdy are actually of quite light construction – in this case, thin sheets of magnesium alloy stretched over aluminium frames, and this helicopter was losing – had in fact already lost – the battle with the front of the tractor, which was still grinding away, pushing the side of the helicopter like a demented tug boat.

From every part of the hangar men came running in the direction of the unfolding drama. They homed in on the noise and movement coming from the tractor and helicopter waltz. The perpetrator of the drama lay on the floor just inside the half closed door bleeding profusely and staining the recently scrubbed deck.

Somebody in the hangar office decided to call the Squadron Flight Safety Officer. The Flight Safety Officer is the Senior Pilot. That was me. Whether this incident came under 'Flight Safety' was debatable but I didn't think we owned a 'Ground Safety Officer' so I thought I had better respond.

By the time I arrived at the hangar things had developed – and they were developing further. The tractor engine had been stopped and the vehicle withdrawn from the tractor shaped dent in the side of the folded helicopter. On the other side of the hangar the broken rotor blade had already been detached from the rotor head and was lying on the hangar floor. Propped up nearby was the former tractor driver.

At this point cars began to arrive outside of the hangar, disgorging various important and senior chaps from other parts of the airfield. There was nothing for me to do so I stood and watched events unfold. The squadron engineers looked unhappy. Senior ratings were crawling in and around the damaged helicopter taking bits and pieces off and examining others. The, now three bladed, helicopter was being pushed back into the hangar, where it should have been in the first place, so that a replacement rotor blade could be fitted. No one noticed as the heavily concussed, bandaged and still bloodstained tractor driver staggered to his feet with a stupid grin just visible through the blood on his face and began to walk unsteadily over to the broken rotor blade. He looked at it, and climbed onto it, giggling quietly. At this point another very important officer arrived by car, leapt out flashing lots of gold braid against his Persil-white summer uniform and spotted the first and nearest thing in his line of sight. The image in front of him, of a scruffy, bandaged and bloodstained young rating, clearly enjoying the damage he had caused, and now walking along the length of the blade was just too much. With an angry roar which would have done credit to the King of the Jungle, he lunged towards the rating – clearly intent on inflicting further damage – or perhaps he thought of it as administering instant justice. Whatever it was, someone had to step in to prevent escalation of the incident to unrecoverable levels. That could only be me. I was the only person near enough. I moved quickly to place myself firmly between my red faced enraged superior officer and the gibbering idiot now tap dancing on the remains of the rotor blade. I could see that I was in danger of taking the clobbering destined for the ex tractor driver. "Out of my way, Pommie Bastard," roared the angry man. I thought at least he's remembered who I am. Holding my arms wide like a basketball player protecting the net, I dodged back and forth while the rage in front of me subsided as quickly as it had arisen. He turned without another word and went back to his car and sat in it. I relaxed and contemplated the headlines which might have been: 'Very senior chap in smart uniform hammers the shit out of dim and deranged scruffy junior rating'.

Then, I turned around in time to see another officer who also had allowed anger to drive out commonsense. He had arrived at the scene from a different direction and was even now clutching the unfortunate junior rating by the lapels, shaking him and yelling imprecations into his face from three inches away. The bloodstained face smiled back serenely. As I moved forward a regulating petty officer – a naval policeman – appeared from nowhere and gently extricated the young man from the grip of the angry officer. I could hear the regulating P.O. saying earnestly, "Thank you for detaining him sir, I'll take him now, thank you sir, thank you," as he led the young man away – initially in the direction of the sick bay, I hoped.

Afterwards I thought about the incident and the instant anger it had raised among the hierarchy. What I didn't know at the time was that this had been yet another silly, unnecessary and expensive accident among a series which had occurred in the other squadrons on the station – and all just before the big inspection. Also, one young fool had just removed 6.25% of Australia's anti-submarine helicopter force.

****

When I arrived home that night I was looking forward to describing the whole sorry tale of the afternoon's drama to Irene but what she had to tell me didn't exactly put the matter out of my mind but it did move it to second priority.

Irene had arranged to meet a friend who lived at Huskisson, a village situated just behind the beautiful Callala Beach, a journey of about twelve miles, mostly along tarmac roads through bush country. It was hot and dry with the beginning of the hot wind from the Centre. The bush fire risk was high and there was a total fire ban throughout the district of Shoalhaven. As she had gone around the house that morning, Spoofy had stayed close by and had not disappeared on his usual morning jaunt. She had a light lunch with Rebecca, cleared up the third of Rebecca's food spread around the kitchen table and watched while Spoofy hoovered up another third from underneath the table. She cleaned Rebecca, searched for and found a small sun hat and loaded the child into the back of the car. She was about to drive away when she looked down from the car window and there was Spoofy gazing back balefully, accusingly, at her. A wave of doggy induced guilt flowed over and through her. She tried to shoo

Spoofy airily away, slipped the car into gear and started forward. Spoofy kept pace, deep brown eyes fixed unwaveringly on the car driver. Irene could not avoid eye contact with her dog, and then she gave in. She opened the car door, stepped out and went to the rear door. The lower half of the rear door opened downward forming a platform. Before this had reached the horizontal Spoofy had jumped on top of it and there he was – in the luggage section of the station wagon.

Irene set off accompanied by little singing noises from the back seat punctuated by monosyllabic barks from the very back. She decided that she had time to take Spoofy for a short walk and Rebecca for a short 'carry' along the beach before calling on her friend. The afternoon rolled on with tea and chats while Rebecca played with Kirsty, daughter of Irene's friend Sally, until it was time to go. The radio was not switched on so both women were unaware of the fire risk broadcast repeated twice that afternoon. Rebecca was packed into the car and Irene then called Spoofy. There was no response and no sign of him. This was of course a recognised hazard when taking Spoofy away from his home territory. He didn't get lost. He just enjoyed exploring new places.

It took another hour before Spoofy put in an appearance. Scolding him as she encouraged him into the back of the car seemed to pass over his head. Still irritated at being delayed Irene pressed on quickly back towards Nowra. After only a few miles, a wild pig ran across the road, being narrowly missed by the front wheels. Within a mile this had been repeated as several other small animals came racing across the road.

Then, at about the halfway point along the journey, Irene smelled smoke. She began to worry and when glancing into the rear view mirror she saw tall columns of smoke curling up from the trees beside the road. She was now seriously worried. She thought she had about five miles to go when a curtain of smoke was blown suddenly across the road from the trees beside the car. She knew she couldn't go back but she didn't know what might lie ahead. She thought she could do nothing but press on. There was no shelter, no water and nowhere to turn off.

The whole tree line to the left of the car was now smouldering and smoking. Streams of sparks were being blown across the road and with a gasp of horror Irene realised that small fires were starting up on the right hand side. The smoke was covering the road like a swirling grey fog and the car was forced to slow. Irene concentrated on peering ahead, straining to see through the smoke when Rebecca started to cry. She shut her mind to this and concentrated on driving the car through burning twigs which were now falling all over the road. Suddenly, ahead through the smoke she saw a great surge of flame on the left, then on the right. The fire had jumped the road. Although all the windows of the car were closed the interior seemed to be filled with smoke and breathing was becoming difficult. As an automaton now, and petrified for herself and her child, Irene pressed on. In the rear view mirror all she could see was a wall of flame and she was convinced she was not going to survive this, when, like a miracle, the smoke lifted and two hundred yards of clear space opened up ahead. She glanced left and wished she hadn't. It seemed that just behind the roadside line of trees there was a red inferno. As she looked, one of the roadside trees burst into flames, the flames and sparks roaring up into the smoke canopy like a giant roman candle. This had to be the end. The fire had jumped the road here and had roared up into the trees overhead, creating a burning tunnel that the road was passing through. One thing in her favour was that the old car was still going strong. Then, did the six cylinder engine miss a beat? Or did she imagine it? Everything was now impossibly hot, even the air inside the car.

Out of the smoke ahead, a big curving left hand bend emerged. Three things happened almost simultaneously. The smoke began to thin, the red glow beyond the road disappeared and she heard an emergency vehicle siren. In about three or four minutes she had arrived among a group of bush fire brigade vehicles. Friendly, smoke blackened faces looked into the car. Irene had never been so pleased to see people. Spoofy uttered his first sound of the journey. "Wooo-o-o, Woof!" He sounded triumphant.

The firemen had water and all three occupants of the car drank greedily. Irene realised that the wind was now blowing down the road instead of coming from the left and, according to the firemen the fire line was at the bend in the road. They quizzed Irene on what she had seen and where she was going, reassuring her that the road ahead to Nowra was clear.

When she arrived home the only trace of the bush fire was the smoky dirt on the outside of the car and the lingering smell of curiously sweet wood smoke clinging to the clothes of the occupants and apparently ingrained in Spoofy's fur.

There seemed to be no lasting effects and when Irene took Rebecca inside for tea, Spoofy trotted off down the road to check that his domain was as it should be. As she sipped her tea Irene wondered at Spoofy's strange behaviour that morning. Normally he wasn't at all bothered about being taken out in the car but that morning he had seemed desperate to accompany Irene and Rebecca. Why? Could he possibly have known that they were going into danger and had wanted to be with them? We will never know.

It didn't take me long to realise that my wife had experienced a much more interesting day than I had.

Chapter 34
Men from Vietnam

The altimeter read exactly 1500 feet, the speed was a little fast, at about 95 knots and the compass heading was remaining within a degree either side of 090 degrees. It was a reasonable night for a basic night flying navigation exercise, with a half moon slipping in and out between the broken cloud layer 500 feet above us. I was at the controls, giving Ben a break, although the sortie was for his benefit, to get him back into the techniques of night navigation over the sea. Our task was to fly a triangular track out over the sea and back again to Nowra. The aircraft were not fitted with radar and so the navigation was back to the basics of flying accurate, timed legs with occasional confirmations of our position from Tacan – a radio system which would give the direction and distance of its base station, in this case, the airfield at Nowra.

I glanced across the cockpit at Ben then, a second later, I froze. I couldn't believe I had seen what I had seen. I checked the instruments again and then looked back slowly and carefully. I shook my head and looked again. Ben was enthusiastically 'colouring in' his section of the windscreen with a blue coloured chinagraph pencil. "What are you doing, Ben," I said, as evenly as I could manage.

"I'm blocking out the glare," he responded, colouring furiously.

"But you won't be able to see out," I said, reasonably, I thought.

"We're on instruments," he shot back. I thought. I decided that the best bet was to avoid making an issue of it and find an excuse to turn back towards Nowra. Ben's behaviour was not rational and he was demonstrating a pattern of behaviour which cropped up from time to time among those pilots recently returned from Vietnam who we were taking through a conversion and re-familiarisation course. They had been through a unique experience and some of them had been very inexperienced when they went to war, learning as they went along.

The nub of the problems we were encountering was the method used by the Australian Navy to identify and allocate those officers that were to fly in the RAN unit based in South Vietnam.

The Australian Government, wishing to support its ally, had decided to respond favourably to the American request to send an independent helicopter squadron to support the American forces in Vietnam. Unfortunately, it seems that the politicians failed to consult the navy, who, it had been decided, would provide the unit. The tiny Australian Fleet Air Arm simply did not have the necessary pilots, even if they denuded all of their other helicopter squadrons. The solution they hatched jointly with the Americans was that they would send batches of young officers to the huge American training base at Pensacola in Florida. But where were they to find these officers?

It is an unfortunate fact that training people to fly helicopters in a demanding naval or military environment is difficult. Typically, the failure rate is likely to be around seventy per cent. If this proved to be the case with the men sent to Pensacola, it would look bad and potentially be an international embarrassment for Australia.

The Navy Office had scraped around for a solution until someone came up with the bright idea of trawling through all the officers' service records to try and identify those officers who might already have gained some aviation experience but who were not employed as pilots. Everyone was very pleased when this scheme started to produce lists of names. Some of these were men who had started out as pilots and then transferred to being observers – the naval term for navigators – and most of these were employed in other flying roles anyway. However there were still plenty of names who had not continued into a flying career from which to select the first trainees.

There was one big snag with this selection method, which was never identified by anyone in the Navy Office. The problem was that all of those who had previous flying experience had obtained that flying experience when they were being trained as pilots, or occasionally observers. The reason that they were not now employed as pilots or observers was that somewhere along the line, in a carefully constructed flying training regime, they had failed. Some had even failed several times. The reasons were manifold. Some became air sick, some were temperamentally unsuited, others could not cope mentally with the task of flying a military helicopter, and some were unreliable or just inherently dangerous. A few had actually done quite well but had dropped out through sickness or for other unavoidable reasons.

It was therefore a slightly unusual bunch of embryo pilots who arrived at Pensacola to hurtle through the sausage machine which would turn them into basic pilots and very often disregard faults and problems arising along the way. At the end of the course they were shipped off to join the squadron being formed in tents and makeshift huts at Phuc Tui south of the Mekong Delta.

They were then pitched in at the deep end. Each pilot was teamed up with an experienced pilot, usually American, and 'experienced' meaning that he had survived for at least half of his six month tour. The attrition rate was high and as the 'experienced' pilots completed their tours the brand new Australian pilots found themselves out front with no one to guide them, no one to correct their mistakes and no one even to care if they made any.

They made plenty of mistakes, but for the most part they survived these errors and they didn't crash or die, so they assumed, naturally, that the way they were doing things was the proper way.

Then they came home and were assigned for refresher training to us.

****

They came in ones and twos and in all shapes, sizes and degrees of competence. In one respect they were all the same. They had about six months' calendar time in their flying careers but they had amassed about two or three thousand flying hours – experience that would normally take several years of mixed flying had been packed tightly into a war setting.

Barry was a pilot who had done an extended tour in Vietnam and had survived a number of close calls. Ordinary life was very tame for him and he tried to deal with this by going off into the bush, trapping and fighting wild pigs. He would return to the squadron scarred and bleeding, but happy. Otherwise he was a quiet and unflappable man who would make his point in his own quiet way. When I put him under pressure to join in the ad hoc painting team who were busy painting everything prior to an inspection, Barry volunteered to paint the 'heads' (the lavatories). Imagine my horror when doing the final check before the inspecting party I looked into the heads to be faced with a sea of pink. Everything was pink – walls, floor, ceilings, windows, lavatories, lavatory seats, light shades and even the light bulbs. I was very careful in what I asked Barry to do in the future, and I resolved never to let him near a paint brush again.

Gray (Graham) got rid of his aggression every weekend on the Australian Rules football field. He would appear on a Monday morning smiling engagingly out of a mess of bruises and plasters to explain to anyone he could corral, the intricacies of Australian Rules and his part in the latest massacre or triumph. Personally I have never understood the game nor found anyone capable of explaining to me an event that seemed more like a contrived minor war.

Jamie was a bigger problem. Tall, dour and with a permanent scowl above his full beard he had been one of Australia's most decorated officers in the Vietnam War. The Americans, in particular, had showered him with gallantry medals which, since they were awarded by a foreign government, he was not allowed to wear. There was no doubt that Jamie had done well in the most trying circumstances. He was a brave and reliable pilot who had snatched victory from defeat on more than one occasion. He had had a good war. But there was a dark side to him. If even half the rumours were to be believed he had been involved in unacceptable behaviour, resulting in the death of civilians who had the misfortune to enter what the Americans termed 'Free Fire Zones'.

In the squadron he was generally unobtrusive but uncooperative and difficult to handle. He played bridge a lot and was known to persuade another pilot to take a sortie in his place if he was engrossed in the game. At weekends he would change from being a smart sub-lieutenant into a 'biker' – a 'Hells Angel' and disappear off down the coast with his similarly attired friends where we believed they would create mayhem.

It was in fact a combination of Jamie's addiction to the game of bridge and his contempt for authority that led to his departure from the Australian Navy. My phone rang to tell me that an aircraft had been sitting out on the dispersal, rotors turning, for about fifteen minutes waiting for the replacement pilot. I checked and saw that it was Jamie. He was, as I guessed, in the middle of a game of bridge, in the crew room. I told him to get out to the aircraft and get airborne. He hardly turned around, as he said over his shoulder, "Won't be long. I've got a good hand." I wasn't having that. I knew a confrontation would come sooner or later so it might as well be now. I swooped my hand over his shoulder and ripped the cards from him.

"Not now, you haven't," I said. He leapt up and spun round, his face, three inches away from mine, suffused with anger and fists already bunched and coming up. Just as quickly, others who had been watching the development sprang out of their seats, almost as though they were expecting the situation to turn violent. They knew Jamie, I thought later, so they probably were expecting violence.

We stood for a few moments facing each other in silence. Then I said to no one in particular, "Get him out of the Squadron and back to his cabin." That was the last time I encountered Jamie. Within hours the disciplinary system had taken over, Jamie's record had caught up with him and he was a civilian within days.

Jake liked wire puzzles. The first time I set eyes on him was when he walked into my office one sunny morning when I was engrossed in the next day's flying programme. He walked up to my desk, placed a wire puzzle on it, said not a word, turned on his heel and walked out. I looked at the puzzle, turned back to my work, looked again and, five minutes later when Gerry came into the office I was still struggling with the puzzle, the flying programme temporarily forgotten. "What are you doing?" said Gerry as he peered over the desk. "Give it here," he said confidently. "It goes like this."

When I left for lunch forty-five minutes after Gerry had arrived he was still wrestling with the wire puzzle. He didn't notice me leave. As I passed the Boss's office I could see him engrossed in another wire puzzle. I learnt much later that Jake was in the habit of bringing the airfield temporarily to a standstill just by strolling around handing out wire puzzles from his seemingly inexhaustible supply. In the way these things go, his nickname was 'puzzle'.

Some weeks later, Jake was flying an Iroquois from another squadron over the bush near Jervis Bay when he put out a 'Mayday' call. The call said his engine had failed and he was going down into the bush. An S.A.R. helicopter was scrambled with a medical team and set off low and fast towards Jake's last known position. They could see the crash site easily as they approached because of the damage to the low scrub trees. The wreckage was sitting about one hundred yards in from the beach line on fairly flat ground so the S.A.R. aircraft was able to land nearby, having first dropped the medics at the crash scene from a low hover. When the rest of the team hurried over from the S.A.R. they found two slightly bemused medics standing looking at Jake who was sitting, still strapped into his seat, calmly smoking a cigarette. The remains of the tough little Iroquois lay scattered around him like a small scrap yard. There was just one problem for Jake. The engine was still running.

****

It was easy to see the strange and funny side of the men who came back from Vietnam, but they had been pitched into a hellish situation at short notice by their government, given the minimum training for a nasty and hot war. By and large they acquitted themselves well, they did what their country asked of them and their fellow citizens had every reason to be proud of them.

There is a postscript to the Vietnam experience. The United States servicemen were very well supported with almost everything they could want, but with one exception. They had ice cream, coca cola, steaks, turkey at Thanksgiving, weapons and ammunition, but they didn't have beer. Due to the influence of the D.A.R., the Daughters of the American Revolution, the provision of beer to 'All American Boys' was frowned upon. On the other hand, when the Australians arrived in theatre they had almost nothing. They were set up in a makeshift camp of tents and rickety rotting sheds with no running water supply and primitive sanitation. One man with an entrepreneurial spirit that would, under other circumstances, have made him a multi-millionaire, changed all that.

Billy, otherwise 'Trader Bill' quickly identified the possibilities arising from the shortage of beer in the adjacent American camps, the poor relation status of the Australian encampment and the copious supplies of beer available to the Australians, delivered regularly by *HMAS Sydney*, a former aircraft carrier now in the role of supply ship. Billy approached the Americans and started by swapping a few cases of Australian beer for some steaks and some coca cola. The rest of the story is based upon rumour and legend but I have little doubt as to its veracity.

After the first few exchanges of beer for high quality food the word spread among the Americans and Billy's operation expanded accordingly. He hit upon the novel idea of trading beer for plumbing fittings and other bits and pieces which could be used to improve the comfort of the Australians. Emboldened by this Billy struck out further afield. More steaks, coca cola and ice cream arrived and the daily fare of the Australians improved steadily. Later on, it was said, Billy was arrested by American military police and was accused of stealing an entire convoy of refrigerated vehicles and their contents. Somehow he talked his way out of this, putting the whole thing down as an unfortunate misunderstanding. Apparently he lost the convoy though.

The pièce de résistance of Billy's glittering career as a trader came when he somehow managed to acquire a complete, brand new, Iroquois helicopter. This was just too much for the boss of the Australian contingent. Apparently, this potentially incriminating and embarrassing trophy was disposed of by being flown up to the huge American air base at Da Nang in the dead of night. It was placed carefully on the end of a line of other similar helicopters recently shipped in from the United States. The crew then climbed aboard a similar helicopter which had escorted the flying embarrassment and they all sneaked off to their own base in the south.

I honestly don't know whether all of this is correct but I heard the same story from so many different sources that I believe it must be substantially true. When Billy came back he resumed the normal career of a naval aviator, quietly and unobtrusively getting on with his job.

Chapter 35
Fun in the Bush

Neither Irene nor Rebecca seemed to have any lasting effect from their experience in the bush fire. Spoofy thought it was just another one of those strange things that humans did. He had his dinner after his adventure and he had his cosy bed in the utility room. What more could he want? He would just look forward to tomorrow's adventure.

By the end of the next week the hot wind had died away and the bush fire threat had been officially downgraded. We had even had an unseasonal shower of rain – which being an Australian shower had produced flash floods around Nowra.

We decided to devote Saturday to following the dirt road along its full thirty mile length, deep into the bush, to visit the disused gold mine at Yalwal.

We set off in mid morning with Rebecca sitting up in her seat behind us with occasional tinkling giggles signifying the moments when Spoofy's big black head looked over her shoulder. We had travelled perhaps eight or ten miles when we saw another station wagon stopped in the middle of the narrow road. There seemed to be a problem so I stopped the car and walked forward. Both front doors of the car were open and the left seat was occupied by a man holding his head in his hands while a woman, presumably his wife, tended to several deep cuts on the side of his face. Irene joined me to see if she could help. The situation seemed to be in hand but although the damage to the man's face had been eased somewhat by his wife's first aid, the man seemed to be traumatised. I fetched some water from our car, and carefully watched by both

Spoofy and Rebecca returned to the other car. We all agreed that the driver needed to get to a hospital as soon as possible so, after a few minutes, when he began to settle, we encouraged him in to the seat, shut the door and I went back and moved our car over onto the rough verge while the woman now in the driving seat of her car carried out an eight point turn before rumbling off in the direction of Nowra.

I learned the full story of what had happened from Irene. The couple had also been heading off to visit the Yalwal gold mine and had been travelling quite slowly along the rutted dirt road when they had spotted an object rather like a blob in the middle of the road. The driver had stopped the car, got out and walked forward to see what the 'blob' was. It turned out to be a good-sized specimen of the tail-less lizard, a species unique to Australia. These are, as the name implies, lizards without tails, which grow up to about two feet in length. They are in fact quite harmless except for one problem. They are shy and timid but like to spend a lot of time lying about sunning themselves. Since they seek unbroken sunlight they often wander out and lie in the middle of country roads, particularly dirt roads where the traffic is slower and lighter. They may, of course lie in busier roads, but their survival rate would be low.

The lizard is also very short sighted, as well as timid, and when it feels threatened it seeks sanctuary by running up the nearest tree very quickly indeed. What happens from time to time and indeed what had happened here was that the unsuspecting motorist who stops to get out of the car and have a close look at the lizard will advance close to the immobile lizard and peer down at it, usually casting a shadow on or near the reptile. The lizard panics, seeks the nearest tree, which with its sight impediment it mistakes for the man standing beside it and with no warning at all the static lump on the road runs up the man, stopping when it gets to his head. This experience is understandably bad for one's nerves and most people are not able to cope calmly with such a situation. The thrashing of the victim usually dislodges the lizard which then seeks an alternative refuge while the hapless victim deals with the deep scratches inflicted by the lizard's dirty claws as well as the hysteria provoked by the incident. Such are the hazards of the wildlife of Australia.

We settled ourselves back in the car, and with all the windows wide open to provide a cooling breeze, we continued our journey to Yalwal. After another hour and a half we rounded a bend to enter a clearing which seemed to have a lot of tyre tracks. The taller trees had been cleared back from the area but there was a lot of scrub encroaching around the edges of the clearing. Beside the clearing was a small lake roughly oval and about three or four hundred yards in length. Dotted around, here and there, were heaps of abandoned detritus from the mine. Bits of rusting machinery with wooden props tumbled over them, the remains of some sort of cart and what the termites had left of a shed. It was a desolate, forbidding place with nothing romantic, exciting or interesting to commend it.

As we hauled ourselves out of the car Irene remarked to me that this looked like good snake or spider country so we kept Spoofy close. I carried Rebecca and I resolved to keep the visit as short as possible. There was a slight breeze whispering through the scrubby eucalyptus trees but the place was otherwise silent. Then we heard, from not far away, the distinctive cackle of a kookaburra. These are remarkable birds and as I shaded my eyes to peer into the trees for it, we heard the same sound from a different direction but closer now. Were there two of them or was there just one moving around us and laughing at us I wondered? As I was pondering and peering, taking in the desolate scene surrounding us, my reverie was interrupted. Irene grabbed my arm and said in hushed tones, "God, look at that!" I looked, the kookaburra instantly forgotten. Swimming along the length of the lake was a creature which at first sight looked like an alligator. It couldn't have been, I thought hopefully, because there weren't any in New South Wales. It was about six feet long, grey in colour and was swimming fast on the surface. As I looked towards the lake I became aware of a rustling noise from the grass and shrubs to the left of where we were standing. That was enough. "In the car," I said. Spoofy assumed there must be something in it for him so, for once, he obeyed immediately. I strapped a protesting Rebecca into her seat, both Irene and I piled into the front and in a sweeping turn, with a cloud of dust we were off back the way we had come. We rumbled and shook along the corrugations of the road which had not been 'graded' for a very long time and within two hours we were back in our driveway, our picnic still untouched, so we all settled down around the back porch and picnicked there. I wondered as we sat eating our pies and sandwiches why Spoofy, most unusually, had responded with instant obedience when I had ordered everyone back into the car. I came to the conclusion that with his bush traveller's instinct he had decided that he did not want to be lunch for a lizard.

That was our only visit to Yalwal.

"Irene at Yalwal".

"We return from the Vet across the road."

"The Author risks a close
encounter with a tailless lizard".

Chapter 36
Fang Bosun

One of the by products of the system of annual inspections that are inflicted upon military and naval units is a frantic scramble for every section and supporting unit to get their records up to date. Inevitably at the forefront of this operation will be the medical department. This brings the unfortunate experience for aircrew, in particular, of being medically examined, tested and checked. Vaccinations are brought up to date, fat aviators are put on diets and exercise regimes, pilots and observers disappear for half a day at a time to undergo the thorough aircrew medical and everybody has to see the dentist.

I was quietly minding my own business and hoping the whole pantomime would pass me by when two nasty little slips of paper landed on my desk almost simultaneously from the internal mail. One required me to report, with flying log book, at the medical centre (generally called the 'sick bay') at ten o'clock the next morning. Thanks for the notice, I thought, sarcastically. The second piece of paper was rather more accommodating in style. I was asked to telephone the dental surgery to arrange an annual check-up and, secondly, to make a routine appointment to visit the dental hygienist. I was pretty confident that my teeth would stand any test imposed by the station 'Fang Bosuns' or 'Tooth-Wrights' so I reached for the phone and within minutes a nice sounding young lady had allocated me a place in the late morning two days hence. She made it sound rather as though I had just won a national competition to be awarded the last available seat at the Sydney Opera House. Still it was better than the rather arrogant and peremptory instruction from the Principal Medical Officer.

I got through the medical examination the next day without any significant problem but inevitably I ended up with at least three vaccination jabs, however I had the all important signature in my log book declaring me fit for a further year. I got down to the more rewarding task of an hour's flying in the afternoon, cleared up a bit of admin and left myself off the next morning's programme. Like the rest of mankind, I did not look forward to a visit to the dentist but if it could not be avoided I thought it was better to get it over with.

I arrived at the dental surgery on time next morning and was shown into an otherwise empty waiting room by a very pretty WRAN dental nurse. The whole place was different from the sick bay. It was bright, quiet, comfortably furnished and, notably absent was all the noisy bustle which seemed to pervade the sick bay. A small table contained magazines – recent issues intriguingly marked 'Wardroom – Do Not Remove'. I had just selected one of these when the inner door swung open and another equally pretty dental nurse positively beamed out at me and in the manner of a courtesan inviting me to the boudoir, she ushered me into the treatment room. I was trying to think of some eloquent remark, and was walking a little taller when, springing from out of nowhere, my hand was clasped by an earnest young man who looked about eighteen but was decorated on each shoulder with the two gold bands of a lieutenant, with a salmon pink stripe between them, identifying him as a Surgeon Lieutenant (D). He told me his name was Garry and seemed as pleased as punch that not all of his customers had escaped, as he led me towards the dentist's reclining chair.

Garry had clearly completed the advanced 'charm and persuasion course' so before I could say anything or complete the fleeting thought about whether he had a special process for selecting his attractive assistants, I was flat on my back in the chair which had tilted back to a position which made any attempt at escape impossible.

"Any problems I should know about?" crooned Garry, as he delved into my mouth.

"Errg, mff mff," I replied.

"Good – good," said Garry. "Upper left three, Isobel," he continued.

I remained silent as Garry went on. "Oh dear," he said, "oh dear." A wave of panic shot across the room, climbed the chair and threw a black cloak of despair over me. This was not going to be a routine in and out job. Something was wrong I thought. Images of drills and probes filled my mind.

"Good – good," said Garry soothingly.

It was a lie – he couldn't mean it. "Yerr, mff mff urg," I ventured.

"Yes," he said. "Not a problem really, soon have you sorted out, be as right as rain."

Frantically, I thought, but I was as right as bloody rain when I came in here. Now, I'm not.

Suddenly, it was all over – at least phase one, I thought.

Garry stood in front of me with a look of deep earnest concern pasted all over his youthful face. Just behind his left shoulder stood his lovely assistant, adding her own expression of equal concern – as if his wasn't enough.

"She has blue eyes," I noticed, as I realised that Garry was droning on about a gingivectomy. I managed to stammer out, "What the hell is that?"

"Nothing to be worried about," said Garry, explaining that it was just the removal of a little piece of gum to get at some infection below the gum line – and film stars had it done all the time – just to give them more glinty teeth.

"Where?" I said.

"Where what?" said Garry.

"Which bit of gum?" I said.

"Oh, all round," said Garry, cheerily. I was doomed!

Garry went on about needing only four sessions, while I died a death with his every word. Four sessions! How could I escape? Could I go on the run?

Then the lovely face of Garry's assistant loomed into view. My God, she really is gorgeous, I thought, before realising that I was still marooned in the dentist's chair. Maybe I can bribe them. This was my last thought before complete mental capitulation. I walked quietly out of the dental surgery gazing with horror at the appointment card in my hand, hoping as strongly as I could that something would intervene to drive it all away, or maybe, could it be a dream? It wasn't.

****

My first gingivectomy appointment took place exactly one week after I had fallen into the clutches of the dental world. With considerable uncertainty as to my fate I walked into the dental surgery. This time I was met by Garry himself who shook me warmly by the hand and led me straight away into his inner sanctum, all the while carrying on a one sided inconsequential conversation. As I eased myself back into the deep leather of the reclining chair I began to wonder where all the other patients were. Perhaps there weren't any? Was I the only specimen to be captured?

As Garry advanced on me with needle in hand I glanced up to the ceiling behind him. There, pasted on the ceiling in large easy to read letters was a sign: 'Patients are reminded that failure to attend for dental appointments is a disciplinary offence'. As the import of this terse announcement sank in, Garry was happily taking me through what lay in store for me. This was the first of four appointments when strips of gum were to be cut away, top and bottom, left and right. Rhetorical questions were occasionally shoved in the monologue and I gurgled incomprehensible responses, just to show that I was still alive. In fact it was a surprisingly short time later that Garry slapped some protective gunge on the fresh wound and announced with irritating good cheer that all was well and he would look forward to seeing me in a week. "Goodbye sir," said his assistant, who, in my mental torment, I realised I had only just noticed. I turned specially to say goodbye, "for ever" I was tempted to say but didn't because I realised it wasn't her fault.

The second instalment was rather like the first, but a bit less worrying. Garry told me he had been up to Lake Eucumbene at the weekend and had caught a lot of trout most of which he had given to the Captain for his cats. I remained mute.

The third appointment went off without a hitch but things took an interesting turn when I arrived for the fourth appointment. I was due at the surgery at half past one on a Friday afternoon and since I didn't want to eat lunch immediately before my ordeal I duly arrived five minutes beforehand, resigned to getting the whole thing over as quickly as possible. I had agreed to the appointment on that Friday afternoon because the whole station was turning out for 'Divisions' and no flying would be taking place that day.

'Divisions' is a big parade involving almost every man and woman in a particular ship or establishment. Everyone is turned out in their finest immaculate uniform and paraded by department – or Division, hence the name. Divisions are inspected by their Divisional Officers, reported correct to the Commander of the Base, who in turn reports to the Captain. The Captain, perhaps accompanied by an even more important and grand personage, inspects the whole lot, everyone marches past a saluting base and occasionally, fine words are spoken before the whole parade is fallen out to go their separate ways.

I had remembered that Divisions was to take place in summer (white) uniforms, but I had forgotten that on completion of the parade it was traditional to declare a 'Make and Mend' so everyone could disappear early on weekend leave – or go to the various mess bars where, in the case of the wardroom, a 'Happy Hour' was announced. In Nowra, Happy Hours were known to extend from lunchtime, unbroken, to late into the night, or even into the early hours of the next day. I had also forgotten that the squadron officers had planned to let their hair down somewhat by descending in force on the wardroom to take advantage of the Happy Hour. As Senior Pilot, they expected me to be with them. Instead I was lying in the dentist's chair with what felt like both his hands and half his toolkit competing for space in my mouth.

I don't know who first remarked on my absence from the bar, but word got around pretty fast that I was captive in the dentist's surgery and so prevented from enjoying the fun and camaraderie of the Happy Hour. Within forty-five minutes, a plan of action had been determined upon by the lads in the bar and they decided that I should either be rescued or at least provided with appropriate refreshment whilst undergoing my trial.

We were about halfway through the delicate oral operation when I saw through the window beside me, the first cars draw up on the road outside. One after another, familiar figures clad in various forms of white uniform, mostly the high collared, formal, 'ice cream' suits they had worn for Divisions that morning, made their way from the cars steadily towards the dental surgery. More cars were arriving by the minute. Each visitor was carrying either a glass or bottle in his hand. The door burst open. Fleetingly, I caught sight of the receptionist as the room began to fill with squadron officers. Garry bravely tried to place himself between the intruders and his patient, unsuccessfully. I stared up helplessly as the first gin and tonic was poured inaccurately into my mouth and down my shirt front. Within a few moments I was covered in the remains of the various forms of liquid hospitality which I had not actually swallowed. The room seemed to have halved in size and the raucous crew were alternately, leaning over me enquiring how I felt, crashing into expensive bits of equipment or encouraging co-conspirators to return for more drinks.

Garry took the initiative. Tilting the chair forward so rapidly that I was ejected out of it, I heard him shout, "We're getting out of here." Then he was off and running, propelling me along in front of him. He had grabbed some essential bits and pieces – I wondered vaguely if he was permanently prepared to be raided in mid operation by friends of the patient – and suddenly we had arrived at my car. "Get in. Drive," ordered Garry.

"Where to?" I said.

"Your place."

"Why?"

"Only place I can finish off the op."

So I drove out of the base, with a bloody mouth and a white protective cloth obscuring the front of my uniform.

Fifteen minutes later, a very surprised Irene was heading a small audience of three – including a big black dog, as I sat on a kitchen stool, propped backwards on two legs against the wooden wall of our back porch while Garry delved inside my mouth and finished off his handiwork.

Amazingly, I suffered no ill effects, both Garry and his surgery survived without lasting damage and by the time Irene had driven Garry back to the base, all the revellers had returned to rejuvenate the party in the wardroom and to wonder vaguely where the Senior Pilot had disappeared to. Me, I was sleeping off the substantial quantity of gin, rum, and Australian brandy that had found its way past two lovely nurses, defeated Garry and me, and poured down my gullet.

Chapter 37
Another Visit

One more interesting event occurred that weekend. We had another visit from our beloved landlady, mercifully without any more horticultural gifts. She arrived without warning in the middle of Sunday afternoon. We had finished lunch which, despite the heat, had been a traditional British Sunday lunch of roast beef with Yorkshire pudding, roast potatoes, carrots, beans, parsnips and rich gravy. Old habits die hard and old traditions are difficult to break – and we had not tried too hard to break this one.

Spoofy was out on patrol somewhere, Rebecca was playing in the sitting room whilst simultaneously watching an afternoon version of *Sesame Street* on TV. I was helping Irene to clear up in the kitchen whilst formulating plans for the rest of the afternoon. We didn't hear the usual sound of tyres crunching down the drive, probably because both of our cars were lined up just inside the entrance. There was a knock on the door which was immediately opened to reveal the face of our landlady – smiling this time. "Won't you come in," said Irene, not smiling.

"Yeh, right, thanks."

I led the way into the sitting room with the distinct feeling that we were undergoing a snap inspection. Our landlady said something nice to Rebecca who, not being used to *Sesame Street* being interrupted by strangers, retreated hastily to the protection of her Mum.

We sat down, slightly uncomfortably from my point of view because it was still a very warm afternoon and I had been looking forward to a stroll in the fresh air.

Mrs Landlady opened the bowling. "Dog not around then?"

Irene's appearance with tea and biscuits interrupted my reply. She said, casually, "No, he's out somewhere. He disappears for ages and really only comes in for food you know."

"Right," said our landlady, dunking a biscuit in her tea, and apparently still looking around for examples of damage or loss. As she spoke, I could see Rebecca peering around the doorway behind her mother. She was clutching crayons in each hand and I said a mental prayer that crayon marks should not now, of all times, appear on walls or furniture. I needn't have worried. Irene deftly removed the tea tray, disappeared into the kitchen and, momentarily, re-appeared holding Rebecca by the hand, Rebecca's other hand was holding two of her favourite picture books – with no sign of crayons.

Our landlady tried another opening shot, proving she was direct, if nothing else. "Your dog destroyed my plants," she announced. I wondered if this was the beginning of a campaign to unseat Spoofy and if so I was not going to let it pass unchallenged, particularly as we now had an agreement on paper from the letting agent allowing us to board one 'outside dog'.

I responded firmly. "Our dog didn't touch any plants." As I spoke, my eye caught movement outside the window behind our guest. 'Our dog' was standing on his back legs peering through the open front window of the old Holden wagon. He was clearly contemplating a post patrol siesta which would hopefully keep him out of the way for a while. We had at least two hours to go before his dinner time.

"He chewed up my pau-pau trees."

"Mrs Bradford," I said, "Spoofy is not a vegetarian. He is not interested in plants. He eats meat and chews on bones."

"He destroyed my plants." She dunked another biscuit.

"I think I know what plants you are talking about," I replied, working hard to keep my tone reasonable. "There were some very small trees planted in the lawn alongside the house some months back, while we were away. When I found out about it I was surprised that anyone would just come in and plant things there without discussing it." Her face darkened as I spoke.

I ploughed on. "The thing is, to help keep the garden in good shape, we hire a local lad to keep the grass mowed, and, not knowing any different, he just mowed the plants when he was doing the lawn." Her face looked even more belligerent, but I was not finished yet.

"In fact I think it was a good thing," I continued quickly, determined not to allow any opportunity for interruption. "Our friends told us that there had been a man around from the Department of Agriculture wanting to know where these plants came from. Apparently he was also on about the rubber trees which I think you put in. He was talking about court cases, they said and plant smuggling over the border. Did they say when he was coming back, Irene?" I continued to lie, with what I hoped was a look of friendly concern pasted on to my face.

Bingo! I had hit the spot! The belligerent stare faded away and was replaced by uncertainty, then worry and craftiness in equal proportions. "Oh," she said. Half a sopping biscuit fell with a distinct plop into her teacup.

"Let me get you some more," said Irene with an engaging smile as she took the cup of 'tea and biscuit porridge' out to the kitchen.

"I'm sure it will all blow over, particularly now there is no evidence," I said with a confidential smile. "I'm sure the Department of Agriculture have got bigger fish to fry." I could see I had won. Game, set and match. There was no more righteous indignation on display, only relief. I really didn't think we were likely to find any more alien plants struggling for survival in our rented garden.

"Gosh, look at the time," said Irene, returning with fresh tea but no replacement biscuits – thankfully! Everyone looked at the clock. Everyone, that is, except me. I was looking out of the window behind our landlady, where I could see a large black dog, yawning as he peered out of the open car window. I considered what to do. I didn't want another contrived confrontation as the 'outside dog' tried to become an 'inside dog' and more than that, an 'inside dog looking for his dinner'. I found myself talking slightly faster as I saw the familiar black shape slide out through the open car window and disappear from view. I feared a looming crisis but I saw, with a wave of relief, as our visitor eased herself out of her chair, that we had been granted a few more moments in which to resolve the situation. The recently reprieved 'outside dog' was now standing on his hind legs, gazing happily through the window at the group assembled inside. He was wearing his big doggy grin and his impossibly long pink tongue was hanging out of the side of his mouth. Our departing landlady had her back to the window so she was blissfully unaware of the developing drama.

Spoofy was on the verge of booming out a reminder of his presence at the window. He liked to look through the window but he also liked us to react to his presence and we had not done so. As I led our landlady towards the front door I prepared myself for a classic Spoofy welcome, which I knew would not impress the visitor and might even result in a dry cleaning bill. Mercifully nothing happened. I made a point of glancing at my watch and with as much haste as I could muster I encouraged our landlady back to her car. It was only as the car was pulling away down Berry Street that Spoofy arrived, happy, boisterous, noisy and licking his lips.

Irene had saved the day. As I had escorted our guest into the hallway Irene had moved swiftly to the window and tossed out the remains of our lunchtime beef. Spoofy wasn't going to pass up a gift like that and although it didn't take him long to devour it, it was just long enough.

I relayed the parting words of our landlady to Irene. "Yeah," she had said. "Take me a couple of hours to get back I guess," then, as she was easing herself into her car, she smiled a bit and actually said, "Yer looking after the place nicely, thanks," and with that she drove away.

"Well," said Irene, "that's the nicest thing she's ever said to us. Perhaps she has a heart after all."

"Yes," I said. "Perhaps she has."

That was the last time we saw our landlady, and the last time anything strange appeared in the garden.

Chapter 38
Snakes Alive

When we first arrived we had been very wary of the insect life in New South Wales but we had never really heard or thought much about snakes. We knew there were snakes around but our attitude was that they were somewhere else, meaning somewhere else far away. Later, we saw that there were frequent reports in the papers of snakebites, sometimes fatal, but nevertheless, we noted with satisfaction, they always seemed far away. A typical news report would refer to someone driving over a snake on a country road, assuming it to be killed but eventually finding an angry snake wrapped around the car's suspension, ready to attack the first thing, person or animal, that it encountered. They were interesting reports but still far, far away. Thus it was that one Saturday towards the end of the southern summer we were strolling along a 'bush trail' near the little village of Vincentia on the edge of Jervis Bay. The sun was shining, it was warm but not hot, Rebecca was toddling along just in front of us and Spoofy was ambling along a few yards further on. Our pace was governed by the pace that Rebecca set, mostly very slow but occasionally she would put on a little spurt and we would quicken our steps to maintain an even distance.

We had been walking along the rough path for about forty-five minutes which was nearing maximum capacity for Rebecca so we were on the verge of turning back, when Spoofy, perhaps eight yards ahead, stopped suddenly. He stood, stiff legged in the centre of the wide path and stared fixedly towards a spot to his left and slightly ahead of him. There was a movement in the tall grass to the left. I saw it at the same time as Irene. A snake. A big one. And it was closer to Rebecca – who had no idea of the danger it posed – than it was to us. I had a rough stick in my hand which I had been throwing for Spoofy until he tired of the game and I brandished it as I moved cautiously towards the snake. Spoofy was now growling ferociously at the snake which for the moment was still. Irene acted more quickly, rushing forward and scooping Rebecca up in her arms. Folklore always stipulated that a snake surprised by humans will invariably leave the scene as quickly as possible. Clearly this snake had not read that one.

Part of the snake was now out on the path. It was a rusty brown colour, slightly smaller than the diameter of a man's wrist and quite long, with the tail off the path and partly coiled. I had to do something to rescue Spoofy who showed no sign of backing off. I realised that this was likely to be a one sided contest and we were at risk of losing Spoofy. I brandished the stick again but I wasn't going to expose myself to the snake so all I could do was keep my distance and wave my stick and rage at it – joining Spoofy in this, who was also raging at it. It was a stand-off.

The snake started to move forward and as I watched a remarkable thing happened. Spoofy lunged to his left across the front of the snake. The snake's head moved right, closing on Spoofy's lunge, but at the same time stretching out its body and tail. With amazing agility for such a big and heavy dog, Spoofy reversed his direction, flinging himself sideways to his right, landing on all fours on the run and as he passed by the snake his head shot to the left and took a mighty bite near the tail of the snake. The snake snapped back like a coiling spring, but Spoofy was well clear, rounding to face the direction of threat once again but the snake had had enough. It was withdrawing back off the path trailing blood. I grabbed Spoofy's collar and thankfully he did not resist. Together we ran back down the path putting as much distance as we could between us and the big reptile. We caught up with Irene who was carrying a now struggling Rebecca, noisily demanding to get down on her feet and see what all the fuss was about.

As we threw ourselves back into the car I recalled, for some reason, a one day familiarisation course in jungle survival I had attended a few years before. It had been held at the Jungle Survival School near Jahore Bahru in Malaysia. In particular I remembered the demonstration given by the super-enthusiastic Australian Sergeant Instructor who was proving his theory that a striking snake only moved at the same speed as a man punching – so to overcome the snake all you had to do, he said, was be fit and fast, and grab it where it wasn't expecting to be grabbed.

Once in the car, we drove off rather quickly and as we did, I wondered seriously whether Spoofy was a graduate of that course.

****

Before we left Australia we had another nerve jangling incident involving snakes. It was early summer during a seasonal leave break and we were travelling around through the country districts of Southern New South Wales, Victoria and South Australia. We didn't have the companionship of Spoofy on these trips as he stayed behind with friends. One of the highlights of this journey was the old colonial town of Swan Hill. This is actually a very realistic reconstruction of the original settlement and despite the name it is located on a bend in the Swan River rather than on a hill. We were travelling huge distances as we normally did on these touring holidays and our plan had been to make full use of the day by visiting Swan Hill in the morning then, some time after lunch, setting out on the three hundred mile journey, much of it across desert, to end up at Broken Hill.

Swan Hill is a fascinating place with things to see, to do and to wonder at for everyone in the family. We all had our pictures printed on 'outlaw wanted dead or alive posters' and saw the little town going about its daily business as it would have done over a hundred years before. We had lunch, mostly ice cream for Rebecca, but otherwise supposedly typical of the fare of the previous century, before checking the water supply in the car and setting off on the long journey to Broken Hill.

As we drove away from the modern version of Swan Hill we passed a sign on the roadside which had said something about a flora sanctuary. Both of us remarked on the sign so I stopped the car and backed up till we could read it. The sign was pointing towards a dirt road which had escaped our attention until now. It read: 'WILGA PARK. FLORA AND FAUNA SANCTUARY. 40 MILES'. We looked at the map we had, assessing whether we had enough time to visit this intriguing prospect or whether we should press on. We had over a hundred and fifty miles of desert to cross and I was keen to complete the crossing before sunset. We eventually agreed that we should fit in a quick visit to this sanctuary because we would be unlikely ever to have another opportunity.

We turned off the main road and set off along the well maintained and recently graded dirt road. After three quarters of an hour and thirty miles we passed a big sign stating proudly: 'You are now entering the WILGA PARK Fauna and Flora Sanctuary'. Almost immediately the road curved to the right around a stand of tired looking trees and a smaller sign pointed in the direction of a dilapidated single storey house situated on a slight rise in the ground about eighty yards away. We pulled off the track and stopped on the open ground in front of the house. Irene unstrapped Rebecca and lifted her out of the car. Together we made our way up towards the house, which, we saw, appeared to be unloved and deserted. It had that unmistakeable dilapidated air about it. There was a raised wooden platform across the front of the house, shielded from the worst of the sun by an extended wooden veranda. Our guess that the place was deserted was confirmed when we saw a small table outside the front door. The table had a faded typed note pinned to it and two large jam jars. The note said: 'Gone to town. Take the guide from the jar, put fifty cents in the other jar and follow the instructions in the guide. Please return the guide before you leave. We only have one copy'.

We obeyed the instructions, deposited a dollars worth of coins, assuming they meant fifty cents each and that toddlers would be free, and examined the stained and dog eared 'guide'. Inside was a hand drawn map showing the house and an arrowed path towards a double row of what appeared to be cages. We set off in the direction indicated and I immediately tripped over a tiny wooden signpost hammered into the ground with an arrow and one cryptic word 'Fauna'. I supposed it was for those who couldn't read or on days when there was more than one visitor.

We trudged through short grass, downhill in the direction of what turned out to be two rows of old fashioned fruit crates – we used to call them orange boxes – mounted on stacks of house bricks to bring them up to a reasonable viewing level. There was a space of about one yard between the rows of boxes: an important point of note as things turned out. The three of us moved in between the first of the boxes and gazed at the first exhibit in front of us. The arrangement was casual to say the least. The wooden box had its nearest side removed and replaced with a sheet of glass which so far as I could see was fixed in place with a series of thin nails. The top of the box consisted of a sheet of hessian sacking stretched over the four corners and loosely tacked down. Looking along the row, I noticed that some boxes had half bricks weighting down the corners.

We stood and looked. This box had a shelf about half way up upon which was crouched a small rabbit. Irene pointed out the bunny to Rebecca who immediately said, "Why is it so sad Mummy?" The rabbit was indeed shivering and looking very unhappy indeed.

"Yes, what's wrong with it?" intoned Irene.

"It's lunch for the snake sleeping underneath it," I announced somewhat harshly. Two pairs of eyes widened in silence. We all stared at the unfortunate tableau in front of us.

Suddenly, we were shocked into action. There was a huge bang right behind us. I whirled around in time to take in three things: an enormous brown snake rearing back in the act of striking again at the quivering glass on the front of his frail wooden cage; a stream of venom running down the glass in front of me, and a small notice pinned to the bottom of the cage/box which declared simply: 'Australian Brown Snake. Venomous. Aggressive'. I could work out the last two monosyllabic statements for myself and had no need of the obscure little notice.

Irene was distressed. "Let's get out of here," she said. Foolishly, I didn't leave straight away. In the brief moment before I answered, the glass, now facing us shook and the box rocked as the brown monster inside struck again. Again I saw the venom slide down the glass. For some extraordinary reason I then insisted on walking all the way down the line between the rows of boxes, possibly in the hope of spotting an animal other than a reptile. All I saw, on each side of me was snakes, snakes and more snakes, of various colours, markings and sizes. None of the 'cages' looked particularly secure and my speed on the return journey between the exhibits was markedly faster than that on the outward journey.

As we three left the immediate location of the fauna exhibit, we spotted another small wooden sign hammered into the turf. We had missed it on the way in and it was probably just as well. It proclaimed that: 'All these animals have been captured within fifty metres of this spot'. We stared at it. No one spoke as the real horror of our predicament dawned on us. Did the inmate's friends also live around here? Did they return to visit? This was not a place to be. Only Rebecca, happily swinging on the end of her mother's hand was blissfully unaware. Still without speaking, I led the way back towards the car, staring hard into the grass before taking each step and then doing a kind of dainty tip-toe dance. We reached the car. Clearly the remaining unfettered reptile population of Wilga Park was out to a meeting or on holiday. The windows of the car had been as usual left open, so before anyone entered the vehicle I opened each door and peered in. I looked in the luggage area and under the bonnet. No snakes. We breathed again. Rebecca looked puzzled by the strange game her parents appeared to be playing.

After examining the ground between the car and the house, I tip-toed over and returned the grubby dog eared guide. I got back to the car and suggested to Irene that since we were here we might as well take a look at the flora. She agreed, demonstrating, we later believed, a kind of collective madness.

Driving away from the clearing in front of the house we turned right following yet another sign declaring 'Flora Trail'. I drove slowly along a deteriorating, narrowing road flanked on either side by groups of blackened, burnt out stumps of trees and other destroyed vegetation. It looked like the main route into hell. As we drove I began to notice that the road surface was turning from solid dirt into loose sand. We both thought that the road should lead in a circle to rejoin itself but there seemed to be no sign of this happening so, with an image of our nice car being stuck in a sand drift for ever I chickened out. "If we get stuck," I said, "no one is going to come and drag us out." Irene quietly agreed. She was worried. Even Rebecca in the back seat seemed unduly quiet.

I stopped the car and put it into reverse. Almost immediately, the heat, which had been eased by the slight breeze of our motion, became intense. A combination of fear, stress and heat caused sweat to run in streams down my face obscuring my vision. I gingerly inched the car backwards along that horrible apology for a road until after a hundred yards, Irene declared that the road seemed wide enough to do a several point turn and reverse our direction. I got out and had a good look at the surface before getting back in and attempting a multi point turn. The long reverse we had done had made the engine heat up considerably so I began to worry about that as well. Eventually the turn was completed and we cruised away back down the road, and past the house, nursing the engine all the way. Mercifully within ten minutes the engine temperature was almost back to normal.

Rejoining the highway was like returning from outer space. We had made it! All we had to do now was to cross a hundred and fifty miles of sand desert to reach Broken Hill. We made it with only one other small incident when we had to stop in the middle of the desert to give Rebecca a drink and some food. It was too hot in the car to get her to eat comfortably and as soon as we tried it outside the flies arrived in black aggressive clouds. Poor Rebecca would just have to wait until we arrived at Broken Hill, which would be another hour.

The desert would have been completely silent if it were not for persistent marauding flies which occupied the otherwise empty space in their millions, producing an intrusive buzzing, like a badly tuned radio. Although the problem of flies is well known and experienced throughout Australia, in the desert we seemed to have discovered their home territory. I mused on the agony that must have been the daily lot of the early pioneer explorers who had nowhere to hide from the pestilence out here in the nowhere land. We could at least retreat into the car.

We drove into Broken Hill tired, dusty, sweaty and fractious. Our intention had been to stay in the camp site on the edge of town but as we drove up to it we took in the chain link fence, the hot concrete covering most of the site and the shabby buildings. On the opposite side of the road was a white painted Spanish style motel with a clear blue swimming pool alongside it and a big sign over the front entrance that said: 'Fully Air Conditioned'. It was an easy choice. We pulled into the motel car park.

****

Long after we returned home, I was prompted to find out a bit more about Australia's snakes. The subject came up while I was listening to Alex, one of our young pilots, who was not given to exaggeration. He was relating his recent experience of having been caught in a flash flood while driving his car one night. The flood water had risen with breath catching speed and he had narrowly escaped from the car as it was swept away. As the flood carried him along he had managed to grab and hang on to a sturdy tree branch. He had used the branch to lever himself out of the torrent. Having done so, he climbed further up into the tree where he settled himself for the rest of the night, waiting for the flood water to subside.

As dawn broke and it became light enough to see, Alex looked around to take stock of his situation. To his horror he found that he was sharing the tree with about a dozen snakes, all sheltering from the flood water. Alex had the presence of mind to remain motionless while the snakes slipped back one by one into the water as the level fell.

Alex had looked into the snake position in New South Wales. New South Wales has about forty different species of venomous snakes and a few more non-venomous ones. They are spread all over the state, mostly in the countryside but they are not unknown in small towns and settlements. Snake bite incidents usually occur because the snake is inadvertently trodden on or otherwise disturbed. Most snakes will quietly slip away when they hear the approach of creatures that are not their natural prey. There are two exceptions to this. Both the taipan and the much larger and more common Australian brown snake are inquisitive and aggressive. The Australian brown snake in particular will seek out, hunt and attack anything.

I believe that our alarming acquaintance at Wilga Park was an Australian brown snake – and we were lucky he was in his box!

"The Author takes a break in the Bush."

"Irene at the cool mountain stream."

"Rebecca goes solo".

"Rebecca's first driving lesson."

Chapter 39
Deployment

When we arrived home from holiday there was a surprise waiting for me in the shape of another small blue letter. I was informed that I was to be reappointed to the front line squadron for the rest of my time in Australia. I would lose the exalted status of Senior Pilot but take on the role of Executive Officer. This was in fact a nice important title but with a limited range of duties. On the plus side I would get the chance to go to sea in Australia's aircraft carrier, *HMAS Melbourne* and visit one or two of the interesting places in what we call the Far East but Australians call the Near North. Sadly I would lose the Higher Duties Allowance that had been so handy when money was tight but free board and lodging with limited opportunity to spend might offset that to some degree. Irene had a different outlook. She would be left to look after our small family of one child and one dog without the immediate support of a husband and with the added pressures of doing it in a foreign country. Such is the lot of naval wives and she simply accepted the situation without comment or complaint.

The move to 817 squadron took place almost immediately and after quickly handing over my duties I took my goods and chattels the few yards to the next door huts, there to begin the process of embarkation in the carrier. As I recall there was no departure party or arrival party. I just moved.

The new squadron was a different world to the one I had left. A front line squadron in the weeks before embarkation for an extended deployment inevitably must spend most of its time and energy ensuring that the aircraft are in a fully fit state to operate from the carrier at sea. This meant that most of the aircraft remained in the hangar where the maintenance crews laboured to get as far ahead on the planned maintenance schedules as they could. The aircrew were left to get through safety equipment drills and necessary courses. Trips were made by road to the Garden Island Dockyard in Sydney where *Melbourne* was completing her final preparations for sea.

In fact my flying log book shows only fifty-one hours day flying and eleven hours night flying in the nine weeks prior to embarkation in the carrier. An average of only seven hours a week is not very much input for someone who is paid to fly professionally. This did have one advantage as far as I was concerned. With so little flying going on it meant I could spend a great deal more time with my family. We lapped up the opportunity presented to us to go for long and pleasurable walks around the Shoalhaven area and along the coast and beaches as far north as the famous Kiama Blow Hole and as far south as the small coastal town of Batemans Bay. We thought of this area as 'Spoofy Country' because we knew that somewhere to the south of Batemans Bay was where Spoofy had been born.

It was during one of the few night flying sessions within the work up to embarkation that I was interrupted by an urgent telephone call from Irene. We had completed the briefing for the second night flying sortie of the evening when the phone rang. It was passed over to me and I took it with some concern because Irene was not in the habit of phoning me at work, so it must be something serious. She immediately began to explain that she had found a massive insect in the empty fireplace of our sitting room. She had captured it by putting a bucket over it and was calling me for reinforcements. I started to explain that I had to go out and start up the aircraft within ten minutes so there was nothing I could do until I returned later that night. I was about to suggest that she should take shelter with some friends who lived just around the corner when Ben intervened.

Ben, who had completed his flying for the night, was an old friend who we knew from his time in England. He said he would go straight away to rescue the situation. I knew, as I walked out to the aircraft, that it must be serious because Irene was not given to fanciful notions. Together we had encountered yard long stick insects on the side of the house, seen giant lizards, frogs the size of a dinner plate and crabs the size of a small car. We had been attacked by aggressive snakes, driven through storms of locusts, listened to the orchestra of cicadas, and encountered spiders of record breaking dimensions. Irene was sensible and I knew Ben's resourcefulness would resolve the situation so as the aircraft climbed away into the night I could concentrate on the task in hand untrammelled by domestic crises.

When I returned to the crew room just over two hours later, Ben was still there. He was, in fact, engrossed in recounting his visit to my house. He had been as good as his word and had gone straight into Nowra. On arrival at the house he had found Irene surrounded by Rebecca and Spoofy, under a kind of siege, with the door to the sitting room firmly shut. Irene explained that the creature, which she couldn't identify but was massive, was restrained securely under a bucket in the hearth.

Arming himself with a long steel poker, Ben had carefully opened the door to the sitting room, switched on the light, examined the periphery of the room and then advanced stealthily on the upturned bucket in the hearth. Crouching to present a smaller target should a tentacle lash out at him and holding the poker at arm's length, he knocked the bucket over and sprang back in case the creature lunged at him. Nothing happened. Ben had moved carefully forward once more where he found he was staring down at a slightly bemused cricket. It was true that it was a very big cricket, but a cricket nonetheless.

I learnt all of this as I joined the other late night coffee drinkers who I gathered were getting the second or third telling of Ben's story.

****

The squadron was due to embark on 20th of July while the carrier was still alongside the Garden Island dockyard in Sydney. We were not due to sail until 24th of July so when I flew out from Nowra, Irene packed Rebecca into the car, having walked Spoofy round to our friends and shown him where his blanket and feeding bowls were now deposited, before setting off for Sydney. She had booked into a local hotel which was already doing a roaring trade from the other squadron wives.

As I descended over Sydney Harbour, I could not get out of my mind Irene's remark a day or so after we arrived in Australia, when she had first seen Her Majesty's Australian Ship Melbourne, dirty, angular and old, streaked with rust and covered in black electric cables mixed with the detritus of a ship in dockyard hands. She had said, "Does *that* actually go to sea?"

From a height of about four hundred feet on a bright sunny day, and set against the background of the famous harbour bridge and the half completed opera house, I thought the ship looked a lot better. The cables and machinery boxes had gone, there was less rust and there seemed to be a competent air of bustling activity about the deck. I was leading in the second wave of four aircraft and I could see the first four already with folded rotors, being dragged to the parking area in front of the bridge. Nevertheless *Melbourne* was an old ship that had spent her operational life batting along at the high speeds necessary to operate aircraft at sea. She had started life in the Royal Navy as *HMS Majestic* many years ago before transfer to her present role as Flagship of the Australian Fleet.

We spent the four days before the ship sailed enjoying life and the comforts of a modest hotel. I dealt with my few duties in the ship during the day and went ashore as soon as I could. We saw some of the sights of Sydney but the high life was somewhat limited by having to meet the needs of a small child.

On the afternoon of the 24th, the ship took on avgas (high octane petrol for the Tracker aircraft) and was moved out to a buoy in the harbour, so that if somebody dropped a match in the wrong place we would not blow up the whole waterfront.

We sailed the next morning for four months of exercises and visits to exotic places such as Manila, Hawaii and Japan. *Melbourne* was not a happy or a lucky ship. The senior officers were remote from the 'workers' and although we worked hard and played hard, most of the squadron people were very pleased to get back to Australia. I thought it was a poorly run ship, which was reflected in a dreadful accident rate. I also found it strange, if not discourteous that, although I was the senior representative of my country on board, I was never invited to meet the Captain or the Admiral – but all that is another story for another day.

Chapter 40
Return of the Sailor

The last ten days of the voyage were relaxed and pleasant. The fleet paused briefly off the port of Cairns in Northern Queensland while a team of Australian customs officers was embarked in the flagship. As we progressed slowly down the coast they proceeded to clear everyone through customs – being extraordinarily generous in the process. From time to time we would airlift them across to the destroyers and frigates to complete their clearance and on the way out or back we would divert to take them on a short scenic trip along the barrier reef or the often spectacular coastline. They were a decent bunch and we enjoyed their company in the evenings in the wardroom.

We approached Sydney and the Carrier Air Group was flown off back to Nowra. The Trackers were the first to go as they had the greatest range. They were followed by the Skyhawks who blasted off as one of the 817 Squadron Wessex hovered off the port bow as Planeguard. Last to go were the helicopters. With all the other aircraft clear we had plenty of deck space so all the aircraft were positioned along the flight deck. Engines and rotors were started almost in unison and, one after another, we lumbered into the air.

As we approached Nowra, the Boss requested and received clearance for a squadron formation flypast. We dropped down over the airfield formed in a large V of seven aircraft with the eighth aircraft in the space between the two legs of the V. As we cleared the boundary, the squadron reformed into a long echelon and returned once more over the field for a progressive 'break' allowing the helicopters to peel off and land individually.

We taxied in line ahead slowly into the dispersal area and I could see hundreds of families crowded along the hangar frontage. I also spotted half a dozen or so men in blue uniforms. They were not navy because, being high summer all the navy people were clad in either tropical white uniform or green flying suits. They were another set of customs officers, unnecessarily present, since we had already cleared customs.

The column of helicopters turned into line facing the hangar and after a few seconds, eight gas turbine engines were simultaneously shut down. As the rotors slowed to a stop I could see Irene and Rebecca waiting, looking pleased and excited almost opposite my aircraft.

An advantage we helicopter aviators held over our fixed wing counterparts was that we had plenty of space in the back of the aircraft in which we could carry our kit with us when changing location. We had all used this space to maximum capacity and as I walked around the front of the aircraft the big sliding door on the side of the cabin was being opened. Inside was a wall of bags, cases, parcels and other bits and pieces. Foremost inside my aircraft was a miniature armchair made of cane and wicker work. A present for Rebecca, obtained after much haggling, from a shop in Johore Bahru.

I stood there beside the aircraft watching a customs officer, a thin, humourless looking fellow, younger than his colleagues, heading purposefully towards my aircraft and as he got closer I could see that his number one target appeared to be the little armchair, still lodged among the stack of packages and cases in the aircraft cabin. He was within a dozen paces when he was overtaken by a tiny figure streaming sun-bleached blonde curls and running at impressive speed, homing in directly on the chair.

Two little arms reached up, heaved out the chair and placed it firmly on the tarmac beside the aircraft. Rebecca then sat proudly and firmly in her chair. Moments later, the customs officer arrived, clasped the back of the chair and attempted to haul it out from underneath my little daughter. Rebecca was having none of it. She gripped the arms of the chair and planted her feet firmly on the tarmac, refusing to budge. A huge, penetrating wail came from the occupant of the chair.

"Daddy!" she yelled, "the bad man's stealing my chair." Every eye focussed on the confrontation between the man in the blue uniform and the pretty little blonde girl stubbornly clutching her miniature armchair. Rebecca repeated the yell, even louder in case there might still be someone in the District of Shoalhaven who hadn't actually heard it the first time. Mr Customs was deeply embarrassed and I felt some sympathy for him because he was only trying to enforce Australia's official paranoia against the importation of any wooden or cane product from the Far East. I was confident that the chair carried no tiny passengers because it had been under my gaze in my cabin for several months and I had seen nothing untoward. It also came with the required disinfestation certificate.

The customs officer was weakening – he said something quietly about confiscation and realized he was now the focus of attention for the whole crowd of welcomers as well as the intense glare from the tiny belligerent figure in front of him – still clamped to the chair.

"Well," he said. "Maybe. Has it got a certificate?"

I produced the Malaysian certificate of 'bug-freeness' from my pocket and this seemed to offer him a way out.

"O.K." he said. "That could be O.K. Yes, right, home use only."

"It'll be exported in three months," I added helpfully, "back to England."

"Well that should be O.K. then," he said, before retiring from the scene with as much dignity as he could muster and no doubt resolving never to tangle with determined two-year olds.

The chair is still in use by my granddaughters, forty years on.

****

We unloaded all my bits and pieces from the aircraft and somehow fitted them into the car. Irene and Rebecca waited in the car while I signed the aircraft in, changed and dealt with the last few bits of administration. Then, an hour after landing we set off for home.

Approaching the turning into our driveway, I could see Spoofy sitting bolt upright staring fixedly down the road as if waiting for our arrival. As we trundled very slowly down the driveway, Spoofy bounced and cavorted around the car, a big black grinning face appearing at the window first on one side of the car then on the other. He was ecstatic with excitement – a mood with an intensity I had never encountered with him previously. I climbed out of the car still under the barrage of Spoofy's welcome. Irene attended to Rebecca and by the time the two of them joined me in the kitchen I was liberally covered in dog-slobber. Spoofy was very pleased to see me back.

Irene told me that while I had been away, Spoofy had become very protective and very attentive. His usual routine of daily patrols had been abandoned and he would rarely leave their sides. He had become quite reactive towards visits by strangers and had spent much more time inside the house. Thankfully there had been no more visits from our landlady.

Chapter 41
The Last Holiday

Over the next few days, as I settled back into the routine of driving daily into the air station and having precious little to do except drink coffee and chat with my colleagues, I found I had time on my hands and I began to plan our journey back to Britain. Almost immediately I received a letter of appointment from the Admiralty in London, telling me I was to be Senior Pilot in the Navy's anti-submarine Operational Flying Training Squadron. I would be flying Sea Kings which would mean a conversion course at Culdrose in Cornwall but the squadron also operated Wessex Mark 3 aircraft – a sophisticated and advanced version of the Australian Wessex. I was due to start my conversion course on the 1st of March which was earlier than I had expected but I was anxious to get my teeth into the new job and anyway I felt my task in Australia was done.

One of the perks of going to Australia on Loan Service was that we Brits were treated in the same way as Australian officers for travel. The Australians were very generous to their officers in this respect and all officers flying to Europe or back are sent first class by either Quantas or British Airways. Alternatively, if individuals are prepared to use an appropriate amount of their leave allowance, then the movements section in Melbourne (the city) would helpfully arrange complete travel itineraries including first class travel by luxury cruise liners.

Neither of us had enjoyed the experience of travelling half way round the world while being waited on hand and foot by the Peninsular and Orient Steam Navigation Company so we were keen to explore this opportunity and I was happy to forfeit the leave required to do this. However before seriously considering our trip back to the United Kingdom we had one more opportunity to holiday in Australia. Having been at sea for four months I was entitled to deployment leave and this together with the annual Christmas break would provide the opportunity for an extended trip. We had already decided that should the opportunity arise we would head off to the south and west, retracing part of one of our previous trips but hopefully getting a little further across Victoria and South Australia.

It was early December when we set off for our last and longest tour of Australia. We had already taken Spoofy along to his temporary home with our friends. He was quite content and had by now reverted to his normal pre-deployment behaviour, taking his daily patrols around the town, visiting his old haunts and occasionally returning with some illicit trophy. Now that the Master was home he had relaxed from his role as bodyguard-dog. As we gathered together our clothes and equipment for the trip, Spoofy had often been seen observing us with the air of one who had seen it all before.

We had actually discussed the possibility of taking Spoofy with us this time but there were too many potential problems and we decided against it. We couldn't really find the space to fit in a big active dog among all the other things we needed to take, and the prospect of Spoofy wandering off in some far away remote place was too frightening to contemplate. Finally we really couldn't come to terms with the likelihood of Spoofy standing in the back of the car and repelling boarders by barking his way round three thousand miles of Australia. It would have driven us mad.

****

We rolled down the Pacific Highway and after a few overnight breaks as we crossed New South Wales we entered Victoria, looked around Ballarat, visited the Ned Kelly Museum and rolled on across the state and into South Australia. A good part of South Australia is devoted to the production of high quality wines and as we wandered around we sampled Bundaberg Brandy, various local sherry brands, dubious Australian whiskey and palatable gin as well as an excellent range of table wines.

Eventually we ended up at the little town of Tanunda in the Barossa Valley. We settled in to the local static caravan park and strolled around the town. The area had been originally settled by German immigrants and they had brought their vines with them. The town itself was a charming copy of a typical small Bavarian town with old-fashioned shops decorated for the most part with German names.

We learnt that two of the biggest co-operative wineries were not far away so the next morning we set out to visit the nearest – pushing Rebecca in her pushchair down the grass covered path to the Kaiser Stuhl Winery.

We entered the winery and joined a small group who were beginning a tour of the works and the wine making process. This didn't take long and everyone then assembled in the long zigzag bar where we were invited to sample the wares. Most of the other people drank a glass of wine and went on their way but the bar staff were quite taken with Rebecca and so we stayed and sampled more of their very palatable wines. After some time drinking and chatting we seemed to have become firm friends of the bar staff who were continuing as the perfect hosts. Rebecca was by now seated on top of the bar tucking in to lemonade and crisps.

We were the only customers left – if that is the right description for people enjoying free drinks – when the door opened and two men dressed in overalls came in. Immediately the party was regenerated. The newcomers plonked packets of sandwiches on the bar and more glasses were produced. It turned out that these two worked for the gas company, delivering bottled gas around the area and this bar was where they usually took their lunch.

The party was going well when, having failed to monitor the amount of lemonade Rebecca was drinking she demonstrated that she had reached capacity by piddling over the bar. We were embarrassed but our new friends thought it was a hoot. One described it as "getting pissed" which we hoped had not registered as Irene took her away to get cleaned up and sorted out. Nevertheless it served gradually to bring the party to an end and we said our goodbyes, making false promises to return, before heading back up the hill to our caravan site for an early supper and a quiet evening.

We travelled widely during that holiday but there were three places which left the most lasting memories with us – Wilpena Pound, Parachilna, and Blinman.

Wilpena Pound is in the centre of the Flinders Ranges. The Flinders are a range of spectacular mountains in a circular formation, situated in the far west of South Australia. The whole area, famous for the activities of cattle rustlers is rugged and remote. The Pound is in fact a huge area of rich grassland entirely enclosed by the mountains. There was only one small entrance which, it was said, had been only wide enough for a single horseman (or a single cow) to pass through at a time. Many years ago, gangs of rustlers had operated from within the Pound, venturing out at night to steal cattle grazing on the pastureland outside. The only thing the cattle farmers knew was that their herds were steadily disappearing. Eventually, of course, justice caught up with them – rough justice in some cases. The whole area is now on the more demanding tourist trail. The one time narrow entrance to the Pound has been widened to allow in a single track road and that is where we headed to camp for a night in the Pound.

We set up the square tent we carried and emptied the contents of the car into the tent. Our sleeping routine was for Irene and I to share a large inflatable mattress in the back half of the car while Rebecca was tucked inside her portable cot across the front seat. Most times it worked well but not on this night.

For some reason Rebecca was fractious. Irene woke up but I didn't until some time later, when I woke to the realisation that I was alone in the car. With all kinds of possible disasters flitting through my mind I tumbled out of the car and, torch in hand, went in search of my family. It took an agonising twenty minutes to find Irene serenely pushing Rebecca in her pram (normally carried on the roof of the car) through the light bush in an endeavour to lull her to sleep. She had just succeeded in this when I arrived and woke her up again. For the next ten minutes we continued our nocturnal ramble around the wilderness while Rebecca dozed off. She happily continued sleeping through the remainder of the night. Unfortunately we did not.

The Birdsville track is the route taken by the pioneer explorers Burke and Wills who were seeking a route from the South Coast through the Simpson Desert to the north. We didn't dare attempt to travel up the track but we wanted to see what it might be like at its beginning. So we set off for Parachilna. Parachilna isn't a town. It isn't a village or settlement. It is just a single building standing on its own, miles from any civilisation but providing a basic waypoint and watering hole for the hungry and thirsty but undemanding traveller. The map shows a road leading away towards the east and this was the route we followed on leaving Parachilna and setting out for Blinman. The distance is about thirty miles but the conditions en route make it seem much longer. The road at first seems to be a reasonable ungraded track but it soon deteriorates until it appears to settle into the course of a dried up river bed.

As the car bumped and bucked along the dry bed of the river, the banks on either side presented a cavalcade of transport through the ages. Every decade since the motor car first appeared is represented by broken down and abandoned vehicles. In many cases the dry atmosphere had ensured that these motorised ghosts were well preserved with not very much wrong with them. We didn't dare to take the risk of stopping to investigate. The reason that they are all left abandoned to their fate is that no other vehicle or organization is going to accept the risk and expense of going in to try to drag them out.

After perhaps the most hair-raising slow drive of my life we eventually struggled out of the river bed to run the last few miles into Blinman. The fact that we completed that drive without leaving another decaying wreck to add to the exhibits says much for the rugged construction of the modern Holden station wagon. And our car was not a four wheel drive model!

Blinman is a ghost town. Built around a copper mine it used to boast a population exceeding 35,000 but now, with the mine worked out, the population numbers just twelve, mostly from one family and mostly living in and working around the pub – the only functioning building among the dozens of decaying wooden buildings fronting streets where balls of tumbleweed are blown through by the desert wind.

We arrived at the pub – the only inhabited building in the town – about ten days before Christmas. More importantly it was the day of the Blinman Pub Christmas Party. We were welcomed into the pub, introduced to the orphaned baby kangaroo which seemed to have the run of the place, taken to a high ceilinged spacious bedroom equipped with mosquito nets and then called downstairs as the pub's diesel generator was switched on, partly in our honour, but also in order to cool the beer for the party celebrations. The temperature outside had climbed well above a hundred degrees Fahrenheit but somehow the structure of the building managed to ease the worst effects of the extreme heat. Our hosts ran a comfortable establishment despite their remote location and they went out of their way to ensure our comfort and provide fitting seasonal hospitality.

As the afternoon drifted on, various 'neighbours' arrived from their 'properties' – cattle stations for the most part, situated up to a hundred miles away. In the evening after Rebecca had been tucked up in bed, the party, which had been kept simmering by the steady arrival of guests, really took off as we all became one big happy boozy family. Irene, who was not a beer drinker, was intrigued by the response of our hosts, who when she was discovered nursing a half full glass it was whisked away to be replaced by a cold – and full – one. She was told that she would not be allowed to drink warm beer.

We enjoyed one of the most unusual and remarkable Christmas parties at Blinman and when we steered the car away followed by a small cloud of dust next day, all of our hosts and the remaining visitors turned out to wave us on our way and wish us bon voyage.

Rumbling along the pot holed dirt road towards civilisation we were struck by the dozens of little ruins near the roadside, usually consisting of not much more than the chimney of a former homestead – representing the destruction of someone's dreams and the end of a way of life. The outback of Australia could be a harsh and unforgiving place.

Chapter 42
Going Home

We arrived back in Nowra a few days before Christmas, after a long dusty drive up the Pacific Highway from Victoria. We had packed a lot in to our holiday, we had seen remarkable new sights, visited many places far from the beaten track which some would describe as the 'real Australia', and we had even managed to spend a day with my aunt and cousins in Melbourne.

When we pulled into our driveway in the early evening there was no sign of Spoofy and no response to the earnest summonses of "Pooo-feee" from Rebecca. Irene was not surprised as she pointed out that it was his supper time and he was unlikely to be far away from his feeding bowl – which was still at his 'lodgings' in the house of our friends.

When the car had been unloaded and an exhausted Rebecca fed and put to bed I hopped back in the car and drove around the corner to pick up Spoofy's nice new bed which we had bought for him, as well as his other odds and ends. I had travelled less than two hundred yards when a familiar black figure hove into view, loping along at a brisk pace and heading purposefully in the direction of our house. I stopped the car and got out, calling to Spoofy as I went to open the tailgate door. Spoofy reacted in character. Within seconds I was once again covered in dog slobber as Spoofy went through his unique welcome home celebration. He hopped in and out of the back of the car, licking and slobbering on me, barking at me, at the car and at whatever else took his fancy. Eventually I got him in the back with the door shut and we set off again on the short journey to collect his belongings – with Spoofy standing four square in the rear compartment, loudly challenging all comers.

When he and I eventually arrived home and he saw Irene, the whole procedure was repeated until he had exhausted himself whereupon he shambled into the kitchen and flopped down on the floor.

****

Our time for departure was drawing much closer and several problems had arisen that needed urgent attention. First I learned from the Navy Movements Office in Melbourne that the travel system had been changed – and not for the better. Instead of a choice between cruising the world in style or being whisked home in first class airline luxury I was to be the first loan officer to be flown tourist class to Singapore and then on home by trooping flight. This decision had come about following the selfish misbehaviour of my countrymen. I had been the last loan service officer to arrive in Australia and I was to be the last to leave. The last few officers to go home had been creating more and more difficulties for the Australian authorities. They had been changing plans at the last minute, missing ships or planes, arguing over the leave needed for sea trips and so on. They had shot dead the golden goose and I was left with the consequences.

Possibly through a sense of embarrassment at my precipitate treatment, the movements office tried to do everything they could for me within the new rules and it was finally agreed that our trip home would include a flight to Perth, staying a week in that city then a flight to Singapore, where we would extend the normal forty eight hour transit break to nine days, before boarding the RAF VC10 for Brize Norton in Wiltshire.

Spoofy was the next major problem needing resolution. His owners had long since arranged with a family in Nowra that they should look after Spoofy for the six or eight weeks between our departure and their arrival back in Nowra. It was the same couple who had let down Sip and Gordon Edgecombe previously, resulting in our guardianship of Spoofy for the last two years. Now they had let them – and us – down again.

Irene got in touch urgently with Sip in England. No solution was immediately evident and Sip even suggested that Spoofy may have to be put down. Irene was horrified and said that she would sooner take him back to England with us.

Meanwhile other preparations for departure were advancing upon us. On the 9th of January the fabulous Australian Navy packing team arrived to pack up all of our belongings that were to be shipped home by sea. Six men under the direction of a 'no nonsense' lady supervisor who appeared to be strong enough to pick up any piece of furniture and tough enough to deal with any dispute with her all male gang. Every item, no matter how small, was carefully packed in layers of protection and then into stout cardboard boxes which were to be fitted into a shipping container. They were superbly professional and when our belongings were eventually reunited with us, not one item no matter how delicate, had been damaged. I was amused when, back in England, the arrangements for the return to us of our furniture and effects were being agreed, the man from the High Commission telephoned and asked me if I would like to keep the container. He said they made very good garages. Unfortunately it wouldn't fit in a married quarter.

We arranged the sale of the two cars, leaving the older one until last, in case we couldn't sell it at all, when it would have been scrapped. We packed up our remaining belongings and prepared to move in with our friends Sue and Chris Olsen for the last few days before leaving. By now the Spoofy situation was getting desperate but at the last minute, Irene achieved a minor miracle. She contacted the family of the Base Engineer, who was also a British officer on exchange to the RAN and who was due to return to Britain three months after us. They had five sons in their family and saw no problem in accommodating Spoofy in their married quarter on the edge of the air station. Spoofy was saved.

On the 3rd of February we locked the front door of our house in Berry St for the last time, said goodbye to Mr Booth and with Spoofy for once in his life on a lead, I said "hup" and he hopped into the back of the old Holden station wagon. We set off for the air station married quarters and handed Spoofy over to his temporary new family. He stood between us for a few moments, Irene shed a tear and I felt a lump in my throat as we both ruffled his ears. He looked up, wagged his tail, hung out his tongue and then gave Irene's hand one big lick. With that he was off across the grass to the five sons of his new family. He knew he was moving on. He didn't look back. That dog was uncanny.

Before we got back into the car Irene took some cine film of our last sight of Spoofy. He was now the leading light in a newly formed six man football team – that is a five boy and one dog team. He was at home. He was O.K. We drove away.

****

The one remaining task we had to do before leaving was to hand over the car to the man who had already agreed to buy it. He proposed to use it to collect logs in the bush and had paid us the fifty dollars it had originally cost us. Our parting advice was that if he ever found a big black dog inside the car to be very careful and diplomatic in evicting him.

We set off by train for Sydney a few days later. At the station in Sydney we piled our luggage into a taxi and departed for Kingsford Smith Airport. The driver, a rough and ready looking gent struck up a conversation as we neared our destination. "Where ya goin?" he asked.

"England," I said.

"Holiday, is it?"

"No," I said hesitantly. "We're going for good."

"Been here long?" he probed further.

"Two years," I replied.

Turning with a sneer he said, "Wassa matter? Can't ya take it?"

He obviously thought we were among the last of the ten pound immigrants. I was not going to give him any lengthy explanation and I had long since understood the Australian principle of 'give as good as you get'.

"No," I drawled slowly. "We really don't need it."

"We are going home," added Irene brightly in an attempt to lighten the conversation.

The rest of the trip passed in silence and when we reached the airport we heaved our own luggage out of the car boot.

****

The remainder of our trip home was as eventful as most of our time in Australia. The flight from Sydney to Perth courtesy of Reg Ansett and his Airlines of Australia was memorable for all the wrong reasons. The pilot couldn't decide whether to go via Melbourne or Adelaide. He decided on Melbourne and, having done that, he left most of the passenger's luggage including our eight cases, standing in pouring rain on the tarmac at Melbourne airport. As we taxied away towards the runway, rows of horrified passengers had their faces pressed close to the windows – identifying their suitcases and bags piled in sad little heaps under the deluge. The onward journey was very bumpy and for the first and only time in my life I heard a stewardess tell an air sick passenger "Aw shaddup!"

When we arrived in Perth four hours late at two o'clock in the morning, local time, we had no luggage and the hotel had lost our booking. We toured the city in a taxi looking for a room which the driver found after an hour. Our luggage turned up soaked a day later and this generated a protracted row with the local airline manager. Eventually he capitulated and agreed to pay for the laundry, dry cleaning and ruined cases. Despite this dreadful introduction we enjoyed our visit to the beautiful city of Perth but we were not sorry to be on our way again, this time in a proper airline – Quantas – to Singapore.

We stayed in the five-star Equatorial Hotel in Singapore which was also one of the designated transit hotels. Our travel instructions told us that the first forty-eight hours would be free to us but we would be responsible for the bills for the remainder of our stay. Ten days later when I came to pay our bill before departure, the young lady at reception would only accept payment for our drinks and laundry. I didn't want to blot my copybook so I argued. She remained adamant and inscrutable. I then consulted the joint ANZUK movements team at the airport, while still unsuccessfully trying to pay the bill. After a short while back came the answer. The receptionist was right and my travel instructions were wrong. She knew the technical difference between an officer on loan service and an officer on exchange!

It was all in the fine print. Under the rules Australian officers were not allowed to pay bills directly. The bills were sent to the Navy Office and recovered subsequently from their pay. As a 'loan' officer I counted as Australian. But the moment my feet touched the tarmac in Britain I instantly became British again with no further Australian connection and my hotel debt would cease to exist. If only I had known sooner.

"The pub at Blinman - on a busy day!"

"Spoofy relaxes."

"The camp in Wilpena Pound."

"Irene in Wilpena Pound."

Epilogue

We lived in a holiday cottage for the six weeks of my conversion course in Cornwall and we waited until the move to Portland and my new job before going to collect Bobby. Sadly he was not the same dog we had left although he was ecstatic to see Irene again. He was of course now in dog's late middle age so he had less energy but he also had less patience for the first few months with us, nevertheless he became part of our family again and a staunch companion to Richard our new baby son.

We went to see Sip and Gordon Edgecombe and gave them a full report on Spoofy as well as showing them the film of him playing football with the boys when we left him.

The Edgecombe family returned to Australia a few weeks later and quickly moved back into their old home where Spoofy rejoined his proper family. He was delighted to be back with his own folks and soon settled into his old ways, protecting the house and occupants especially the ladies of the household. He was a friendly biddable easy going family dog but he took his duty as guardian quite seriously, seeing off potential intruders with an impressive display of blazing eyes, white teeth and red gums when he thought the occasion demanded.

For years afterwards he remained a familiar figure on his patrols about the town, dominating the lesser dogs of the neighbourhood and often returning home to deposit yet another knuckle bone in the garden, obtained from an unknown source.

By the late 1970s, age had begun to catch up with Spoofy and although just as willing, just as determined to look after his people, Spoofy began to slow down. His glossy black fur had turned very grey around his face and he spent more time sleeping in the shade of the garden or by the fire in the winter. His liquid brown eyes were still warm and friendly as his impossibly long tongue lolled out of the side of his grinning jaws, but he was an old dog.

In 1980, when he was by then about fifteen years old, the infirmity of age became too much for this wonderful companion and eventually, because he was by then suffering from cancer of the mouth, Gordon took Spoofy on his final trip to the vet. His brown eyes closed and his old tail wagged one last time.

I am sure the memories of that unique dog will live on with many people in Eastern Australia as well as with a few in England. He lived an itinerant life; full and fun. For the two years of his life shared with us he made every day different and he lit up our world.